P. L Groome, Bros Thomas

Rambles of a Southerner in Three Continents

P. L Groome, Bros Thomas

Rambles of a Southerner in Three Continents

ISBN/EAN: 9783337403560

Printed in Europe, USA, Canada, Australia, Japan

Cover: Foto ©Andreas Hilbeck / pixelio.de

More available books at **www.hansebooks.com**

Yours truly,
P. L. Groome.

Rambles of a Southerner

IN

THREE CONTINENTS.

"I must also see Rome."—*Paul.*

"... An altar to the Lord in the midst of the land of Egypt, and a pillar at the border thereof to the Lord. And it shall be for a sign and for a witness."—*Isaiah 19.*

"In the way going up to Jerusalem."—*Mark 10.*

P. L. GROOME.

SECOND THOUSAND.

GREENSBORO:
THOMAS BROTHERS, BOOK AND JOB PRINTERS.
1891.

To Col. JULIAN S. CARR,

The Friend of Universal Man, the Beau Ideal Philanthropist,

and to

WASHINGTON DUKE, ESQ.,

Who has done for my Alma Mater what was in my heart but beyond my ability to do, this volume is inscribed.

By the Author.

We Thank Them All.

In addition to his own observations, the author is indebted to many writers for valuable suggestions in preparing this volume; the following have been specially serviceable: The Standard Histories; Geikie; Farrar's Paul; Conybeare and Howson's Life and Epistles of Paul; Thompson's Land and the Book; Josephus; Dr. Young; Bishop Marvin's East Via West; Col. Gorman; Dr. Buckley's Writings on Foreign Travel; Dr. Olin; Dr. Fisk; Bayard Taylor's Views Afoot; Lee Merriwether; Mark Twain; President Winston's Continental Letters; Dr. De Haas; Dr. Menzie's *Turkey, Old and New;* Dr. Hamlin; Wood's Ephesus; Hamilton's Works on the Turks; George Ebers' Works; Encyclopedia Britannica, and all the guide books *in loco*. When more than suggestion is used the text is borrowed with due credit.

For illustrations we gratefully acknowledge the kindly services of *The* (Epworth) *Alliance Herald, Pittsburgh Christian Advocate,* Col. J. B. Gorman and Miss Lehman.

To friendly critics and a generous press the first edition owed its rapid sale.

May we not hope that enlargement in volume, revision of text, and illustration will secure for this the favorable reception accorded to the first edition?

CONTENTS.

CHAPTER.		PAGE
I.	FROM NORTH CAROLINA TO NEW YORK	9
II.	CROSSING THE SEA	16
III.	FRANCE	25
IV.	PARIS TO ITALY	31
V.	GENOA—"PEARL OF THE SEA,"	36
VI.	PISA, FLORENCE	41
VII.	ROME	52
VIII.	NAPLES—"WANTON BEAUTY,"	59
IX.	EGYPT	71
X.	FARTHER UP THE NILE	85
XI.	DOWN THE NILE TO CAIRO	96
XII.	ODDS AND ENDS	105
XIII.	ON SUEZ CANAL	113
XIV.	THE OLDEST SEAPORT	118
XV.	FROM JOPPA TO JERUSALEM	125
XVI.	MT. CALVARY	138
XVII.	IN AND ABOUT JERUSALEM	145
XVIII.	AROUND, ABOVE, BENEATH AND IN JERUSALEM—MT. MORIAH—GETHSEMANE	156
XIX.	TRAVELING IN PALESTINE	167
XX.	NORTH OF JERUSALEM	175
XXI.	MT. TABOR, SEA OF GALILEE, NAZARETH	184
XXII.	MT. CARMEL AND THE COASTS OF TYRE AND SIDON	190

CHAPTER.	PAGE.
XXIII. BEIRUT	197
XXIV. THE LAND, THE PEOPLE, THE MAN	205
XXV. AMONG THE GRECIAN ISLES	215
XXVI. SMYRNA AND EPHESUS	221
XXVII. FROM ASIA TO GREECE	237
XXVIII. AMONGST SAVANTS	247
XXIX. THROUGH THE HELLESPONT TO THE SUBLIME PORTE	254
XXX. IN AND ABOUT STAMBOUL	260
XXXI. CONSTANTINOPLE AND THE TURKS	267
XXXII. THROUGH ROUMANIA, BULGARIA, SERVIA, HUNGARY AND AUSTRIA	277
XXXIII. VIENNA	283
XXXIV. THROUGH GERMANY DOWN THE RHINE	292
XXXV. HEIDELBERG, WORMS, DOWN THE RHINE TO COLOGNE	299
XXXVI. THREE WEEKS IN LONDON	306
XXXVII. SIGHTS IN LONDON	315
XXXVIII. SCOTLAND—ABBOTSFORD, EDINBURGH, GLASGOW	327

LIST OF ILLUSTRATIONS.

Frontispiece....................................	
St. Peter's Cathedral............................	8
Ship—La Gascogne	19
Leaning Tower..................................	45
Loggia Dei Lanzi—Florence.....................	51
The Colosseum.................................	54
Naples, Bay, Vesuvius...........................	58
Pompeii as Dug Out............................	65
Exhumed Bodies................................	63
Hon. Elihu B. Taft..............................	66
Mill, Bakery, Wine Jar of Pompeii...............	79
Taking a Drink of Water.........................	73
Sakieh for Raising Water........................	74
Cairo from the Citadel..........................	77
Section of the Great Pyramid....................	82
Pylon, or Gate to Egyptian Temple...............	93
Scene on the Nile...............................	98
Water Carrier...................................	106
Slave Boat on the Nile...........................	112
Joppa or Jaffa...................................	119
Women "Grinding at the Mill,"..................	130
Jews' Wailing Place.............................	154
Mount of Olives.................................	164
Jerusalem from the South Side of Olivet..........	171
Sea of Galilee...................................	204
The Acropolis of Athens as it Was................	243
Constantinople..................................	259
City Road Chapel—Wesley's Church, Front View..	316
Interior of City Road Chapel.....................	317
Wesley's Tomb..................................	319
Interior of Westminster Abbey—Choir............	322
St. Paul's Cathedral, London.....................	324
Sir Walter Scott's Monument.....................	330

ST. PETER'S—LARGEST CHURCH ON EARTH.

CHAPTER I.

FROM NORTH CAROLINA TO NEW YORK.

"I have always supposed that the gospel narratives would be more interesting and better understood, and that the instructions of our divine Teacher would fall with more power upon the heart in the places where they were first delivered, than where read or heard on the other side of the world; and to a limited extent I find this to be true."—*The Land and the Book.*

At five or six years of age I read "Peep of Day," in which graphic descriptions of scenes in the life of our Lord awakened a desire to travel over the Holy Land; subsequent reading and education only intensified this desire. And I have often prayed for the privilege and believed it would be afforded. A kind providence anticipated my most sanguine expectations, removing all barriers in the autumn of 1888.

So by January, 1889, preparations for the journey done I went over to Trinity College to see Professors Armstrong and Price, who had spent some years abroad, for such kindly suggestions and advice as they might make, and much to my delight and profit. Dr. Crowell placed a very valuable book in my hands that served me in studying the conditions of things in Europe.

At Archdale I had the good fortune to meet the Rev. Rufus King, who had been to Palestine, and who gave me several valuable hints. Bishop Granberry very kindly gave me a letter commending me to the confidence of such Christian communities as I might visit, with the assurance that I should have his prayers in my behalf, all of which were most cordially appreciated. Dr. Young wrote me a few days ago, to go first to Egypt and Palestine, as the " mercury would soon be too high for comfort there." I never did like mercury and purposed to follow his advice.

Farewells said at home, with a valise as my only traveling companion, I turned my face toward the North.

By way of Richmond you reach Washington at 11 A.M., leaving Greensboro at 8:40 P. M. Our engine killed a very fine cow just before reaching Washington—we stopped and all went back, exept the ladies and children, to see her.

In Washington I called first at the State Department for my passport, after which, it being Wednesday, and Mr. Cleveland's day for receiving visitors, I called at the White House with about one hundred others to be introduced to the President. It is an informal affair; the President stands in a doorway leading out of the East room, and visitors come up to him, say " howdye do, Mr. President?" and pass out. It is simple and does a little good perhaps and no harm. It adds a proportion to American citizenship denied the subjects of most other countries.

I admire the public buildings of Washington enough to write a whole letter about them, but many of my readers have already seen them, and others have written them up in better style than I may hope to do. In all the travel before me I do not expect to see any one building more magnificent than the Capitol of the United States, nor any city more beautiful than Washington, with its fine buildings and parks. Being detained in the White House, I had to wait till four for a train, but the loss of time was more than compensated by the acquaintance of a Mr. Miller, of New York, son of a Presbyterian clergyman. He says in their church they have the Y. P. C. E. S., *i. e.* the Young People's Christian Endeavor Society, and that it works admirably. It is the same thing about which I wrote an article in November. I formed one of the same at Mt. Tabor, on Granville circuit, with twenty-four members. It gives each something to do. We are all very fast learning the fact that, to take stock in anything or expend labor, prayer or thought to further a cause, identifies us with that enterprise as we cannot otherwise be. *

I reached Jersey City at 11:35 P. M., Wednesday, and New York next morning at nine o'clock. I have now been here two days, stopping at the International Hotel, Park Row, opposite the post office first, but as our Steamer leaves to-morrow morning at six, I came down to the Palace Hotel, one square from the pier.

My first care was to put a portion of my cash into the hands of Messrs. Brown Bros., whose letters of credit are honored all over the world where there is a Bank. But they required that I be identified; and Dr. Deems was the only man who knew me in the city. I purposed calling on him for letters of introduction, advice, etc., and called at his house, but he was not at home. I could not find him. But sometimes when things can't be done one way they can another, so I succeeded by the other.

The Cunard and Inman lines send vessels to-morrow to Liverpool, also the Red Star Line to Antwerp. But

---
*It is gratifying to know that since writing the above, the General Conference of our Church has provided for the same thing, calling it the Epworth League. But I was the first to organize one in Southern Methodism.

I chose the *Gascogne* of the French Line to Havre. This is the largest and finest boat in the harbor, capacity seven thousand tons. I chose this also because I might pick up a little French on the way.

I presume I need not dwell on this city much. Everything is done on a magnificent scale. Many of the buildings on Broadway are from six to ten stories high, with high pitched rooms. A. T. Stewart's old property occupies a whole square, and is built of stone as are hundreds of others. The Brooklyn Bridge is the largest suspension bridge in the world. The main span is 1,593 feet 6 inches long, the entire length is 5,989 feet. It is eighty feet wide, and ninety feet high, and would hold altogether fifty thousand people. They have several lines of elevated steam railways, capable of carrying 200 passengers each at a trip; they go about every sixty or seventy seconds during the morning, and the cars are full in the morning and late in the afternoon. They stop every few blocks to let passengers on and off.

Cooper Institute is a magnificent brown stone building, opposite the Bible House, Eighth Street and Bowery. Here is a free reading-room, one hundred feet wide and two hundred long—I am guessing—with a dozen copies each of scores of papers, and thousands of volumes of books; tables with chairs, and desks for standing are plentifully provided for the thousands who come here yearly to read and obtain the knowledge they are too poor to buy elsewhere. About one hundred and fifty were in when I called. Free lectures are given also. Paintings and statuary are on free exhibition. I felt a thrill of admiration for the beneficent founder when I departed. I saw the statue of the Father of his country, in Wall Street at the treasury building, where he took the oath of office as the first President of the United States. I visited the Stock Exchange, where men are made paupers and millionaires by telegraph. And although I have attended many scores of revivals of religion, I have never witnessed such antics as I saw cut there. Men yell and scream much, I imagine, as Indians celebrate a victory won, or Cannibals the dance of death; but others have written up New York.

I noticed a very few colored people in New York, not over a dozen or twenty perhaps. Too cold or too something for Sambo up here.

Another thing: I have seen less smoking on Broadway than one would in a town of a thousand inhabitants, perhaps, in North Carolina. I have seen less than a dozen boys with cigarettes—this I thought remarkable and very creditable. The habit may be smoking at home, I don't know, only I have not seen it to any extent, hardly, in public.

I must relate what will seem to be a narrow escape. It may be serviceable to some young reader expecting to visit the Metropolis. The morning I arrived a familiar looking chap accosted me with, "Hello, Groome, you here!" "Yes," I replied. He endeavored to draw me into conversation, but being in a hurry I escaped him, but to be encountered a few moments later by a more successful accomplice. The first had learned of my home, name, etc., and reported to the second man who said: "I am from Greensboro, and felt as if I *must* speak to you; my name is ———," giving the name of one of the first families in North Carolina, "and we are going to put up a cotton factory in Greensboro; I am here to buy the machinery for it. Let me give you my card and show you our fancy label." He being so well related, and from Greensboro, and putting up a factory, I supposed it was the knitting factory that was going up about that time. I hated to appear so disinterested as to refuse his card and pictures. "They are just here," he said, leading me across Broadway and on a square, chatting very pleasantly. I began to feel, this man is presuming very much to thus waste my time, and the thought occurred to me, he is a "sharper," but I followed him two squares, and he stopped at a very nice looking second class office: "Walk in, Mr. Groome." I paused at the door, he passed in and said to a gentleman writing at a table and in front of a screen: "Is the printing done?" "No," replied the scribe, "sit down and I'll send over for it." "Come in, Mr. Groome, it will be done in a moment, and we will go." "No, thanks, I'll stand here," I said. He then came out and insisted that I come in, wished to know if I were in a hurry, etc., etc. I looked across the street, and a gentleman shook his head violently and gesticulated his warnings. I had already started away. After listening to the proposition of another confidence man to visit a clothing store, I looked straight at him and said: One of your men tried that game on me yesterday! "I don't understand you—what do you mean, Mr. Groome?" Oh, nothing, I replied, except it seems when a man comes to the city looking rustic, he finds himself surrounded by a set of new friends, who—"Good day, Mr. Groome," he said excitedly, and was gone.

These fellows go in pairs; one learns the name and place of residence, reports to the other and thus catch up unwary visitors. They are called "Confidence men."

Once inside of their dens, the door closed, and you may be robbed if not murdered.*

At six o'clock Saturday morning we went aboard.

"The sails are spread, and fair the light wind blows,
As glad to waft him from his native home."

*Since reaching home, two North Carolinians have told me of being swindled in the dens of "Confidence men" in New York.

CHAPTER II.

CROSSING THE SEA.

Before the gangway was pulled ashore and the ship cut from her mooring I penned a few lines, in the early morning light, to loved ones at home, and felt a sensation of fear and peril, new to me and strange, possibly common to those about to cross the ocean for the first time. What lies before me on this waste of water? And if I return not what of the little group that I left weeping a while ago? What right had I to leave any way? Had not one Jonas tried the same with disastrous results? And was he not an example to men of like habits? Are there any other preachers aboard who, like myself, are going forth to widen and deepen their knowledge of men and things that they may bring to the church's service better equipment of both body and mind, who may be a sort of guarantee to me, that God's good providence will guide us safely over? No, not one can be found on the roll, save a Hebrew Rabbi.

About six o'clock, on Saturday morning, a small steam ferry boat that had been fastened to ours, began to move her out towards the channel of the river and turn her prow towards the ocean. So small was the motion that only by sighting distant objects in a line with the opposite end of the vessel could one see her move, but when she at last got into position, and turned her mighty engines loose, her screw churned the sea behind into a foaming whirlpool. We dropped our pilot about the same time as one of the Cunarders. Our engineers determined to run out of sight before night, and did but damaged an engine, causing several hours delay; during the night the tortoise passed the hare, but we afterwards passed them to see them no more.

This is the sixth day we have been out, the first was bright, only one passenger sick, but the second was windy and the usual tributes were paid to Neptune. Sunday night blew a gale. Monday was stormy all day, nearly everybody was sick. We had a musical crew, but no singing.

Lying in our state room the water rising above the ports looked green at first, but when a great wave struck her we would be in the dark. When at last I essayed to go above, the sublimest scene I ever witnessed met my view. The legions of the storm swept the crest from the waves until a fancy net work seemed to be spread out over the sea. Our ship rolled heavily from one side to the other and all movable commodities changed sides accordingly. The storm beat from the starboard quarter, the waves sometimes running over the rail "leaped on the deck like charging giants." She proudly lifted her head, careened to the larboard, shook them off and rushed through the tempest, but to be again attacked by the furious storm king and but to conquer him. When her screw was lifted by her plunging a jarring tremor ran through the ship, but like a thing of life with a goal in view she went groaning, creaking, yet careering on. One can recall but not relate how the wind shrieked through her masts, spars and cordage. It may be weakness, but to see the sea rising above your ship like mountains and sweeping down as if anxious to engulf her, to see her rise momentarily as if by magic to escape certain death, far above, to be plunged again into the deep, the sea ever and anon breaking over, sweeping all movable things from the deck alarms one for the time. You know that death would not have to go far from his course to take you. I was a little more fervent, if no more sincere in my devotions. I renewed my pledges of service, to greater length than at the usual hour of prayer. Thursday morning the storm was gone and we have since had fine weather.

Our ship, *La Gascogne*, is a gallant barque, four masts, and iron from mast to keel. Her entire length is 546 feet by 36 feet wide, capable of carrying 1,500 passengers though there are less than three hundred on board. She was built in 1886. She is a fast boat, has crossed from New York to Havre in seven days. We expect to be out eight days this time. Her draught is 26 feet. When at full speed, on a smooth sea she generates a wave on either side about six feet high, the two aggregating in bulk about what she displaces. These waves stand at an angle of about 40 degrees, and between them and the ship is perfectly smooth. She is driven by three massive engines, aggregating eight thousand (8,000) horse power; she burns one hundred and sixty tons of coal per day, in thirty-six furnaces.

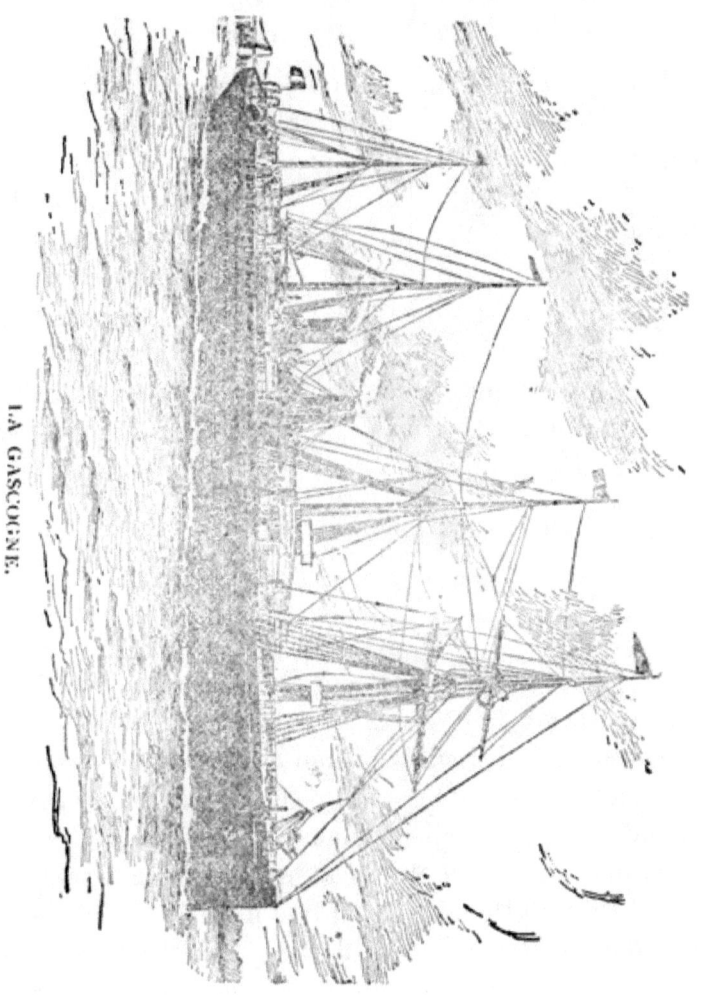

LA GASCOGNE.

Fare on *La Gascogne* is high because the distance is greater than to Glasgow or Liverpool, her ship's crew is larger, and the line, "Compagnie Generale Transatlantique," to which she belongs, has a monopoly of the travel from New York to Havre. She carried on this trip three hundred pouches of United States mail.

The seabirds attended us all the way across. Sometimes they light on the water for a short while and rise to pursue us again. What power of endurance must be locked up in the tiny muscles of their tireless wings. I have

"Marked the seabird wildly wheeling through the skies,"

and considered that,

"God attends him, God defends him when he cries,"

and felt secure.

You never get tired looking at the sea, it is so suggestive, as well as so wonderful. The universal receptacle of the washings of all continents, with their city sewerages, and yet one of the great health giving powers of the world; all the rivers run into it, yet it is not full. Its floor may be covered with the corpses of those who have essayed to traverse its plains, yet it seems at times harmless and inoffensive. You may become familiar with a thousand of its secrets, yet ten thousand are concealed, "emblem of the infinite God, vast, unsearchable, unknowable." Verily, they that go down to the sea in ships, in time of storm, "See his wonders in the mighty deep,"

"When the Almighty's wrath is glassed in storms,"

the highway of all nations, it in turn requires tribute of

them all, type of the Maker's power, type of his love, as it embraces every land, small and great, disbursing its beneficence to all, inspirer of ambition, eloquence and song, paralyzing with fear and dread, when Neptune drives abroad to wreak vengeance on his foes, or soothing to happy dreams, when

"Rocked in the cradle of the deep,"

or one lounges in the shade, some quiet summer evening, near the beach.

"Down by the deep green sea."

What stories could it relate of piratical deeds, of lost and starving crews, of bloody encounter, prosecuted by ambitious thirst for power, covetous thirst for gold and unholy revenge, and not a few of sighing lovers.

"Roll on thou deep and dark and wondrous ocean, roll."

I have formed some pleasant acquaintances; an art student who has studied in Naples, Rome and Germany, and spent a year in New York, is on his way to the Julien School in Paris; two Greeks returning to Sparta, a wealthy Italian, who promises to serve me in Turin, and a Jewish Rabbi from Jerusalem. All these have spent some time in America and acquainted me with many facts relative to the objects of my tour. I have also had the good fortune to be invited, while in Genoa, to the house of an Italian importing merchant, who lives in the same street Columbus did. There are many garrulous Frenchmen aboard, but as yet I have not become acquainted with any of them.

Yesterday and to-day we saw in the North two beautiful rainbows, their reflection on the surface of the water reached almost to the ship. Our artist went into raptures over them. He is sketching almost everything, has got me down in black and white.

And I will tell our young readers how illustrative sketches are made: first, outlines are made with an ordinary graphite pencil, these are filled with a pen and ink, this is photographed on a plate of gelatine, making a *fac simile* of the illustration, this plate is after this submitted to acid treatment, when all is eaten off except the photographed impression, which now projects above the other surface; from this is made the stereotype plate, from which any number of pictures may be taken.

About 1 o'clock P. M., Sunday, the 8th day from New York, *La Gascogne* dropped anchor a mile from the wharf at Havre. But we did not go ashore till 4 P. M., when we were told that the train then in waiting was the only one that would carry us on our tickets to Paris. The alternative was presented of losing the fare or traveling on Sunday; we reluctantly and perhaps unfortunately chose the latter.

CHAPTER III.

FRANCE.

No one expects to go to Europe without visiting Paris. She has learned to project herself into the thought of every civilized people. As Apollo was consulted at Delphi, the goddess of Fashion sits on the tripod and dictates here. God Mars likewise has long held his court here, in the *cite* in the Seine, and here only is learned the par excellent *code de cuisine*, (way to cook).

The transformations of her civil and social life exhibit all the variety of the kaleidoscope, now grave, now gay, humorous, stoical, ancient, modern, full of churches yet irreligious, surpassing all others in contributing to life's reliefs and indulgences, yet the most reckless in sacrificing life, to-day it is *vive la roi*, to-morrow it is the guillotine. Strange, beautiful, mysterious metropolis, we will enter thy gates, walk thy streets and boulevards, visit thy cathedrals, *cimetieres* and gardens, thy palaces, towers and temples and briefly study thy pleasure-loving people. It was 9 o'clock P. M., when we reached Paris. It was Sunday and election day. Gen. Boulanger had just defeated Jacques, Radical. The citizens thronged every square of the magnificently illuminated capitol, and wild shouts rent the air at every item favorable first to one contestant and then the other. Fatigued, we sought our couch, but the enthusiasm without was unabated for hours. On going abroad next day we found that Paris was painted red, yellow and green with large posters representing the various claims of the rival candidates to represent the district of Seine in the House of the Deputies; at least one hundred thousand circulars varying in size from four feet square and under were posted in the city, and from what little French I am able to read, I think the same methods are resorted to here to defeat one's opponents as at home. The friends of one candidate would cover the posters of his opponent with their own; these would be covered again until they would be forty deep, one for Jacques, one for Boulanger throughout. They were pasted on everything that would hold them by the thoroughfares, but all were cleaned off nicely on Monday. I made effort to visit the Senate and House of Deputies also, but failed, as considerable red tape is required, which I discarded, rather than lose the time.

I visited the *Place de la Bastile*, which is occupied by a monument commemora.ing the bravery of "French Soldiers in 1827, 1828 and 1829."

The base and pedestal are marble, the column proper is bronze, on top is a bronze figure representing the Genius of Liberty holding in one hand a torch, in the other a broken chain, the ascent is by a spiral stairway of two hundred and twelve steps, and from the top one has a fine view of the city. There is an interesting history connected with this column. It is on the site of the prison by the same name, which was built over five hundred years ago by Kings Charles V. and VI., not used at first for a prison, but afterwards was used to confine persons of rank. It was destroyed at the beginning of the French revolution, July, 1789. The present column was well nigh destroyed by the commune in 1871.

Hotel de Ville is one of the finest buildings in the city.

It contains the town hall and offices of the municipal authorities, but is not yet completed on the interior ; the facade is very imposing; in niches of the second, third and fourth stories are statues of the Celebrities of Parisian history. Here also was a rallying point for the revolutionists in 1789; to this place Louis XVI. came from Versailles in procession, testifying his submission to the will of the National Assembly. Here the two Huguenot Chiefs died by order of Catherine de Medici, after the massacre of St. Bartholomew. Here Foulon, treasurer, and his son-in-law were hung to lamp-posts during the Revolution, and here perished many another victim.

The Palais Royal is near by, built by Cardinal Richelieu, in the early part of the seventeenth century. It also is connected with many a tale of royal dissipation, faithlessness and misery. It has been owned in turn by French and German kings and people. It was also well nigh burned down by the commune in 1871, but has been since rebuilt. Here one sees the finest display of jewelry in Paris; in one window are hundreds of bracelets, selling at fancy prices; watches, chains, charms, ear-rings, pins, etc., etc., with diamonds worth thousands of dollars. They are arranged in rows, in rings, in stars, in pyramids and all manner of fantastic forms, all pleasing to the eye. Occasionally one sees the sign, "English Spoken," but I find it often not so; if "one speaks English" you are the one, yet any of them can make a trade; in fact every article has marked on it the price in francs. There are more restaurants here than any other kind of shops, and living is cheap or dear, according to what you wish. One can dine anywhere for five cents or five dollars, as one pleases. One notable thing about bread is that it is all baked alike, in long, light rolls, one to five feet long. I have seen scores of persons carrying bread in their arms, exactly as a boy carries a turn of wood. Occasionally t is carried in baskets, mostly in hand, arm or apron. Lee Merriwether remarked that they sell bread here "by the yard;" another author says by the "ell (as in Cambridgeshire they sell butter by the yard)."

Paris contains a reading people, judging both from the number of book-stores and news-stands, and the number of papers published daily at one cent each. As far as I could judge, I think much wine is drunk, but very little whiskey or cognac.

I visited the churches of Notre Dame, St. Sulpice and the Holy Sepulchre. St. Sulpice, a very large structure, four hundred and sixty-two by one hundred and eighty-three feet, by one hundred and eight feet high, supported interiorly by thirty-two stupendous columns rising to the height of seventy or eighty feet, they support an arched ceiling of marble or stone. This church contains eighteen chapels, beside a nave where the faithful were worshiping during my visit; this is the second oldest church in Paris, Notre Dame being the oldest.

This church is on the site of a church of the fourth century; it was consecrated in 1182, but the nave was not completed until the thirteenth century. The finest part of the Cathedral is the facade facing the West; the three portals are adorned with the finest gothic workmanship. There is one window in this church said to be fifty-four feet high. Notre Dame is five hundred and seventeen feet long, one hundred and fifty-six feet wide, and the vaulting in the nave is one hundred and ten feet high. It has passed through the revolution and witnessed much bloodshed; within its portals reason has been deified and the true light seemingly extinguished. To the credit of Napoleon it was opened, by his order, for Divine worship again.

I spent a day in the Louvre, situated in a place once infested by wolves, when this was a forest; hence its name. It covers several acres of land; it contains the largest collections of paintings in the world, besides a large collection of relics from Babylon, Ninevah and Egypt; immense Sarcophagi, Statuary Mummies, etc. Here is a dinner table in mosaic, displaying ducks and fatted fowl in gorgeous colors, yet the pieces of stone of which they are made are often no larger than a pin-head, many thousands of pieces are required for one bird, yet the picture is complete in every detail, and the surface of the table is as smooth as a pane of glass. The cost must have been many thousands of dollars. Among the Statuary I believe the Venus de Milo is thought to be the best, though now time-worn and abused by handling.

I spent much time in the SALLE of the Italian School; a novice can discern the superiority of these in outline and faultless blending of colors. One becomes intoxicated with admiration, and dazed before the splendid panoramas.

Passing still down the beautiful quay you enter the Jardin des Tuilleries, once reserved for Royalty alone, it is now a public esplanade, enjoyed by happy lovers, gay soldiers, nurses and hundreds of romping children rolling hoops, spinning tops, etc. Next is the *Place du Carousal*, where Louis XIV. gave an equestrian ball, 1662, and where fetes have been held ever since. The

Arc de Triomph now stands there, and is small in comparison with its surroundings. Next is the Court of the Tuilleries which, with the Jardin, and *Elysees Champs* transcends the most lofty ideas I had conceived of their beauty, on farther at *Place de Concorde*, where thousands of gay and idle denizens assemble every afternoon, is the Obelisk brought from Egypt, with its silent eloquence. I turned aside to see the Panorama—siege of Paris in 1870-1, but was disappointed; it was inferior as a work of art to the Battle of Bull Run, as seen in Washington by the same artist, Poilpot. Up the same Boulevard, one and one-half miles farther, though it does not seem half a mile, is *Arc d' Etoile*, begun by Napoleon I., after his Austrian campaign, and finished twenty or thirty years later; he is the only cognizable figure on the facade. He is being crowned as a conqueror.

I visited the *Hospital des Invalides* and saw many of the wounded soldiers of their last war. Near by is the Tomb of Napoleon I. which I did not enter, it being closed, but which I presume is the most colossal tomb that has been built in a thousand years. The dome and cross on top are bronze; around the silent chieftain hang the tattered colors riven on many a gory field. A spell hangs over the place and falls on the intruder into such a presence.

I visited the cemetery *Pere La Chaise*, and saw the tomb of Abelard and Heloise, whose pathetic history has been read around the world. Their effigies lie in state upon two sarcophagi under a small canopy, and if in life divided, they are in death united. Here lie many others once famous in letters, eloquence and diplomacy.

The Palace of the Luxomburg, built by Mary de

Medici is a magnificent structure combining Tuscan, Doric and Ionic orders of architecture. It has been occupied by kings, consuls and socialists. It is now a museum of art.

I was greatly interested in *Jardin des Plantes*, founded by Louis XIII., where I spent a morning. Time would fail to tell of the reptiles, fossils, birds, beasts, savage and tame, carniverous, herbivorous and omnivorous. Here were bears, lions, tigers, cats, hyenas, wolves, etc., etc., from Africa, Asia and America; storks and cranes tall as a man, pelicans, with sacks large enough to hold a gallon under their bills, ostriches, hawks, and the giant condor from South America; one white bird had a green tuft on the back of its head from my stand point, like a bunch of grass. Here are seals, antelopes, bison, reindeer, kangaroo, deer, zebras, etc., *ad infinitum*.

The *Jardin des Vivants Plantes* was closed, but one could see the vast collections through the glass sides, and by it a cedar of Lebanon about three feet in diameter.

I went to the markets and priced a good many things to ascertain the comparative cost of a table support with what it is in North Carolina. The difference is small. The meats are of a fine quality. They have jack rabbits three times as large as any in North Carolina, and they are plentiful.

One is pleased with the fine Norman draught horses used. One horse carries over a ton of coal, often two tons on a cart, about the streets; two horses haul ten to twelve tierces of molasses often. On one omnibus forty to fifty persons will go, drawn by two horses till a grade is reached, when a third is hitched in.

I visited one branch of the McAll Mission and conversed with a missionary about another, Le Bruin.

They are prosecuting a vigorous work, have services every day at the dispensary; free lectures are delivered every day to the invalid poor, who receive free treatment. Many young women are educated and afterwards given employment, and homes are found for the destitute. They claim that the school was asked of God in prayer and given by Him in answer thereto—and in the anteroom many verses of scripture are quoted on the walls as proof of the legitimacy of their position, and which all Christians with much experience can believe. They are prosecuting a vigorous work and will be perceptibly felt in that gangrenous capitol.

The weather was fair and considering the brevity of my stay, I had a fine opportunity of studying French outdoor city life.

They are a gay and contented looking people, and notwithstanding the words, "*Libertie, Egalitie, Fraternitie,*" are engraved or painted over the portals of every public building the iron paling, fifteen feet high around them, and the jail-like defences in front of private windows tell that up to this time a commune was not only a possibility, but a probability at any time.

The poor had a way of exposing themselves in order to be hurt by passing vehicles, as they were supported during convalescence. The custom became so general as to require an ordinance fining anyone who was hurt by such means. Of course few were found willing to pay a fine for the luxury of being run over by a cab.

Hotel Haute Loire, 203 Boulevard Raspail and B. Vard, Mt. Parnasse is a good one, and convenient to the Exposition grounds and places of most interest, and English is really spoken.

CHAPTER IV.

PARIS TO ITALY.

Having spent several days in Paris, visiting the various places and objects that claim a stranger's notice, as the *Louvre*, depository of the most famous works of Art from the most ancient to modern times, *Jardin des Plants*, where perhaps the largest collection of plants in the world are to be seen, a very large exhibit of animals, birds, reptiles, fossils, &c., &c., *Jardin du Luxembourg, Tuilleries, Champs Elysees*, Boulevards, Arches, Towers, &c., &c., the most comprehensive exhibit of goods for the shambles extant, I left this city so famed for displays, for men of science, learning and war, for its love of the beautiful and blood for Italy. We soon ran into the green gardens that feed the vast population on vegetables. We see thousands of plants under glass vessels about gallon measures, to protect them from cold, and going up the Seine, we soon run into the wildest scenery, seemingly, "where mortal foot hath ne'er or rarely been," but find it is only a park which has doubtless been preserved by the decéndants of some feudal lord, it is here the large hares of which we saw so many are grown. Up the Seine we fly, now over a bridge now under one, all of which are built of stone, beautiful villas adorn the brows of the hills, and grassy meadows lie between, green to the very water's edge, even in mid winter. We are now at the head of navigation; here is a dam thrown across, ah, no, there is a lock, and boats can pass; here is another park and balsams and other evergreens are thick; we emerge from the forest and here is another villa, where once a Feudal Baron lived in State upon the hard earnings of his serfs. Not all the griefs of the feudal system are gone from republican France yet, as the little patches of ground, the thached roofs that cluster about some pretentious mansion, as well as other facts of modern history testify. We see the washer women down by the river bank with their goods. This is the custom both in France and elsewhere in Europe. I met with the same trouble in leaving Macon that Lee Meriwether had in getting there, I could find no one speaking English, nor any one who could understand my French, *ou est le convoi pour Modane?** said I to a number of men; they would all tell me something, but I could not understand, finally I got on the right one. The real trouble was this; I found the right train but the wrong side, they would show me the one and motion round, I would go round and try to take another and say, *ici pour Modane?* One can enter the cars from only one side at any one station. Sleeping a few hours I awoke to look out upon snow-capped mountains. Soon we enter a valley and the mountains begin to look higher and higher, on we sweep through a dozen tunnels up a beautiful, sinuous stream. We reach *Lac de Bourget*, a beautiful sheet of water, clear as crystal with a greentint at the bottom that renders it with mountains beyond and strip of fog and solitary farm house and flying duck all reflected on its quiet face a picture fit for any artist's pencil.

The public road up this valley surpasses anything of its kind I have ever seen, graded as carefully as the railroad with stones set to mark every mile, and round

---
*Where is the train for Modane?

stones every few feet to guard the trees planted every twenty or thirty feet for shade in summer. I heartily wish every road maker in America could see it. The bridges are all of stone or iron.

By the falls in the river beside the railroad, I know we are rising fast, as well as by the snow, which is now deepening on the ground. Thousands of feet above the threatening craggs look down. High up as material could be carried the mountaineer has fastened his cottage, the eaves seeming to be buried in the mountain on the upper side; why they should have been put there, all beyond being inaccessible, approach to them almost impossible—except to the birds or the chamois—is as great a mystery as to tell how their children can be reared without falling out of doors and rolling over the precipices to the valley below. Soon we will reach Mt. Cenis tunnel, no, we stop at Modane till midnight.

Modane, at the State boundary, is a pretty little Italian town. I learn here the way they have of making a passenger pay for his ticket and enough besides to pay the government tax on the railroads; five *centimes* above the price stamped on the *billet* is the universal custom. On the mountains around Modane many cannon frown upon all the avenues of travel, defying any other Napoleon to pass these mountains to surprise and capture a lethargic land.

Custom-house officers, which are found at nearly every town of any size, expect *pour bois*, or drink money, for the pains of searching through your baggage. I begin to practice on these border Italians, with the purpose of paying just as little cash for having my valise emptied as possible, so I appear not to understand what they mean. I say "English," "no understand." "*Non parlo l'Italiano!"* To all their pantomimes, which really mean, pay me a *lira*, I look like a dummy and pass on.

It is after midnight on the first day of February when the cars leave Modane *gare* (station) heading towards Turin. The ground is covered with snow, and our compartment is warmed up by two large zinc tanks half filled with hot water. One can rest his feet on these and keep warm; they are changed about every two hours for hotter ones. In case of an accident there would be no danger of fire except from the lamps, but they are altogether insufficient for warming travelers as our American cars do.

There is a long step outside reaching the whole length of the coach; along this the officer running the train sometimes walks to see if all is well, and in some European States to collect or punch the ticket.

There is a large number of officials at every station; only one or two employees on each train. The porters and ticket collectors are at the stations. It is difficult to leave the train without their aid. The advantage of having them at the station is that fewer men can do the work.

From Paris to Rome there is a train every hour or two, and the same agents attend to them all, besides doing local work. The cars have eight or ten doors opening on the sides to compartments having two seats each perpendicular to the course of the train, the passengers occupying them being *vis-a-vis*. The doors are doubly fastened on the outside and one can scarcely reach the fastening from within. When you wish to descend you have to beat the door and yell for a porter. One is seldom asked for a *billet* (ticket) while aboard, but when leaving the train the passenger has to pass through a gate, where his ticket is demanded. In Italy without a ticket one has to pay four times the price of one. If one rides on a first class car when he has a second class ticket, three times the difference between the fares is required. So I learned from fellow travelers. The class is marked in large I's, thus: First class, I; second class, II; third class, III, on the door to each compartment.

Some trains are only first class throughout, others first and second classes, again they are mixed, and when they are the classes of coaches are mixed sure enough. They are coupled together regardless of order, and the mail is coupled in the rear. There are no conveniences on any trains run for the public in Europe.

The style of these cars is favorable for murder or robbery, being in compartments as elsewhere described, so electric bells are provided in case of foul play, which has occurred on some English railways.

At five o'clock, passing Mont Cenis tunnel, we are in Turin, called by the Italians Turino, a beautiful city and once the capital of Piedmont. We go from this place to Pisa and Florence.

CHAPTER V.

GENOA—"PEARL OF THE SEA."

About sun up we reached the Po, on whose classic banks still weep the unhappy sisters of the rash, unfortunate Phaëton, who, alternately freezing and scorching the earth while driving the chariot of the Sun, was cast by Jove down headlong into this stream. At least Ovid so told us when a boy. We ascend a ravine down which plunges a beautiful rivulet, on whose banks are many villages, through another tunnel about two miles long, and down another gorge towards Genoa, called by the Italians Genova. It is the wealthiest city in Italy, containing with its suburbs 180,000 people. Half of the males of proper age are soldiers; half of the male passengers on the cars are soldiers.

On reaching Genoa I was met at the train by ——, a host of porters, and men and boys wanting to help me, ready to take one's valise, either with or without his permission.

The first thing that greets one's eye on entering the street is the statue erected to Christopher Columbus, the figure of America kneeling at the base of the statue, and the allegorical figures of Religion, Geography, Strength and Wisdom seated around, and between which are reliefs of scenes from the discoverer's life. It was built about twenty-seven years ago.

I worshiped on Sunday at the English church, and

heard an average sermon from Math. 8:24, after which I introduced myself to the rector and inquired about Protestant religion in Genoa. He and a Presbyterian minister have four churches which are useful chiefly in affording seamen and travellers with church privileges. Italians do not take to Protestants. To their mind it is like "carrying coals to New Castle." I heard the Waldensian preacher, however, preach a sermon in Italian to a crowded house, and the Holy Spirit seemed to rest on him and his people throughout the service.

I was favorably impressed with the Genoese; there is quite a contrast between them and the French; if anything they are more ostentatious, and are a much better looking people.

And historians say all their energies have been concentrated on making money, whence it has come to pass that she is the wealthiest city in all Italy. She has not been rich in the Arts nor Sciences, but has contributed indirectly to their encouragement.

Some say Genoa derives its name from the likeness of the bay on which it is built to a knee, called in Latin, *genu*. The mountains press close down upon the sea, giving but little level land on which to build, but if they could not build wide they certainly built high. The average height of the buildings of the entire city is probably six stories. Many of the streets are very narrow, not over eight feet wide.

The police of Genoa are a very fine looking set of men; they dress finely, wearing silk hats and their clothes cut in the latest styles. Both in Paris and Genoa a peculiar kind of dray is used—two long skids, say thirty feet long, between which at one end stands the horse, for they are both for shafts and body to the dray, are balanced on the axle about two feet apart, and braced together from end to end; on these poles or scantlings the load of boxes, bags or barrels will be packed to the amount of two or three tons. When the load is too heavy for one horse another is hitched in front of him, a third in front of the second, and so on. Such gearing is inconvenient, and often on turning corners the horse next to the load is thrown down, often the load pitching forward preventing him from rising. No place on earth needs a law preventing cruelty to animals worse than Genoa.

I arrived on Saturday—blue Saturday. I was amazed to see thousands of windows full of clothes hung out to dry, until I reflected, there is no where else to dry them, except by the fire. So it was the raggedest town I ever saw. While Genoa is so wealthy the majority of her citizens are poor. There is little to do. I saw nothing to indicate that they were lazy. On the wharves men stood around waiting for ships to come in, anxious for a job. Others were sweeping the streets for the sweepings. There were few or no gossiping groups. They are striving to improve their people morally, have many institutions of charity, asylums for destitute children and abandoned women, and a statute was enacted during my sojourn with a view of suppressing as far as possible the existing lewdness. Copies of this ordinance were carried through every street next day and thousands of copies distributed.

I should not have been able to glean so many facts but for the kindness of the Italian merchant previously referred to. He showed me the churches and explained the events connected with them—the monuments, walls, palaces, and the institutions of the city. I saw the house Columbus was born in, and also that which his father was born in; they are near together. The first is seven stories high, while those on either side are eight. It has a brown stuccoed front, and is perhaps 1,000 years old. Near by are the old city walls, on which for some years hung the chains taken from subjugated Pisa, but restored when Italia was united under one government, and which I saw hanging in Campo Santo at Pisa. In a small museum here are exhibited the instruments of torture used during the inquisition, and life-like figures in wax showing the marks made upon martyrs of those days; one for clipping off the end of the tongue, one with iron teeth in a band fitting around the head, the band being in two sections with arms like tongs, which enabled the one using it to apply lever power for pressing the iron teeth into the skull, chills the beholder's blood.

The church of St. Lorenzo is built of alternate layers of black and white marble, the interior is finely decorated with paintings and statuary and is very impressive. This church is said to contain the body of John the Baptist in a gold coffin, taken from the Venetians. By paying one of the sextons a small fee he will take you around to the rear of the chapel of St. John (the church contains several chapels) even during service there, strike a match which makes even more weird the ghostly light of the place and explain how that this (marble) coffin is not the other (gold) one, that contains the real body of John, and for the privilege of seeing which you paid your money, and which can be shown by him after the visitor, by much ceremony, obtains a special permit. As we expected to visit several other cities where John Baptist has bodies, we desisted from further effort to see this one.

St. Ambrose is the oldest and wealthiest church in the city, and had many worshipers in its chapels during our visit on Monday.

The Exchange was about as busy as that in New York, though not so wild; here is the marble statue of Cavour, the great statesman, who died endeavoring to unite his countrymen into one commonwealth. He triumphed, but like most others whose lives are given to the development of great schemes, he did not live to realize the benefit of his endeavors. He is represented as seated, giving counsel. It was for a long time the dream of Italian statesmen to unite their country, but the difficulties of locomotion previous to railroads, together with local prejudices and popular ignorance forbade the feasibility of such a project. The application of steam to facilitate and so to multiply production, travel and commerce will not only unite larger territories, but establish a widespread homogeneity, gradually introducing similar manners the world over. Clothing houses in London now supply retailers in all the large cities of the world. The shoes worn here now would be styled by a certain modern Southern evangelist "tooth-picks."

The toga of the ancient Roman is modernised into a cloak or talma reaching to the knees and folding twice in front of the wearer, the border passing over the shoulder and falling down the back. They look graceful.

Costa Agostino, my Italian friend, gained admission for me into some of the principal palaces. We visited that of Duke Galiera, who gave 24,000,000 *lirae* to improve the harbor by building about a mile of breakwater. It was made of stone and blocks of hydraulic lime and sand weighing some twenty tons each. This wall rises nearly thirty feet above the level of the sea and is about thirty feet broad. Result: one of the best harbors in the world, while it is the busiest in Italy. The walls are in two sections, between which vessels enter port.

The authorities have police cruising near the shore all the time to protect the fish from dynamiters.

Galiera's wife built the hospital of St. Andrew, capable of succoring two thousand inmates, I judge, at one time.

The palace of Spinola on Via Roma contains the portrait of Andrew Doriá, once the Princeps of Liguria, also his statue in marble, together with portaits of a dozen of their pristine chiefs; bird's eye views of the principal cities of Italy are painted on the walls of the upper halls. It is used for government offices partly.

I saw the daughter of the woman who saved Garibaldi by concealing him three days in* her house. A marble slab above the door in *piazza di Sarzano* marks the place. It happened thus: He advocated a republic; the King sought his life; he hid in the house of a coalseller; on the third day he shaved, put on the coal dealer's clothes, took a bag of coal on his shoulder, passed out the city gates and was safe.

The Mazzini palace is the *Palais Royal* of Genoa. The exhibits there quite equal those of Broadway, N. Y.

They have a small but very pretty park in the center of the city called *Vilatta di Nigro*. From the elevated summit of this beautiful place I first saw the blue Mediterranean, whose history would be almost a history of the world. As I gazed I pondered on stories of Jason and of Jonah, of Xerxes and the Greeks, of Troy and Anchises' Son, of the Phœnicians, Syracusans, Carthaginians and Colombo.

Millions may rest in the Necropoles of Egypt, but who could number the shipwrecked victims asleep with the Mermaids there!

In this park is the statue of Joseph Mazzini in marble, twenty feet high, and the equestrian statue of Victor Emmanuel, the first King of United Italy.

Leaving Genoa the road winds through the Riviera towards Leghorn for three or four hours nearly half the time under-ground, suddenly you dart out into a villa prettier than any picture, and scores of them rivalling any residences on Fifth Avenue adorn the hills facing the sea.

The grandeur of such scenery is more easily imagined than described in which beetl'ng crags, barren or crowned with verdant shrubbery now swing over our flying coach, now are penetrated by it or recede far up in proud disdain, the terraced sides and valleys between, clad in vines, olives and chestnuts, while on our right the sea in mimic combat charges almost into the windows of our car, but the surf is lost in spray or recedes, to be swallowed up, the sun sinks into the gilded bosom of the deep and the kaleidoscope revolves to show by twilight's milder ray what "Heaven hath done for this delightful land." We leave the coast run up the Arno and are soon in Pisa, where we stop for a day.

CHAPTER VI.

PISA, FLORENCE.

All the way from Alessandria to Pisa the most luxuriant gardens are to be seen. I counted thirteen different kinds of green salad in one near Genoa and have seen scores like it.

Pisa is an average looking city with massive walls and iron gates, still kept closed at night, as when they were a republic, or a kingdom. Pisa, you know, was founded by Pelops, the grand-son of Jove, and son of Tantalus and Phrygia, and was once the most war-like of any of the Italian states. They whipped the Greeks once at Constantinople. She boasts the oldest university of any country, giving to the world Galileo.

His lamp still swings in the Duomo; but has never suggested a new idea to a mortal since. There are four buildings which all foreigners passing this way think it worth while to visit. The Duomo, the Leaning Tower, the Baptistery and the Campo Santo.

The Duomo was built largely of the spoils of the Saracens of Palermo, in the expedition undertaken A. D. 1063. There are seventy-two columns in the interior of the church, of granite and marble; vast amounts of *verde antique lapislazuli, porphyry, bronze* and *gilt* adorn this temple. The design is by Michael Angelo, and is in the shape of a Latin cross, the style is a mixture of the Grecian and Arabic. The floor is marble mosaic—curious designs; ceiling black and gilt; the main altar is separated from the nave by a marble balustrade about seven feet high; within is a black cross with the figure of Christ upon it, suspended from the ceiling about sixty or seventy feet. The cross is about four by six feet. There is a marble piazza about twenty feet wide all round the outside of the Duomo, and the green grass in the campus renders the whole a fresh and pleasing object to the eye.

Immediately to the rear of the Duomo is the Baptistery, built by one florin from every citizen of the republic in the thirteenth century. Here is a large font of Parian marble and one of the finest pulpits in the world. The peculiar attraction of this structure is the echo: sing a few notes and pause, and they are heard far up in the dome, and after a few moments still farther up, but fainter; so, says a gifted writer, "good deeds, hardly noted in our grosser atmosphere, awake a divine echo in the far world of spirits."

We went from the Baptistery to Campo Santo (sacred camp, or cemetery). The earth in the old portion between the walls was brought from Jaffa, when the Tuscan Knights made their memorable pilgrimage to the Holy Land: it was put in their boats for ballast; it is claimed that it will decompose any human body in two days. The walls around this form a rectangle and display many frescoes of the fourteenth century, with sixty-two Gothic arcades.

I had always thought the Leaning Tower was on a hillside and leaned toward the West; it is in a great plain, as is the whole city, and leans toward the South. I ascended to the top, where Galileo so often surveyed

LEANING TOWER OF PISA.

the planetary worlds. The whole is of marble and granite. There is nothing to prevent one from falling from the first seven stories except about eight feet of railing in front of the doors. The top has an iron rail all the way round. Here one has a fine view of the Carrara mountains, supplying a good quality of marble, of the winding course of the Arno to the sea and upwards many miles towards Florence, the city lies at our feet.

Just out of Pisa we noticed factories making cotton cloth, of all the gaudy styles.

Nearly all of the rich, alluvial bottom land of the Arno from Pisa to Florence, (called here Firenze) is planted in grapevines. The land is laid off by ditches into irregular rectangles; on each side is a row of trees, cut off six to ten feet high and allowed to grow, but kept cut short; these support the vines and at the same time supply thousands of twigs, annually, for willow-ware; between the ditches, say forty yards, the land is cultivated in wheat, gardens, &c. They turn it mostly with a spade. They drive heifers large as ordinary oxen; also a car-load of them was being shipped, all milk-white.

At Florence many donkeys are driven to buggies and drays; the horses are all, or nearly all, very poor, and seemed to be driven almost to death, and poorly fed.

Their dogs are all either muzzled when on the streets or led by their masters or mistresses. I saw, for the first time a woman in our hotel here smoking a cigar. In all the cities visited since leaving New York, nearly every square has little booths where all the papers of the nation are on sale. These are a reading people, they have dozens of book-stores and libraries; every *caffè* is expected to have a dozen papers on the tables for customers to read while sipping their coffee, milk or wine. All their daily papers sell for one cent each. It is only a question as to who holds the helm, to determine whither the ship will drive.

There are many unsettled questions in Italy yet, but the decline of the papal power is not one of them, and looking at papal Italy in one of her strongest holds, I do not think any great nation of the world has anything to fear from this source, except that deadness to spirituality which seems to rest on her votaries. Compromising on forms, she gives ease to the conscience of many who are spiritually dead.

At S. Spirito Annunziata to-day, filled with worshippers, many on their knees, followed visitors around the church with their eyes; one man on his knees was talking to another standing up. One no doubt pious woman dropped her penny into the contribution box, by the door, and stooped and kissed it as she retired.

This church and the Duomo have remarkable resounding qualities, and the priests with their choristers and responsive readings, make a noise about equal to a dozen hives of swarming bees.

The church, whose worship is a strange compound of Jewish and Pagan customs, and whose doctrines pander to all the natural propensities of fallen human nature, has run to great extremes. I was reproved by a Catholic for singing, "Let the Saviour in," as wanting in reverence. Yet he frequently took God's name in vain, and swore continually. He was, however, no doubt, sincere in his reproof.

The Duomo engaged the greatest architects known to fame. Across the street from the Dom two figures in marble are seated, one holding a trestle-board on which designs of the building are drawn and at which his eyes are gazing as if he contemplated changes. This is Brunelleschi. Hard by this sits Michael Angelo, with face upturned towards the dome. He studies it as a model for St. Peters.

We went to St. Croce to look upon the tombs of the Popes, Cardinals, Poets, Sculptors, Architects and great men whom the Italians and Catholics have delighted to honor. We found the inscriptions on many a gravestone worn smooth by the feet of many visitors. Galileo's tomb is a sarcophagus of variegated marble. He sits on it with telescope in hand, and gazes into the heavens.

> "In Santa Croce's holy precincts lie
>   Ashes which make it holier, dust which is,
> Even in itself, an immortality,
>   Though there were nothing save the past and this,
> The particle of those sublimities
>   Which have relapsed to chaos; here repose
> Angelo's, Alfieri's bones, and his,
>   The starry Galileo, with his woes;
> Here Machiavelli's earth returned to whence it rose.

We do the *Uffizzi, Palatine, Buornorotti, Ancient and Modern* galleries, the *Piazzas*, Gardens, &c. I will let the Rev. J. M. Buckley, D. D., Editor of *The Christian Advocate*, New York, who was in Florence about the same time as myself, and who calls this city the shrine of Art, Science and Literature, speak for me as to the impression made by Florentine galleries. He says:

"After several days spent in the galleries and palaces of Florence I found my eyes 'dim with excess of light" and my mind in a confused state—basins of porphyry, portraits of Samson, banners of Italian cities, mosaics and ceilings painted in imitation of mosaics, Judith and Holofernes,, Madonnas and saints without number, the Magi, Venus, Bacchus, St. Paul, Cæsar, tombs, cherubs, Laocoons, satyrs with gaps in their teeth, Cupids on a dolphin, Amazons fighting, small gray birds with red crests, heads of the Medusa death of Virgin Mary, angels with mandolin, massacre of innocents, Luther's wife, kings on horseback, gamblers struck by lightning, columns of oriental alabaster, vases of rock crystal, portraits of popes and cardinals and of Pluto, men with apes upon their shoulders, boar hunts, ancient bronze helmets, spurs, lamps, old manuscripts, vaulted aisles and statues of the archangel Michael, all thrown together, with the names of Van Dyck, Reubens, Correggio, Raphael, Da Vinci, and Titian indiscriminately applied to them. I was intoxicated with art. But after a few days my vision clarified, and there came out a score of paintings and statues as distinctly impressed upon the mind's eye as the most vivid perception of the physical orb. All the rest is lost in the *milky way* of finite memory, but those which remain will shine on until the canopy is darkened with the shadowing of the oblivion in which our most delightful sensations, as well as those which are painful, are lost."

By a fortunate accident I was permitted to see Pitti Palace, where the King resides, when in Florence; the walls of each room are covered with silk, and the color and design of each is different. The upholstery corresponds with the finish of the walls, which in the King's bed-room is lemon-colored silk, filled with rich designs; the Ball-room, King's Reception, Bed-room, Budoir, and Throne-room, the Queen's Reception-room and Bed-room, the royal Dining-room with chairs set for sixty-six were shown; Victoria and Dom Pedro *et alii* ate here last year at a great reception given by Humbert I. We were shown through the rooms of the Prince of Naples, then through the archives, in which were stored thousands of pieces of gold and silver plate.

The day was done and returning to our hotel we queried, "Will the world ever get what it needs?" viz:

Men of brains and prestige and means to go to work for man? Yes, possibly these will be forthcoming, when the church and society following shall put a proper premium on that kind of labor, rather than on a selfish monopolizing, yet tipping plutocracy.

Only let Christians of means indicate in their intercourse with the poor that the religion of Christ is a source of more enjoyment than earthly possessions, that a man's life consisteth not in the abundance of things possessed, but in enjoying sunshine, air, water, sleep, digestion, domestic affection, social intercourse and in mutual service, in serving one's generation according to the will of God, and a simple reliance upon the Lord Jesus Christ for everlasting life. Let it be shown until the restless striker shall see that there is no monopoly of all the best things and cannot be.

How many more decades will poor human society torture her children before the Golden Rule so well fitted, if obeyed, to perfect all conditions of society, will be read and believed?

Let those with the light lead the way.

LOGGIA DEI LANZI—FLORENCE.

CHAPTER VII.

ROME.

I must *also* see Rome.—*Paul.*

From Florence to Rome is about six hours on the fast train; I found a good hotel near the station, and set out to see Rome, old and new, in company with Dr. Tagert, of Chicago. We started first to St. Peter's, the largest church on earth. The Egyptian obelisk seen in front of the church is 82 feet 9 inches high, and is said to be the only ancient monument in Rome that has not been overthrown. The entire outlay for columns, fountains, buttresses, statues of saints, of which there are 162, with the pavement in front of the church was over $1,000,000.

Before the end of the 17th century this church had cost $50,000,000; the new sacristy cost $950,000; the yearly expense is $37,500; and the church is not yet done. But one is met on the threshold, in the aisles, under the colonnades and on all sides by filthy and ragged beggars, and that in abundance.

In the gallery is a bronze statue of Hercules, for which Pope Pius IX gave Baron Righetti 268,000,750 francs, about $53,200,150, and it was impossible for me to separate the idea of such extravagance and luxury from the existing want and ignorance of the bulk of the Romish church and Catholic Italy. It is but one of many thousands of the statues, paintings and relics that crowd the galleries and museums of the Vatican palace, purchased at enormous prices.

Rafael and Angelo gave all their genius to the church. Not only the dome of St. Peter's but the Sistine chapel belongs to the latter, and the Loggia and Stanza of the Vatican to the former, with thousands of feet of canvas besides. I saw no picture anywhere more eloquent than Rafael's Transfiguration. The Church of Rome honored her sons, as she still makes immortal the writer of fiction who knows how to weave in his web some threads of which Nun's veils are made. It is a source of comfort to belong to a church that has not turned aside from constantly proclaiming God's will to exhaust its vitality upon political schemes and its resources in gorgeous mausoleums above its fallen leaders.

From the Vatican we visited the tomb of Tasso, and were shown his chairs, table, desk and the leaden coffin in which he was said to have rested for three hundred years, (this we doubted as it seemed too small.)

We concluded the day with a visit to Piazza Pincio, and a visit to the Colosseum by moonlight. I have visited the Colosseum four or five times and the grandeur of the the structure grows on one at every visit. But looking at this amphitheatre of Vespasian, there is no good ground now for the lines so often quoted by tourists:

> "While stands the Colosseum, Rome shall stand
> When falls the Colosseum Rome shall fall,
> And when Rome falls, with it shall fall the world."

For all the mighty group that cluster about the Forum speak from their desolation, and speak loudly that all the unhallowed toil of man shall perish.

If one could describe how entire the ruin here how

THE COLOSSEUM.

great the change, it would be difficult to gain the credence of the reader and impossible to give any adequate conception of it. Standing on the brow of the Capitoline hill and looking South-east what an array of fallen greatness rises before the eye! To the South is the Palatine hill, with ruins of the palaces of the Cæsars, at our feet stands the column of Septimus Severus over the Via Sacra, the column of Phocas the tyrant, Byron's "nameless column without a base," (that being buried when he wrote his poem.) Here are remains of the Temple of Concord, Temple of Vespasian, Porticus, Temple of Saturn, Rostra, Senate House, where "Great Cæsar fell," Forum Romanorum, Temple of Castor and Pollux, Rostra Julia, Temple of the Vestal Virgin, Temple of Julius Cæsar, Temple of Antoninus and Faustinae, Temple of Rome and of Venus, Arch of Titus, Arch of Constantine and the Colosseum all are open to the eye at a glance. Of the hundreds of columns which once supported fretted frieze and cornice of marble, porphyry lapislazuli or giallo antico or bronze scarcely one remains intact; one sees granite and marble columns four and five feet in diameter broken up into sections of every length from one foot to twenty. I cannot conjecture how the iconoclast performed his task so thoroughly, but it is done, was it of God?

In one minutes walk of the Forum is the *Mamartine*, traditional, prison of St. Peter and St. Paul, you are shown the indenture made by Peter's head in the stone, the spring of miraculous origin, at which they baptised converts, the stone pillar to which they were chained, &c. It was in this same subterranean vault that Catiline was strangled, there is a passage leading under ground from it to the Forum.

Of course I visited the churches that contain the head of St. Matthew and the teeth and fingers of Sts. Paul and Peter, the stone that shows the foot-prints of the Saviour, Peter's bones and table and Paul's house in the church of St. Sebastian, the Scala Sancta, where several monks were ascending on their knees as Martin Luther was doing when the truth illuminated his soul. Our readers will remember these are called sacred because it is claimed that they are the steps on which Jesus ascended to Pilate's judgment hall, they are marble, covered partially with wood and are twenty-eight in number.

There are many hundreds of Catholic priests here; they all wear long robes or frocks, much like female attire, except the binding at the waist; some of them go barefoot, except sandals; some wear ropes around their waists, and all look serious. Hundreds of them are young theologues. Rome is papal. The spirit of Christianity has modified the current of civilization here chiefly from without, I think. The refined selfishness of other days, the bloody æstheticism that could bind Prometheus to the rock, if forsooth the last shadow borne to the visage from the expiring soul might be transmuted to canvass, expresses itself now otherwise. If a dominant animalism found expression in *Templum Veneris* and the Thermæ of Caracalla, and if the Colosseum and its myriads of victims, savage and human, represented the tragedic, and Rome in flames the melodramatic Romans of other years, there is now the anomaly of a Christian nation, the mother of the rest, with resources in the ends of the earth, literally giving her children stones (to gaze at), when they ask for bread, and contrary to the expectation of the Book she holds in her hand, minimizes life's necessities by turning plow-shares into swords.

During our stay a revolt was threatened. The people, exasperated, hungry and restless, determined to change affairs from *statu quo*. The mob created quite an excitement, by breaking out some windows and threatening further mischief; but the military being on hand all soon became quiet, and many of the insurgents were shipped to the country.

The dazzling splendor of kings, the pageantry of power, as set forth in the world's cumulating history, represent much oppression, much blood and tissue vainly consumed, the counterpart exhibits rags for robes, ignorance and ignominy, instead of knowledge and glory.

The factors whence these antipodal extremes have sprung are abuse of official prerogative above and misuse of God-given prerogative and endowment below.

A notice posted in every museum, palace, gallery or garden forbids, in four languages, the giving of gratuities, but we have found only one who refused; the fact is, many of these bankrupt lords are supported by these same gratuities. Sometimes the keeper gets more than he expects and thanks profusely: again, receiving less he looks grum. The common people have become so used to servility and meniality that they seem to have no conception of self-respect, and a gentleman dressed like a lord will take a *soldi*, one cent, and thank you as if it were a dollar. We hired a carriage to take us to the Catacombs of St. Calistus, on the Appian way, one and a half miles from the city, our guide contracted with us for two *liras* but required three at settling time, we paid him, but took his number and left him; he soon came running after us, to pay back what was due us: On the way we visited the church of *San Sebastiano*, said to contain the impress of Jesus' foot when he met Peter about to fly from martyrdom. Peter said, *Domine quo vadis?* Whither goest thou? Jesus replied, "To Rome to be crucified again." Peter turned back. The semblance of of a track is shown, also St. Sebastian's body in stone stuck full of arrows.

This church is at the entrance to the Catacombs of the same name, but as they are all alike we only visited one. These subterranean passages are said to aggregate five hundred miles, cut through tufa stone about thirty inches wide, they have receptacles on either side for receiving the dead, one recess above another like shelves in a store: often all that is left of the corpse is a white streak in the dust where the last bone mouldered back to the earth whence it sprung. These corridors often intersect one another, and occasionally open suddenly into an underground chapel where the early Christians used to worship, when Rome was in the hands of the Cæsars.

The author of Ben Hur says they were constructed with Ben Hur's gold, as an asylum for persecuted Christians, and some think they used it as a cemetery to prevent cremation. No guide will touch one of these bones on pain of excommunication.

St. Peters looks magnificent from the grounds.

NAPLES, BAY, VESUVIUS.

CHAPTER VIII.

NAPLES.—"WANTON BEAUTY."

Naples is renowned for its close relations to Herculaneum and Pompeii rather than for its own achievements. Its population in 1885, was considerably over half a million. While there are other characteristics peculiarly Neapolitan, observable in the priests, merchants and merchandise, artisans and the humblest citizens, there are fewer large and princely palaces. While they have some very elegant squares and fountains, they are very limited in number. They have excellent street cars and a carriage any moment to take one to any part of the city for *una lira* (20 cents.) Like all the cities we have visited, they seem to have excellent police regulations. But the beggars are legion;

some of our party have suggested that if you look at many of them they expect a gratuity. They are brought up to it from childhood.

Sometimes in a very thickly settled part of the city a dozen children will beset one, crying *"signor! signor! datemi soldi! datemi soldi!"* (give me a cent); the philosophy of their conduct is this, if they get something, it is so much made; if not, nothing is lost, and this disposition to beg grows with their growth. There are quite a number of merchants here who have a sign, *prezzo fissi*, price fixed; many others who will sell you a piece of goods for one *lira*, tie it up and declare it is two *liras*. Only to-day we took luncheon at a restaurant, inquired the price of coffee before ordering, was told so much, when we were ready to settle it was double. An incident which occurred one day in a restaurant whither we had gone for coffee, illustrates one or two phases of Italian city life. Hotels sometimes give their guests only lodging, sometimes breakfast, and sometimes all three meals. We were at one of the former kind, to which the restaurant mentioned was attached. We had called for *coffe lotte*, coffee with milk, and knew not why we had to wait so long, until an Italian came in with a large female goat, which had no sooner stopped than he stooped down behind the faithful nannie and began to fill a very small mouthed bottle with milk, for which our host paid him three cents, and for a spoonful of which put into our coffee we had each to pay him three cents extra. They often carry a bag of water in the sleeve to empty in the vessel of milk, a sly cheat.

We have a few times stepped into their shops or stores and priced articles as if we purposed buying; often we were asked three, four and five times what we could really purchase for. They do not read as the Florentines and Romans, nor is much now doing for education in general.

Were the travel to Naples to stop entirely for two years there would be fearful suffering, I believe. The English, French, Germans and Americans drop hundreds of thousands here yearly.

Italy has produced some of the first musicians, poets, painters, architects, and sculptors. She possesses one of the most delightful of climates. Naples has the finest of the bays. "See Naples and die." All these are the heritage of those now living there and holding in fee simple their lawful patrimony. They have preserved in a praiseworthy manner the works of art left to them, as the safest and never-failing source of revenue. What the nation claims as reward for its care is not excessive, but every native feels the patrimony to be his individually, and would fain be enjoying, while you are passing through, the portion of the bounty that falls to him.

Land rents near about Naples for $20 to $30 yearly, and house-rent is pretty high; good living is high, but the poor live very cheap. Macaroni seems to be the chief staple of support, and it is made here by the carload.

The first day of our stay we visited the National Museum, admission one franc (20 cents), catalogue forty cents. The contents are about as follows: Mural paintings from Herculaneum and Pompeii; the finest collection of bronzes in the world; marble sculptures (some master pieces); inscriptions; Egyptian antiquities; Mediæval antiquities; crystals; bronzes; ancient terracottas; Papyri from Herculaneum; engravings (seen only by permission); Pompeian relics; food; domestic

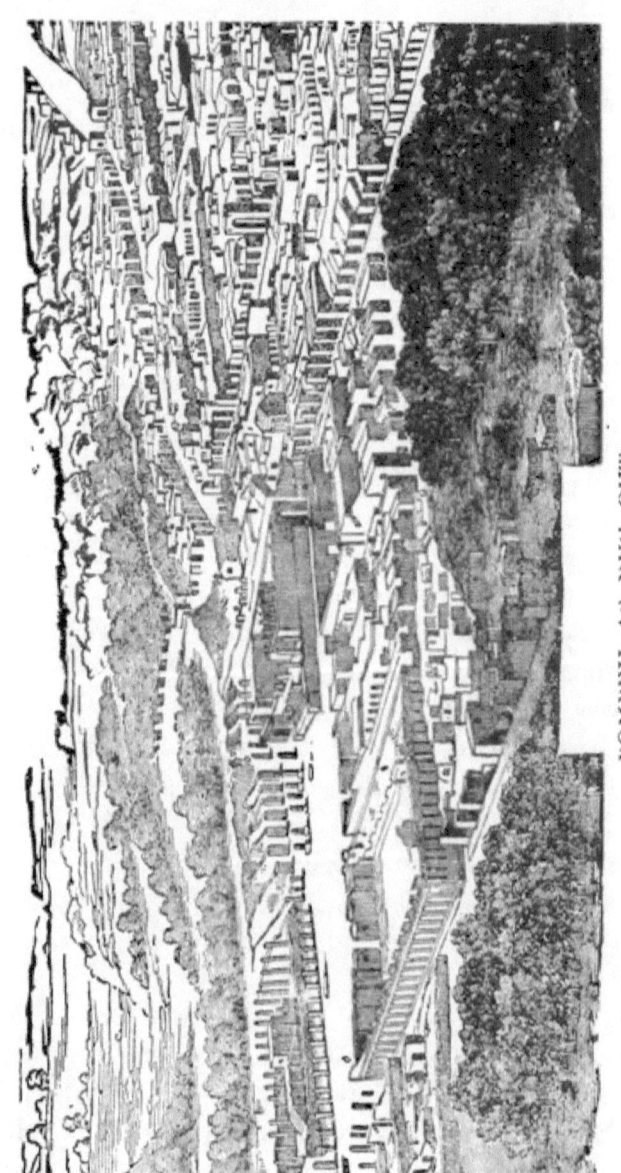

POMPEII AS DUG OUT.

utensils; ornaments; coins; vases; picture gallery; library of 200,000 volumes; 4,000 MSS., some of them rare and of great interest.

We visited, the second day, Pompeii, which was destroyed A. D. 79 by an eruption of Mt. Vesuvius. The excavation was going on the day we visited the buried city, but the principal part has been exhumed for many years. All enter by the *Porta marina* or sea-gate, for the

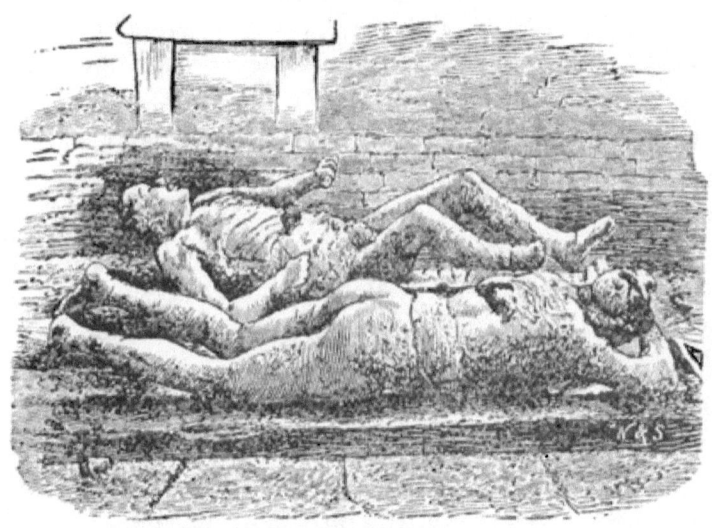

EXHUMED BODIES.

sea, which is now several furlongs off, once reached within a few feet of the city walls, (admission forty cents), a guide is furnished by the government. A museum here contains several plaster casts of human bodies found in the streets and houses—giving a pretty fair reproduction; also a dog, which makes almost a perfect cast. These casts are made by filling with soft plaster the vacuums found in beds of cinders, where the wretches who perished with their city lay till they were entirely roasted. The plaster gradually becomes hard and remains a permanent heritage.

The general plan of the place is about the same as that of ancient Rome. Here is the Forum, about it are the Temples of Venus, Jupiter, Mercury, Fortuna, Basilica, Pantheon, and not very far off the circus and amphitheatre. One is shown also the houses of Sallust, Tragic Poet, C. & E. Rufus, Orpheus, Lucretius, Faun, &c. I can easily believe this city was destroyed for its wickedness as was Sodom by divine appointment. It is strange to a visitor to see the people now building far up on the side of Vesuvius, half way at least from Pompeii to the top. They have two or three cities, as large, perhaps, as either of those overwhelmed in the year 79 not over half the distance from the very crater.

Leaving Pompeii at 11:30 in company with Hon. E. B. Taft, of Vermont, a Californian, and our guide, with a horse and two ponies, we started to ascend the Volcano. Our route lay through Torre Annunciata, a city of 12,000 inhabitants. Mr. Taft had a turn for fun, and mounted on a good horse, he put out at full speed through the town, to the consternation of everybody on the streets. Our guide, divining his intentions, seized the horse's tail as if to hold him back, it being impossible for me and Mr. G., an old gentleman of three-score and more, on our ponies to do more than keep in sight of our illustrious leader, who went careering around the street corners, much, I imagine, like Mazeppa in his excursion from "Bangor to the dismal swamp." Our little steeds fairly spread themselves, but 'twas of no use, the leader had the longest legs and thinnest flanks, besides he was a cavalry horse, on the retired list and had good wind. I should have expected that we would all be arrested, for riding at a gait to endanger our own lives and those of persons on the streets, but how could we be arrested? What prospect would a pursuer, even on a fast horse, have of ever seeing us after the passing minute, and as policemen do not ride, we were safe. Mr Taft bent on fun, and we on catching him and the guide, still holding the horse's tail, and looking as they swept around the street-corners like small boys at the end of a whip-cracking game that scatters them far and wide, flew on at Gilpin speed. It soon grew monotonous to the guide and the martial steed with his double load, and we came up in time to hear the guide say, as best he could, for his breath was about gone, that if that was the way we purposed going he would let us go on without him. I was sorry for him, but had not got near enough to be heard before.

It ill became the dignity of a State Senator, a sexagenarian and a Methodist preacher on their first visit to a town so to astonish the natives as to call all the people from their dwellings into the streets, and have them to follow us as long as they could see us, some laughing at the fun of the thing, others terrified, not knowing what was about to happen. If we had been coming from the mountain instead of going to it, and the air had been filled with smoke and thunder, and the earth with trembling from the restless monster as on that fatal day in 79, our conduct would have been appropriate, but under no other circumstances. But all is well that ends well, and we take it more leisurely as we begin the ascent in the suburbs of the town. Still the guide and the boy sent to hold our horses, hold on to the horses' tails all the way up to the hitching place. This a great help to one walking up hill, I afterwards tried it myself. Leaving town, we enter a vineyard two miles wide, pass a few scrubby pines, about large enough for walking canes, and vegetation ceases.

The soil is about the color of black lead, with a brownish hue. The surface of the ground for the first few miles is covered chiefly with gravels about the size of

HON. ELIHU B. TAFT.

peas. We ride to within one and a half or two miles of the crater, where a boy helds the horses, and men who met us returned to assist us in climbing up. The horses and guide and boy cost seven francs for each person; if you take a man to help pull you up from the place of dismounting, it costs 4 francs more; if you take a cane it costs 1 franc more. Mr. Taft was heavy and took help. Mr. G. and I did as well without. After going to within a quarter of a mile of the top, we found hot stones that had just rolled down, and every few steps more stones and hotter; presently they were red hot; a hundred yards further and we saw one roll down as large as a barrel. We sat down to rest, and down came one, red hot, rolling down an angle of forty-five degrees, going at the rate of several miles a minute, and another; we could see them in time to dodge from their path Now we kept on a ridge of them some ten feet higher than the track down which they were tumbling, and which seemed to be a kind of highway for them; soon we came to a sluice of red hot lava, twenty feet wide and several feet deep, running down like thick molasses. We could not go nearer than within ten feet of it, too intense was the heat. Our guide offered to imbed a penny in a molten piece for a franc. Mr. Taft had him to put two pennies in two pieces. He did so, but it was unsatisfactory, the impression of the coin being so vague. I got one of them, however, as a souvenir of our meeting and Vesuvius.

The fumes of sulphur and gases well nigh stifled us, and so dense was the smoke that all stopped short of the entire journey save myself and guide, who protested against going further, but not expecting to come this way again right away and being so near, I was determined to look down the throat of this heaving, stewing thundering monster. On the summit one feels the mountain tremble like an old mill when it is grinding. So the guide, fearful of losing his position and gratuities, went with me to the top, and my ambition was satisfied. I felt it to be risking my life, and my stay was short; you see where a whole mountain has fallen in, to fill the vacuum made perhaps when Pompeii and Herculaneum were buried ; and it is probable that the thousands and millions of tons since belched forth, have left an immense cavity, which may cause a falling in of the sides at any time. I hurried back through smoke and fœtid gases, sometimes almost suffocated and every moment fearful of being overtaken by a block of heaved-out lava. It was very disagreeable on account of the snow, some of which was melted and made with the pebbles and ashes a muddy track. It was smooth, however, and in a short time we were on our steeds again. As no one has given me any adequate idea of this volcano, so I do not hope to do better for others. Long ridges of scoria, several hundred yards in length, sometimes twenty feet high and from twenty feet to one hundred feet wide, seem to have been placed artificially and but yesterday. They are of many colors mingled, from the black slag to the dura petra nearly white. On the South side the mountain has kept active so long, sending out matter which hardens often near the summit until it is very high and sharp, the ascent for the last several minutes being about 45°. From Naples one sees clouds of smoke ascending from the crater during the day, and at night flames of fire are ever shooting up as if from some distant burning building.

The animals we rode were very diminutive as are nearly all the equine species seen in Italy. Mr. G. who is an elderly gentleman started with Beefsteak but not liking his qualities offered to swap with me. Of course I accommodated him ; but after trying Macaroni, he concluded he had cheated himself and wished to trade back and we traded again. He then thought he was cheated again but determined to take vengeance out on

Beefsteak by whipping him. The animal was so short he struck clear by and missed the object of his ire every time. He then contented himself by abusing the Italians.

We left next day for Brindisi, the ancient Brundusium of the Romans, whence we sailed to Alexandria. Brindisi has nothing of special interest except its name, which means the antlers of a stag, the promontories that jut out into the water there being in appearance very much like a stag's horns, and the pillars that stand there to mark the terminus of the Appian Way paved from Rome three hundred and fifty miles. Only one of these, however, is left now, the other having been thrown down by an earthquake.

On the way to Brindisi we passed Bari where St. Nicholas is buried and where the pious Greeks of Russia go yearly to buy a bottle of precious snow water which is thought to have miraculous medicinal properties. This is specially holy in their esteem and sometimes sells at fabulous prices. We went down the Adriatic coast and in sight of Greece.

There are seven clergymen aboard the steamship Cathay, of the P. and O. (Peninsular and Oriental) line, of whom four are Presbyterians, one a Baptist, one an Episcopalian, and myself, a Methodist. Two of them are missionaries, one representing the *Christian Guild*, of Scotland the other the church of England.

From Brindisi to Alexandria is 900 to 1000 miles and requires three days and nights to complete the voyage. Our captain said he had never seen higher winds. The storm that wrecked the steamers at Samoa came our way.

MILL, BAKERY, WINE JAR OF POMPEII.

CHAPTER IX.

EGYPT.

Who can adequately describe landing amongst Arabs? They throng about the gangway ere it connects the ship to the wharf, precisely as hungry hogs do about the trough where swill is emptied, nor can two or three policemen arrest or check their persistence. They cry their good qualities and crowd one another, pushing and beating opponents until a stranger is surprised that many are not killed every day. When the gangway is secured they overrun the vessel's deck, thrusting their heads under one's hat brim, yelling in English, French or German, as the case demands, for your patronage. So much is paid them for every customer got into a carriage or hotel, besides *baksheesh* for handling baggage. One is impressed at the abundance of the survival of the unfittest.

We landed at Alexandria about 8 o'clock Thursday morning, and taking a ride through the city went to Cairo the same day.

The ride up the Nile was the most interesting of my life. While the objects along the way were not just such as I had expected, they were not below expectation. The railroad crosses the Rosetta and Damietta, arms of the river, and several canals, while every spot of ground is covered with the rankest herbage. The soil is a dark brown, almost black, loam. This deposit of the Nile is 30 to 60 feet deep. Its capacity to produce is limited only by the time required for plant maturity and irrigation. Along the road are hundreds of towns made of sundried brick—not a single one made of timber. We passed many thousands of Arabs on the road, most of whom were riding donkeys; these are very diminutive, being only 3½ to 4½ feet high, yet I often saw two men on one donkey. They sit so far back on him that the only chance for the second man is to get before; you *can't* ride *behind* one of these men on a donkey. A great many camels are used also.

The first things that impress a stranger in the towns are the dress of the people, their want of decency, and their commercial habits. Often one can only tell a male from a female by the beard and a veil worn by females over the nose. Married women also wear a stick or brass tube, about like a number 12 cartridge, between the eyes—thus the face is entirely concealed, with the exception of the eyes, and the hollow tube admits fresh air for respiration.

Their stores are only a few feet deep, and sometimes all their goods are on the floor, even when their stock is bread, and the floor is often mother earth. They sit often on the ground seemingly indifferent to customers, smoking pipes that will hold a whole package of Durham smoking tobacco. They all smoke, and nearly all gamble, just where they sit to trade.

Alexandria and Cairo have many water carriers; the men sell, the women donate. The men carry it in large skins—goat skins—holding about 10 or 12 gallons, price about five cents per gallon of filtered Nile water, which is very good; they cry as they go, *miyeh! tiyeb miyeh!* water! good water! Powdered almonds is said to be put into the slightly muddy water, precipitating the argillaceous and other substances, leaving it pure and sweet. I need not remark upon the excessive filthiness of these people when it is remembered that it seldom rains here—about eight inches a year at Alexan-

TAKING A DRINK OF WATER.

dria, less than two in Cairo, and none further south, one has an idea of the dust that is made by the travel of thousands of donkeys and camels, cows, goats and sheep daily over the highways. It is very hot; a little toil fills one with perspiration, they go into the canal with their beasts, and all lave together, after which they fill their water jars. You can see fleas crawling about upon them; often one sees a dozen flies in their eyes; many of them are half clad, many entirely nude. It is said there is either a cow, camel, goat or donkey for every acre of land in the Delta, and a person for every animal. I believe the true estimate puts one person for every two acres of land.

I suppose they irrigate their land much as they did five or six thousand years ago, or earlier; for I cannot think of anything more primitive. They raise it by a

SAKIEH FOR RAISING WATER.

system of sweeps, like our sweep-wells, only shorter levers are used; sometimes four sets are required to raise the water 20 or 25 feet high, each set lifting a basket full (flag baskets) five or six feet high, where it is emptied into a large cavity in the bank and again carried up. They call these *shadoofs*. Another way is to have a perpendicular and horizontal spur-wheel geared together and turned by a cow or camel blindfold, or person.

This puts in motion an endless chain, with jars fastened at proper intervals (*Sakieh*); they raise the water, which empties into a trough connecting with a ditch, and so is carried for miles over the fields, which are level as far as the foot h'lls. I believe they are a little lower at the base of the hills than at the margin of the river, owing to the greater deposit near the stream during the annual overflow. This facilitates the irrigation, as the water flows down an inclined plane from the start. Small dams are made around little squares to hold the water until every plant on the cultivated area is wet in season. The water is turned into and out of these squares by the bare foot of the *fellah* (farmer.)

When one sees the fertility of this valley, the sweetness of the Nile water, he is not surprised that ancient Egyptians, without a knowledge of the true God, should have deified the stream to which they seemed to owe all their support, especially when the manner of its overflowing and enriching the land annually without any rains, so far as they knew, was so mysterious and wonderful.

I am told that each farmer has to give $5 per acre yearly to the government as tax. In some places two-thirds of all the yield are taken; the government owns the land largely; they raise three and four crops yearly, consisting of barley, sugar, rice, clover, beans, &c. These crops, however, are measurably affected by the rise in the Nile. The tax is levied according to the same.

The Government often reports the Nile to have reached the normal height of 23 or 24 feet when it has not, so as to excuse a high tax. There are raised large herds of cattle and sheep for Alexandria and Cairo markets, and I judge other cities also.

The city of Cairo is now the centre of the world in more senses than one. It is not only the seat of the Khedive's dominions in the North of Africa, but the season is on, and tourists from the Continent, Great Britain and America are here in great numbers. I met two young gentlemen of the U. S. Man of War Essex (I think) now on the way home from a tour round the world, Mr. Scales, of Greensboro, N. C., and Mr. Russell, of ——, N. C. There are travelers from nearly every American State. They have an English quarter, a French quarter and perhaps a German quarter.

Everything looks like spring; everybody seems happy, and Cairo, already numbering 400,000 inhabitants, keeps booming.

We visited the Citadel, on Mt. Mokattam, where the finest panorama in all Egypt lies out before the spectator from the South side of the Mosque of Mahomet Ali. We stood on this terrace for an hour or two, studying Cairo, every part of which is visible, with hundreds of mosques and minarets and palaces; the Pyramids of Ghizeh, eight miles to the west, of Sakarah, "the city of the Tombs," 15 or 20 miles to the south, and Old Cairo, a few miles to the south, enrich the landscape with

"The river gleaming and winding away from the dim south into the blue distance of the north, the green strips of cultivation on its banks delighting the eye amid the yellow sands."

There is the arena where were enacted many of those tragic scenes recorded in the first two books of the Bible. There unknown, obscure little Joseph began and developed into a man of wonderful power, and made himself a home at which he royally received his father and kinsfolk. Hither Jacob came, with trembling step, for life, as Abraham, his grandfather, had done before, and

CAIRO FROM THE CITADEL.

blessed his son's benefactor and beneficiary, and his children and grand-children. There toiled the subject race for four hundred and twenty years. There Moses, brought up in the King's palace and educated yonder at On, returned to work his miracles before the King. Yes, that river was once blood. The blackness of those heavens could once be felt. Those streets were thronged by frogs, and swarms of flies, and other pests tormented the wretched monarch. O, the history enacted on that plain! Egypt, thou wast the nurse of the Hebrew people. Silent, mysterious, wonderful land!

We visited here the Mosque, which is of Alabaster, and contains the body of Mahomet Ali: lamps are kept burning by it all the time. The floor is covered with the finest Persian carpets and rugs, on which the worshipers sit instead of on pews. It was Friday or Mahometan Sabbath, and one solitary Arab sat cross-legged, swinging back and forth and repeating in a whining song verses of the Koran. I think the howlers instead of the dancers worship here. Christians are not permitted to enter the enclosure after the hour for worship to begin. Sandals were provided for visitors, for which *backsheesh* is required. We then visited Joseph's well, which is 290 feet deep, from which pure water is elevated by donkeys at the bottom. This well is square and 15 or 18 feet in diameter; in the solid stone, around the main shaft, a stairway leads to the bottom. We descended partly down, far enough to get a good idea of the whole. We passed out by the narrow defile in which Mahomet Ali had 450 Mamelukes, with their leader, Ibrahim Bey, killed in 1811, for fear of their revolutionary plans; 800 more were killed in the city. Emin Bey escaped by leaping his horse over the battlement. His horse was crushed to death, but he escaped. The eastern terrace, 100 feet high, from which he leaped, is called *La Saut du Mameluke*. The fact of the leaping is questioned.

We rode out to Cheops, 4,060 years old, and the Sphinx, 140 feet long, plus 50 feet for the paws; the head is over 100 feet in circumference and the body 40 feet in diameter. We ascend Cheops alone, without help, (this is quite a triumph) especially when harangued by a dozen Arabs before and behind, and all around; the usual method of ascent is for two Arabs to precede and pull while a third from the rear pushes up the climber.

They try to alarm the novice by pointing out many dangers to which he is exposing himself, saying:

"American no find way. Hawaji (Mr.) head swim. Hawaji fail, get killed."

And the ascent is perilous to one without a steady nerve. Reaching the top when my companion was scarcely half way up I began to muse:

This is Cheops, built some think for the habitation of a single corpse, whose reign had been so oppressive that his body had to be conveyed away secretly, and his name never called by his subjects, fulfilled the words of truth, "the name of the wicked shall rot." What varied scenes have been enacted here, when this pillar was being erected, of toiling serfs and cruel taskmasters, making the world great and miserable! the leeks, radishes and onions consumed by the workmen aggregated $1,700,000. What a celebration when the "chief corner stone" (the apex) was laid! What a history has been made beneath its shadow, what untold thousands of Egypt's sons have passed by with gallant tread, going to foreign wars against the mighty Cheta under Rameses and Thothmes (Napoleon of Egypt), some to bring many captives home, more whose blood enriched the enemies, lands. What unnumbered hosts have marched hither to return no more. Just there Napoleon concentrated an oration into one phrase : " Sons of France forty centuries look down on you!"

What a strange place is this! To the west is endless death, the desert sands, brown and red, interminable, say, "Leave hope behind who enter here!" To the east the fertile and happy valley with the smiling Nile seem as contented and peaceful as if there were no death, and ——"backsheesh Hawadji!" "America give good back sheesh!" "Give New York back sheesh," "Give Yankee-doodle back sheesh!" "Give it! give it!" "Howadji buy mummy! genuine antique! worth 6 shillings," (about the size of a man's finger, a poor imitation of a mummy case). "It is not genuine, I fear," said I. "Genuine antique, Howadji, give it four shillings." "Too much," said I. "How much you give it?" "I will give you a *piaster* (4 cents) for a pair of them," said I hoping to disgust, and get rid of their pertinacity. "Well, give it, give it." "No, I don't want them." "*Give* it, GIVE it." "Miyeh (water) Howadji." "*Tiyeb miyeh,*" (good water). "Buy it, buy it!" and you have to buy it. "Want see do Mark Twain?" "What is that?" "Arab go down pyramid, up 'tother pyramid and back here in fifteen minutes for one shilling." Mark Twain said he hired him in hopes of seeing him break his neck, but Arab triumphed. They call it, "Doing Mark Twain."

By this time my friend had reached the top exhausted. The summit is twenty-four feet square, and there are blocks of stone on this area four hundred and sixty odd feet perpendicular that weigh many tons.

I descended, went into the interior, into the King's and Queen's chambers, both of which have been written much about. I hesitate to say more than that the entrance is fraught with the greatest danger, being by a descent and then an ascent over stones worn smooth as glass. The king's chamber, 34 feet by 17 feet, and 16 feet high, is the most reverberating of any hall I ever entered. It contained a mutilated, lidless sarcophagus or coffer, about whose purpose there is much conjecture. Some say it is a coffin, some, a treasure chest, some say it was designed for a universal standard of measure corresponding to the laws of the Hebrews, others say it is the pillar spoken of by Isaiah 19: "In day that shall there be an altar to the Lord in the midst of the land of Egypt, and a pillar at the border thereof to the Lord. And it shall be a for a sign and a witness unto the Lord of Hosts in the land of Egypt." As our carriage approached the base we noticed men on the summit of the pyramid, and they looked like toy men on a mantel. This optical delusion was owing to the great bulk of matter just beneath. Cheops covers nearly thirteen acres of land, and has been computed to contain enough stone to build the city of Washington, D. C., government buildings and all. It is about an hour's ride by carriage from Cairo, on the foot of the Lybian range of hills bordering on the Lybian desert.

When we were returning from the interior of the pyramid, my Arab guides stopped short before me at the critical turning from the shaft descending from the king's chamber to the shaft or tunnel leading to the well 90 feet below the base of the pyramid and called the bottomless pit, at the point K, (see cut) It is difficult to get from one to the other, and perilous even with

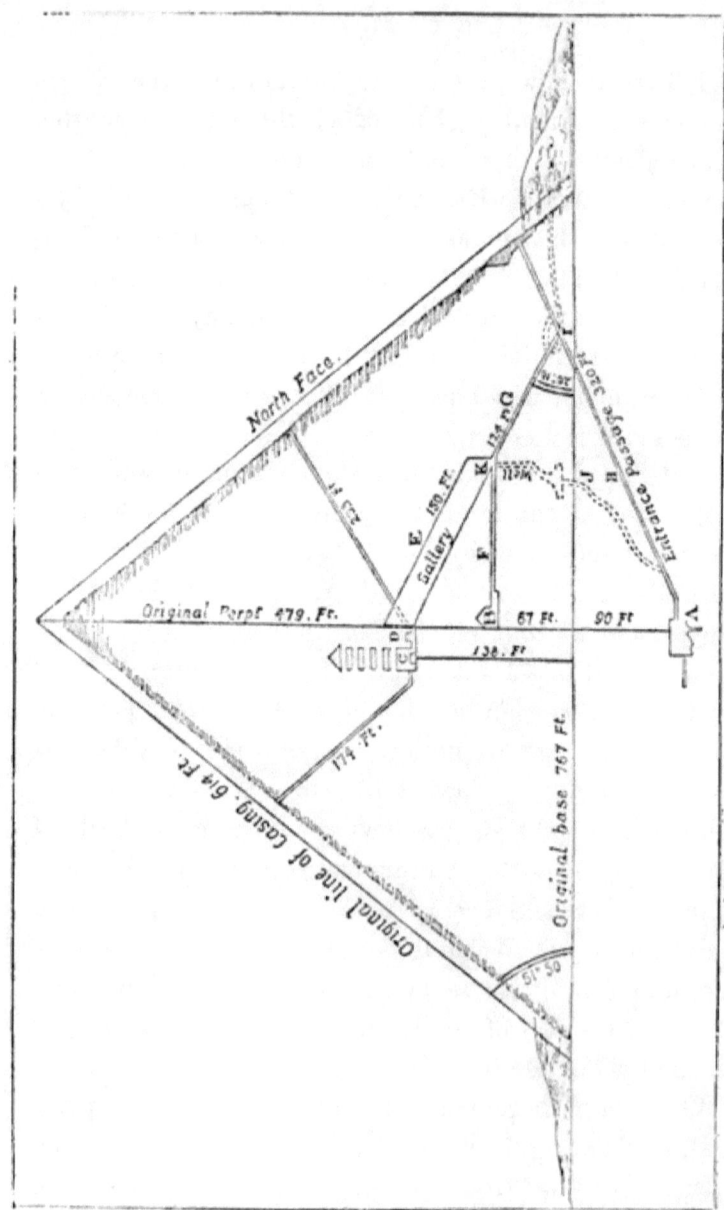

SECTION OF THE GREAT PYRAMID.

good light, but here they extinguished their candles and mine, and I knew not what was next, for I had left my friend on top, who said he did not care to venture within. A man thinks rapidly when unexpected danger suddenly confronts him. So I. What does it mean? There are a hundred of them outside. What can my friend do alone? He was afraid to come in with me, much more will he fear to do so now; besides, what could he do if he should come? Will they kill me and drop me in the deep well they showed me a moment since, that is just behind me?

These, with many other apprehensions, shot through my mind like electricity. I had not been in Egypt over twelve hours; I did not understand the Arabs. Everything I had seen of them disgusted me. I had heard and read of their treachery, but felt safe in sight of Cairo, of English troops, with an English gentleman on the top, especially since I had paid the *sheik* three shillings for the privilege of penetrating this "miracle in stone" that was as much mine as his. Every one who has traveled among the Arabs has anticipated me, I know, when I tell them that "*backsheesh, Howadji!*" was the first sound that filled the darkness. Yes, they wanted this job settled for then and there. An old, useless Arab had followed me up the mountain down again and inside, saying repeatedly: "I make you satisfied, you make me satisfied." So he yelled again and I responded in the vernacular of the place, "Yes, make me satisfied and I'll make you satisfied." I told them certainly I would give them plenty of *backsheesh*—they lighted up and in another minute we stood from under. And for the first and last time (though amongst them for two months afterwards) satisfied them with *back-*

sheesh. It was now sundown, but my friend, seeing me safe outside, determined to try it himself, with an experience similar to mine.

"This mighty structure stands immortal in its greatness, lifting its brow the nearest to heaven of all earthly works (1877), and asserting in every feature something more than human. With all of man's workmanship that went before it in utter ruin, it stands only the more readable from the damages of time, the grand and indestructible monument of the true primeval man. Upon its pedestal of rock, battered by the buffetings of forty centuries, it stands, upspringing like a tongue of fire kindled of God to light the course of time down to its final goal and consummation."

"Old Time, himself so old, is like a child,
And can't remember when these blocks were piled,
Or caverns scooped; but, with amaz'd eye,
He seems to pause, like other standers-by,
Half thinking how the wonders here made known
Were born in ages older than his own."

Next day we went through many of their bazaars, in which they sell fruits of Egypt and other countries—cane, dates, oranges, bread, eggs, cheese, birds, fish, etc., etc. All manner of fabrics of cloth, carpets, rugs, etc., from Arabia and Persia; pipes and tobacco and cigarettes, boots, shoes, slippers and fezes, hardware, and flagware and jars by the ten thousand, and everything else almost, and all on the ground in the streets on a rug, each man or firm just having what they can conveniently take away at night.

CHAPTER X.

FARTHER UP THE NILE.

I had arranged to take the trip up the Nile with Drs. Whigham and Black on Cook's steamer, but being a little careless about securing a berth, found when I did make application that all had been taken. They wished to register me in Rome for this excursion at £50, also at Naples for the same price, but at Brindisi they offered me a ticket for £25 sterling. We went from Cairo over perhaps the dustiest railroad in existence, 247 miles to Assiout. No water is found on these trains unless the thoughtful traveler carries a cruse or water jar holding about one quart, which costs, jar and water, about two cents. At Assiout we took the government postal steamer and were enabled briefly to study the country in its resources, its institutions and population.

We learned that the Copts, about one-eighth of the inhabitants, hold about one-fourth or more of the offices, they are more competent, and being weak in a military sense are awake to their interest, and try to educate themselves. They hold nearly all the positions in civil service, while the military positions for religious reasons are given to Mahometans. The Copts have only one wife and are all Christians. They never intermarry with Arabs.

The stations of the postal service are all on flat-boats

anchored to the shore because the banks and level of the water are ever shifting under the annual overflow of the Nile. At these stations hundreds of Arabs gather on the arrival of the boat with cane, bread, eggs, cheese-curds, vegetables, pigeons, &c., &c., to sell, sometimes a hundred crying their wares at once until however much you want a thing, your only chance to get it is to catch the eye of the vender, who, calling the name of the goods he sells, says: "God will lighten my load of oranges;" "God will forgive thy sins." At the same time from twenty-five to fifty are crying *backsheesh*.

At Abooteeg all others gave way to an old blind man who yelled enough for a dozen. Our captain said his words at first meant, "Oh, my Lord." This he repeated some scores of times; he would then vary, and finally appealed to our idea of the ridiculous by barking like a dog—"bow! wow, wow!" so rapidly and with such frantic jesticulations, and leaping so as to permanently monopolize the attention of all, and secure his *backsheesh*.

At the next station was a blind boy, who appealed only to the emotions and promise of reward for benefactions he had memorized those passages in the Koran suited to his purpose, these he used with great effect. The Arabs were moved as by the spell of eloquence and contributed, as did also the Christians.

The valley of the Nile from Assiout, 393 miles from Alexandria, is between the Lybian hills on the west and Aabian on the east. They rise suddenly from the plains 500 feet high, presenting a barren front of limestone and begin the deserts of the same names. The valley, sometimes 20 miles wide, is, on an average, about six or seven, and all under cultivation. The river will rise again in four months and in those sandbars left bare now they are planting water-melon seed. There are plenty of tomatoes, peas, beans, &c., of this season's growth. We saw also water-melons in Cairo. They have harvested their sugar cane, and our captain says one acre will make three barrels of sugar. They also are harvesting barley which often only grows eighteen inches high but as thick as can well stand on the ground. Flax is maturing.

The Khedive owns many sugar factories along the Nile, making the best standard brands, and the price is about the same as with us. There are also very large jug and jar factories here, as all the vessels used for water are earthen-ware. We saw perhaps fifty thousand at Farshoot.

Our boat, the Akashea, carried us among the most unique scenes we had ever witnessed. The skies above were cloudless by day and by night. The sun shone with intolerable heat by day, but when he retired behind the Lybian hills, the evaporation from the Nile soon cooled the air, and stars invisible in other lands sent twinkling rays down through the translucent atmosphere. When it is hot the buffaloes come down in the river to wallow. The women wade out to fill their ponderous water jars, a boat laden with jars, sheep, wheat or cane for market passes every now and then, the banks are lined with men working at the shadoof, in a state of nudity, except the poorest excuse of a breech cloth, their sweeps creaking on the axle, as with uniform swing they land the life-giving liquid.

The *Ibis religiosa* venerated as divine by the ancient Egyptians is extinct, but many a flock of ducks evades the hurrying boat and every town furnishes thousands of pigeons.

On the morning of the third day we reach Thebes—our destination.

When we landed none of the objects of our visit were in sight, although I stood in the midst of Thebes, well calculated to "fascinate, appall, stun, defy the imagination and confound the reason." 'Twas indeed "like entering a city of the giants, who, after a long contest had all been destroyed, leaving their vast temples as the only proof of their existence." Her magnificence once justified Homer in singing:

> "Not all proud Thebes' unrivalled walls contain
> The world's great Empress on the Egyptian plain
> That spreads her conquest o'er a thousand states,
> And pours her heroes through a hundred gates.
> Two hundred horsemen and two hundred cars,
> From each wide portal issuing to the wars."

From Luxor we went to the tombs of the kings and the temples of ancient Thebes, four miles west of the river. Twenty-five of these tombs are up a defile Bab-el-Molouk, in the Lybian Mountains about one and a half miles from the plain and are all near together; they are tunnels open at one end, and descending sometimes at a small angle, sometimes very steep, and are divided into a great many chambers, the principal one being for the king's sarcophagus and remains. One we visited, No. 17, of Sethi I., descends 180 feet below the entrance, and the bottom, which is nearly four hundred feet distant from the entrance, is more than five hundred feet perpendicular from the top of the hill under which it was dug. The walls and ceiling are full of carved hieroglyphics except No. 17, which, much superior to the rest every way, is done in *bas relief*.

"On entering the tomb (of Sethi I.) the visitor finds himself actually transported into a new world. . . . All has become, so to speak, fantastical chimerical. The gods assume strange forms. Long serpents glide hither and thither round the rooms or stand erect against the doorways. Some convicted malefactors are being decapitated and others are being precipitated into the flames. Well might the visitor feel a kind of horror creeping over him if he did not realize that after all, underneath these strange representations lies the most consoling of dogmas, that which vouchsafes eternal happiness to the soul after the many trials of this life. Such, in fact, is the meaning of the pictures which adorn the walls of this tomb. This legend must be understood in an allegorical sense. The judgment of the soul after being separated from the body, and the many trials which it will be called upon to overcome by the aid only of such virtues as it has evinced while on earth, constitute the subject-matter which cover the tomb, from the entrance to the extreme end of the last chamber. The serpents standing erect over each portal, darting out venom, are the guardians of the gates of heaven—the soul cannot pass unless justified by works of piety and benevolence. Thus the tomb is only the emblem of the voyage of the soul to its eternal abode . . . from room to room we witness its progress as it appears before the gods and becomes gradually purified, at last in the grand hall, at the end, it is admitted into that life which a second death shall never reach."—*Mariette.*

I took copies of the hieroglyphics from several of these tombs but the raised letters copied much the best. We lunched in one of these, and rode through the Necropolis to the temple-tomb (of marble) of Queen Hatasou and the Ramesium—Temple of Rameses II. "erected in the very center of the district of the dead, the monument where after his death his subjects should come and evoke his memory and wherein he naturally displays his piety, his glory and, as a matter of course, his campaigns."

"Rameses should have been pleased with his temple, for it was not built by his descendant, but by himself self and for his own honor."

We visited the Temple of Medinet Habou and the Memnonium of Strabo where a few foundation stones and the gigantic colossi alone remain. One of these is said to have greeted Aurora with a song each morning; the expansion caused by the sun's heat (it being shattered) no doubt has at times made noise enough to attract attention and give rise to the legend. They once stood at the entrance of a temple nearly one-fourth of a mile in length. Many of the columns of the temple of Rameses the Great still stand with the Osiride images *in situ*, but much defaced. The most important thing here is the statue of Rameses. It is a monolith of red granite, representing the king sitting, hands on his knees, at peace with his enemies.

It was originally 57 feet high and over 22 feet 4 inches across the shoulders, and is estimated to weigh 1198 tons. It has been thrown down and much broken, many millstones having been taken from the very face, but from the armpits up it is entire, except exteriorly much mutilated, and is above ground, so as to exhibit "just what it was, the largest statue in the world." But how it became so broken to pieces no man knoweth. This is No of the Scriptures:—"Thus saith the Lord God: I will also destroy the idols, and I will cause their images to cease out of Noph; and there shall be no more a prince of the land of Egypt; and I will put a fear in the land of Egypt. And I will make Pathros desolate, and will set fire in Zoan, and will execute judgments in No. And I will pour my fury upon Sin, the strength of Egypt; and I will cut off the multitude of No. And I will set fire in Egypt: Sin shall have great pain, and No shall be rent asunder, and Noph shall have distresses daily. The young men of Aven and of Pi-beseth shall fall by the sword: and these cities shall go into captivity." "At Tehaphnehes also the day shall be darkened, when I shall break there the yokes of Egypt; and the pomp of her strength shall cease in her: as for her a cloud shall cover her, and her daughters shall go into captivity. Thus will I execute judgments in Egypt, and they shall know that I am the Lord."—Ezek. 30: 13–19. And I turned and read up the prophecies and decrees of God against these idolatrous cities and I saw that they are literally fulfilled. We went one mile south to the Temple of Medi-inet Habon, where the only naval battle of the Egyptians is recorded on the walls. Here is a great succession of temples representing much history and probably great devotion: the victors are cutting off and counting the hands of the vanquished. Once a Christian church was in the precincts of this temple, in the very court where we now stand. All the works of art here have been destroyed nearly. Theodosius, anxious to root out idolatry, ruined much, perhaps jealous and envious conquerors, more. All these temples, while at a good elevation above the Nile's overflow, are still underground, except where reclaimed by scientists. The people clustered around these deserted temples after their overthrow and lived in them and built around them until debris accumulating, they built on the tops of them, and so they became buried, and there being no communication about such things between the inhabitants and lovers of antiquity, some of these cities and temples were long lost. There are miserable mud towns all around every one of them now.

PYLON, OR GATE TO EGYPTIAN TEMPLE, 80 FEET HIGH.

The next day we visited the Temple of Karnak, the most imposing in the world, whose walls 25 feet thick and eighty high, are penetrated by four splendid pylons still standing: it contains the tallest obelisk in the world, 108 feet 10 inches high, of red granite. As we sat in the shadow of this obelisk a strange being suddenly appeared before us whose approach had been unobserved. He is so correctly described by another that I copy, omitting one or two sentences:

"In the Temple of Karnak, amid the grandeur unparalleled, was a scene so strange and weird, so horrible yet fascinating, as to surpass the wildest fancies of Dumas or Eugene Sue. It thrilled, repelled, yet held the gaze until nature, half-paralyzed by the spectacle, asserted itself and compelled the removal of the object. A creature in the form of a human being, paralyzed, mute, naked, except for a rag tied across the loins; with shaven head, apparently seventy years of age, perchance not more than fifty, perhaps nearly one hundred, exactly the color of the ruined columns and the doorway, crawled out from under the broken pillars and huge monoliths, as a lizard might emerge from a pile of stones. A mumbling, inarticulate sound emerged from his lips; he moved sideways and tried to rise, and held out his hands for alms; * * * some of the Egyptian attendants seemed to stand in awe of him, and hesitated to drive him back into the obscurity whence he had emerged. And when at last two of them lifted him up to move him, he exerted what strength he had and broke from them, falling upon the ground and moving off with the sinuous sideway motion with which he had approached; but whenever he fell the hand which was held out to receive alms always came into position. Nothing human have I ever seen in collections of deformities and idiot asylums so peculiar; nothing which appeared to efface humanity and so transform a man into a beast.

"I departed with an intensified sense of the greatness and of the littleness of man."—*Observations Abroad.*

Here stands the most massive and well preserved columns; one court alone contains 134 columns, twelve

feet in diameter and sixty feet high, with capitals of
open and closed lotus—called the forest of columns.
The whole is 1¾ miles in circumference, and dating, a
part of it, to 3064 B. C.

As we wandered through the ruins of this temple,
covering 90 acres and gazed in bewilderment upon the
time-defying obelisk, massive pylons and cyclopean walls,
and above all, the magnificent forest of columns, in imagination we repeopled these plains with a race superior
in civilization to these moderns, laid off the vast plain
into streets and stood dazed in the old, proud "Empress
of the Egyptian plain."

The ocean by its vastness and power, the mountain by
its lofty seclusion awe us, but not less so these stupendous, mysterious ruins. These stones were quarried
and strangely freighted from some far-away mine, and
by the greatest of architects reared for the glory of their
city and worship of their gods, ages before Columbus
sailed in seach of America or the cornerstones of London
or Rome or Athens were laid, before the children of Israel
crossed the Red Sea, or Moses was born, when all the
nations that now exist lay back in the womb of barbarism.

The air seemed "heavy with history." With what
exultant pride the ancient builder stood apart to look
upon the labors of his hands! Was he not a worshiper
of nature's Architect whose templed universe suggested
the pattern for this temple on the Nile! O, wonderful
men of old! O, silent yet most eloquent pillars that
defy the marvelous sweep of Time that has vanquished
all your contemporaries of old! What countless myriads have come and gone since the chisel decreed you to
be so grandly beautiful' I thank you for the spell, the

inspiration, the dread engendered only in such presence.

We stopped at Denderah returning, and found a temple entire. Mariette says this temple was in course of completion while Jesus was living in Jerusalem. It consists of not less than 27 halls and chambers on the first floor; others above are reached by two flights of stone stairs. This temple was not a place for the people to meet and worship, it was penetrated only by the king, priests and their special attendants, no dwellings exist for priests as in the temple at Jerusalem. "It was a sacred depository, a place of preparation (for fetes) and of consecration. Here processions were organized and the sacred vessels carefully stored away; if inside all was dark and sombre and nothing indicates the use of artificial light—that darkness was intended to intensify the mystery of the ceremonies, while it secured the only mode known of preserving the precious objects and the sacred vestments from the ravages of insects and flies, from the penetrating dust and from the scorching sun." The cathedrals of Rome, some of them, might trace their pedigree this far up the Nile if not farther.

CHAPTER XI.

DOWN THE NILE TO CAIRO.

The Nile, one-fourth to one-half a mile wide, increases in volume from its mouths upwards for fourteen hundred miles, owing to the vast quantity of water used for irrigation and evaporation, and the fact that through all this distance it is without a tributary. The water is muddy, a seal brown, but when filtered is clear and cool. Besides the steamer, two or three other kinds of boats ply on the bosom of Sihor, as the ancients called the Nile. The largest of these is called the *dahabeah*. It has state-rooms like a steamer, but is moved by sails and oars. They are often fifty feet in length, perhaps eighty or a hundred. One-half of the *dahabeah* is devoted to state rooms, saloon, &c., the other to cargo, deck, and for the liberty of those managing sails and oars. Other boats (Markebs) using sails when the wind favored and long heavy oars, laden with wheat, sheep, water jars, &c., went down to Cairo and Alexandria and returned well nigh empty or with merchandise for countries south of Egypt. As every nation that uses ships has a peculiar sail with which to drive them, so the sails of any Egptian boat are like birds' wings drawn out and up, the points farthest from the mast being sharp. They are stretched on booms and sheets supported by a long sweep balanced on an upright post rather than masts, and at such an angle as the sailors choose. Sometimes half a dozen

Arabs tugged them slowly up the stream by a long rope, sometimes in the water, sometimes on the bank. We have noticed their boats and cargo covered over with a network that allowed the cargo of water-jars to reach several feet beyond the sides of the boat. The wheat was poured out in the boat without sacks, as it was upon the ground when they reached market.

Thousands of natives almost entirely nude raise water to irrigate the lands for from one to three *piastres*, five to fifteen cents, per day. Herons fly round us all the time and fine large ducks, while hordes of tame uncouth monsters called here buffaloes come down and wallow in the Nile like hogs.

In the morning and evening it is pleasant on the Nile, but in the middle of the day it is hot, no clouds protect one from the sun during the day. At night overcoats are needed; many natives wear them all day.

Returning to Cairo I visited On or Heliopolis, where Moses was graduated, about six miles north-east from Cairo. I went alone as my companions had gone to the pyramids, which I had visited previously. The price of a carriage was ten shillings, having proved their excellent qualities of locomotion in upper Egypt I determined to ride a donkey, as he would cost me, with a donkey boy, only three shillings. There is always a crowd of boys and men with donkeys to hire on the streets of Cairo, and as soon as they learned that I wanted one, twenty or thirty surrounded me, each proclaiming the superiority of his animal. I did not want to go at that moment, so crowding to the margin of the mob I ran as fast as I could down a side street. One of them gave a signal to another company ahead of me, and they started to meet me, the former following, and so hemmed

SCENE ON THE NILE.

me in between the walls, full forty of them, each with a donkey to let, and each determined that I should ride his. Seeing no way of escape, I took out my knife and began hacking as if I would cut them to pieces and trying to look as desperate as possible, but all to no avail; they never noticed the knife more than if I had had none, so I took a donkey and am sure the worst donkey boy in Egypt, and started to see the remains of Egypt's old university town. On the road I passed a cemetery where they were burying a babe without a coffin, as they have no timber out of which to make coffins. It was wrapped up very tightly, rather I should say bound up, laid in a recess on one side of a shallow grave and the sand and gravel poured in upon it. I was ordered to quit the place before the interment was complete, which I afterward learned was because I was *unclean*; being only a Christian I had no right, and they determined not to suffer me to pollute the sacred place.

On leaving I saw a woman veiled and seated about fifty yards away weeping aloud. I asked my donkey-boy the cause of her weeping; he said she was the child's mother. I asked why she was there alone. "She does not want the men to see her face," he said.

It was my fortune to witness two other funeral processions the same day. One was that of Haggar Ali, evidently a man of distinction and popularity, by the style and size of the procession, and the fact that ten widows were following his bier, over which most gorgeous banners floated high in the air.

Another corpse followed by a large concourse and five wives, had been no doubt a man of importance, whose name I never learned; both had been entirely too much married. The procession accompanying these corpses made vocal and martial music, wherefore I judged them to have been government or army officials.

We passed on the way to On a multitude of Arabs formed in a circle about thirty feet in diameter. We paused to ascertain the cause of the excitement. A snake-charmer had two striped snakes about a yard long, which were crawling about over his bare shoulders, arms and neck, and he was making his little boy, about five years old, handle them in the same way. The boy very reluctantly undertook his part, whereupon the father (if he were a father) would take a clamp made of iron, spring it open, run one end in the boy's mouth, the other resting on his cheek and pressing so tightly that the blood would ooze out, while he would stand off and deliver an animated speech in Arabic to the delighted spectators, not seeming to notice his boy, whose anguish was expressed in wailings and tears. I could not willingly witness such inhuman conduct and hurried away.

Nothing of interest remains at On save the obelisk, 66½ feet high and the oldest one standing. said to have been erected "1740 B. C. by Usertasen, under whom Joseph came to Egypt,"—*Wilkinson*,—at which Moses and Joseph before, must often have looked, and perhaps criticised the hieroglyphics on it. Under its shadow Plato studied Philosophy, and our Savior in infancy may have looked at it, as the tree called tne "Virgin's Tree," where the holy family is said to have rested, when they fled into Egypt, is nearly in sight. It is an old sycamore, similar in appearance to a mulberry, cut and scarred by vain tourists, standing about eighty yards from the highway; it is reached by passing through a gate and the walks of a lovely garden, where *bachsheesh* is wanted when you enter, while you stay and when you leave; in fact the gate-keeper refused to let me out until I had satisfied some half-dozen urchins who seized my donkey's bridle and tail when I mounted to start and wanted more; but after all you can often satisfy half a dozen of them with a dime, while again they will clamor until they have gotten two or three times as much as they have earned, and the only way to deal with them satisfactorily is to fix the price of everything before starting with them, pay this only at the end of the journey, or they will never complete it.

I went with a gentleman of Dr. Whigham's party to the pyramids the first day we were in Cairo. We bargained to give fifteen shillings for a carriage and guide, he unwittingly paid him before reaching our hotel, and because we did not give "backsheesh," he stopped, we paid him a shilling to go on, he drove about fifty yards and stopped again, wanting more "backsheesh," and we could not urge him farther. We reached the hotel on foot. It was our first day amongst them and we had not learned their tricks. They are superlatively filthy, though some are scrupulously cleanly. We saw hundreds of them lying on the streets asleep in the scorching sunshine. In the main they are very healthy looking; they live on bread and vegetables, rice and buffalo milk.

There was a fine mission work being prosecuted here in Cairo, under Dr. Lansing and Dr. Bliss (who has since died) of the Presbyterian Church. We visited them and heard them relate how they had moved on from a small beginning to large success. We saw about one hundred young Arab men belonging to their school in a debating society, discussing some query in quite a lively manner, but it was all Arabic to us. The missionary at Luqsor was absent while we were there, but we met several of his pupils which are more or less creditable to him. I think he is doing a fair work. How they can endure the summer here is more than I can understand. Life must be in great peril later in the season. But when the Lord said, "Who will go for us?" the love of Christ and souls constrained them and they said, "Here am I, send me."

I and Mr. Merrill went to the Boulac Museum, the the most important of any in the world on some accounts. Here are the best preserved and most numerous works of art of the ancient Egyptians and the most illustrous mummies that now exist or perhaps ever will. Julius Cæsar or even Alexander the Great, would be modern beside these hoary monarchs. But here they are in a state of excellent preservation.

Here is Sethi I., whose tomb we explored at Thebes done in bass-relief from the entrance to the most remote recesses, at a cost, no doubt, reckoning on our basis of valuing time and labor, of millions of dollars. Fully ten thousand square feet of surface was filled with raised hieroglyphics. He is the Pharaoh, whose daughter found little Moses, at whose table Moses ate, on whose knees he sat, these same hands no doubt smoothed back the curls from his parched brow many a day when he came in from play. He is a little above the medium height and very bright. Just beside him is his son, Rameses the II., commonly called Rameses the Great. He is dark, owing probably to the discoloring effect of the embalming material. He began to rule on the throne at 11 years of age, and waged war at 7 years of age, he ruled 67 years altogether; he was three years younger than Moses and no doubt they had many a boyish joust and turn down in the Nile. He is that Pharaoh who was angry at Moses, when he heard that Moses had taken an Egyptian's life, and he sought to kill him, and Moses fled from his face and from Egypt until Rameses was dead; he is the author of the largest Monolith image ever made; under him Egypt obtained quiet from all her enemies.

He is known to Egyptologists as the Pharaoh of the oppression (of the Israelites.)

Beside these is Thothmes the 3rd, known as the Napoleon of Egypt, because he was the greatest of her warriors. Under him Egypt " placed her frontier where she pleased." "On the beautiful stela of victory of Thothmes III, at Boulaq, it is written: I Amon have spread the fear of thee to the four pillars of heaven."—*Ebers*.

Standing in the presence of these old monarchs of antiquity and thinking of the changes since their day and how they laid the foundation to so large an extent of all subsequent civilization, it seems as if the ends of the earth were come together.

As I looked down upon their upturned faces that did not seem more than a decade to have suffered by the ravages of time, I thought of the poet's words:

> "The cloud-capped towers, the gorgeous palaces,
> The solemn temples, the great globe itself,
> Yea, all which it inherit, shall dissolve;
> And, like this insubstantial pageant faded,
> Leave not a rack behind: We are such stuff
> As dreams are made of, and our little life
> Is rounded with a sleep."—*Tempest*.

One is awed in the presence of the universal slayer's

mighty victims. Could those silent lips but speak, what stories could they relate! What light cast upon the dark and distant past, about our fathers who went down into Egypt, and sojourned there, in a strange land; about these old tombs and temples, obelisks and pyramids, through which the antiquarian wanders, and ponders, vainly trying to make them reveal their secrets. Could it be authoritatively announced that on a given day they would rise in their coffins and tell their experiences, what a pilgrimage of *Savants* there would be. Every additional item of knowledge, however, only confirms our sacred records. The sight of these old kings was well worth the journey to Egypt, and had I seen no more should have felt myself to be well repaid. I said rest on old heroes to wield the sword of truth more mighty than the ones of steel that gave you such renown; let your shrivelled hands, though palsied by death, crush the mighty king's of error, who fain would rob us of the heritage bequeathed us by Moses; you sought his life then, but remain to defend his teachings now; your lifeless bodies, if not worth more to the race than your ambitious spirits challenge, at least, an equal place.

If man has acquired the skill of thus preserving from decay the perishable body of his fellow-man, what an easy task will it be for the great Creator to summon the scattered particles of those who have not been preserved by the embalmers art, on the resurrection morning!

"Why should it be thought a thing incredible that *God* should raise the dead!"

CHAPTER XII.

ODDS AND ENDS.

I noticed in Cairo two footmen dressed in white frocks to the knees, bare-legged, with long tasseled caps on their heads and bearing long sticks as soldiers carry arms. They trotted about twenty steps in front of a carriage in which an English lady and gentleman were seated. These fellows will hire as footmen to run all day for two and a half cents per hour, or even less. Cheap p ges.

On the way up I noticed the natives cleaning out a canal; fully one thousand of them were at work, most of them without a shred of clothing, which fact seemed not to embarrass them in the least. They did not have a spade, a wheel-barrow, nor cart, but standing in rows of five, six, seven and eight, or nine, the first in the bottom of the canal cut out a chunk of mud weighing ten or fifteen pounds with his hands, passed it on to the second and he to the third up the bank until it reached the top, where the last man took it and cast it as far as he could. Some of them were standing two and three feet deep in the mud. Their manner of ditching was about as primitive as that of North Carolinians in working the public roads, in some counties.

The clover of Egypt grows about three feet high, is very nourishing to herbivorous animals, and is cut with a knife. I did not see a mowing scythe in the country. One can sit down and cut as much as he can carry without moving. They carry camel loads (about five hundred or six hundred pounds) and donkey loads of it to the towns every day. These loads of grass borne by donkeys often present a laughable sight—

WATER CARRIER.

nothing but the feet of the animal is seen, or possibly a pair of ears and a tail and feet; the rest is enveloped in a great mound of green clover. One can buy enough of it to support a donkey or a horse for a day for three or four cents.

On all the highways great numbers of women can be seen gathering dung, which is made into cakes, dried in the sun, and stored away for fuel, with which they cook. They are driven to this extremity because no timber except for fruit and shade is found.

The Arabs have a market day every week; on that day every one who has anything to sell, or who wishes to buy, will go to the bazaar, often with long trains of laden camels fastened tandem. The first is ridden or led, a rope halter with an iron piece under the chin of the second, hurting him if he pull back, fastens him to the saddle of the first; the third is in like manner fastened to the second, and so on till a caravan is easily managed by one driver. If they live near the city they pause on the suburbs, as there is a tax on everything that passes the city boundaries. One often sees as many as a thousand, and half as many donkeys and camels, all seated on the ground, (except the donkeys) with all the products of the country and every article imported into the country for sale. On market day only will you find them there. If they are far from the city they have a meeting place in the country, where they bring horses, donkeys, sheep, goats and cattle, and spend the day trading.

As priests in the Greek and Catholic churches are distinguished by their caps, so the different sects of Mohammedans are also. The ordinary Arab wears a red fez with a black tassel in the center of the crown. I have read that families were once distinguished by the color of the fez. I was told that those who have made the pilgrimage to Mecca are afterwards entitled to wear a green fez. The Dervish wears a gray fez with double the altitude of an ordinary red fez and four times the bulk or thickness; in fact it is made of the same material as a saddle blanket and as thick.

There are two sects of Dervishes—the Dancers and Howlers. The first sway their bodies to and fro and whirl around on tip toe, singing, and saying "He is one. He is God," *Lah-Illah-Allah!*, until exhausted.

The Howlers will sit cross-legged on the floor and repeat verses of the Koran and whine as they sing or read from their book, swaying their bodies back and forth. None but the Dancing Dervishes allow Christians to be present during the hours of worship on Friday. But they worship anywhere any day, in a railway carriage, on the roadside, on the deck of a boat. They generally spread down a handkerchief or blanket on the ground, get on their knees, put their forehead three times to the earth, rise and stand, face towards Mecca, touch the lower tip of the ears with the ends of the thumbs, fold their hands across the breast, kneel and touch their forehead the fourth time to the ground, usually taking about three minutes to worship.

A fellow traveller told me a story of an Arab, which is true to life. A physician had taken a very poor Arab to his house and treated him for some disease that promised to prove fatal, but the medical man succeeded in making a cure. When the doctor told his patient that he was well enough to return home, the good mussulman thought that the doctor was under lasting obligations for the privilege of having had such a subject to practice upon, and before leaving told him he thought he (the doctor) should bestow some nice backsheesh (present) by which to remember him. "The only gratitude they know is a lively desire for greater favors."

Said Joseph was our guide to the tombs of the Kings. He had two wives. We asked him about a multiplicity of wives. He said, "Two wives no good." When the husband maltreats one wife she carries the case to a judge, who calls the rascal to account and extracts pledges of good behavior. The punishment of the wife is left to the husband, who is often very brutal.

We noticed excavations going on around the temple of Luqsor—one which Joseph is supposed by some to have built. The Arabs were reclaiming, under English or French engineers, I did not learn which, this most wonderful seat of ancient worship. About two hundred Arabs were carrying the earth off in flag baskets. Many children were engaged on the job. I pointed out one little girl about five years old, crouched in a sunk place on the bank of the river, lying as flat on the ground as possible. Said I, she is hid to keep from work. We stopped about where she was concealed; the overseer looking at us discovered her, called her out, abused her, if he did not beat her. She was exhausted no doubt, and obeyed the voice of nature within her that called for rest. The overseer looked, with a flail in his hand, like the pictures we have seen of the task-masters put over the Israelites of old. These living wheel-barrows get from two to fifteen cents per day.

The American Consul at Luqsor is an Arab, Morad Ali. His son speaks English very well, having been educated at the Mission school there. We were invited to dine with him one day and accepted the invitation. We were there to learn. Now in every place one visits in the east, there are antiquity venders, "*Geniwine antique, Howadji!*" Antiques vary in price according to the success the manufacturer has had in making them look old, worn and dingy.

Our Consul had a large store of antiques. And dinner over, his son invited us to look at them. That was the secret of the invitation to dinner. He had a museum indeed, worth a great deal to look at. He sold mummies and mummy cases. He had mummy cats thousands of years old, hawks, and scarabs worth ten and fifteen pounds sterling. And whatever you priced was high, many times the price of the same article sold by one who had no claim to our patronage. So we bought enough to satisfy him that his invitation was appreciated and not extended in vain.

The donkey-boys are equally shrewd, and if their patrons are Americans they name their donkeys after some famous American, if he is English, after some English Lord. If French, after Napoleon, Boulanger, &c. We have rode on Buffalo Bill, Grant, Abraham, Mahomet and Solomon.

The following paragraph is from a sermon by my comrade, Mr. Merrill, after his return to America:

For hundreds of miles, beyond where the railway ends and foreign energy stops, you see no separate house upon the land, the sign of ownership and independence. Only villages of mud rising here and there out of the plain, where the dwellings of the people look like the burrows of animals in a bank of earth. At every landing where the boat touches, are crowds of people. half fed, half clothed, wholly unwashed, indolent, squalid, beggars and blind, indifferent, crushed in all their hopes by the miserable government over them, paying two-thirds the price of all products in taxes and often robbed of the rest. With no capacity to enjoy anything beyond the leeks and black bread that appease their hunger for the hour—with not enough spirit to raise their hands and brush from their faces the swarm of flies that gather there under the torrid sun. You would not expect in that torpidity, in that lotus eating life, any growth of hope or any desire for something better beyond the borders of the Nile, but I found it even there. I had on the last day at Karnak and Luxon a donkey boy who had learned a little English and had, with much enterprise, named his donkey after a certain president of the United States. As he ran beside the animal during the day he asked much about America, and I answered all his questions and asked him if he would like to go there to live. "Yes, yes," he said, "me go with you!" He found out that I was to leave on the steamer at 6 o'clock in the evening and just as I got on board and was looking down upon the deck I saw Hassen, the donkey boy, running down the bank and pushing through the crowd with eager eyes called "you take me! me go with you!" I wanted to take him but could do nothing. Tossing him a bit of money I answered, "No." His face fell and he was silent, but in a moment after he was gesticulating and calling me again to take him, saying "he would work hard, be good boy and never leave me," and the last view I had of Luxon, as the darkness fell and the steamer moved away, was of the young Arab, Hassen (the acquaintance of a day) reaching out his hands in the darkness and imploring that he might be taken to America. It seemed to me it was but a repetition of that old cry and of that deep darkness and bondage out of which God once led the Hebrews into the promised land — a darkness and a bondage that has prevailed for nearly all its history over the face of Egypt.

SLAVE BOAT ON THE NILE.

CHAPTER XIII.

ON SUEZ CANAL.

Following backward the course over which earthly kingdoms have passed, we go from the home of the greatest of the first nations.

As we flew along through the land of Goshen towards the Suez Canal, and I read again how God dealt with Pharaoh—the man raised up to show what long suffering and authority belong to God—the story of Joseph, the finest and most succinct delineation of human nature, of the domestic affections and the strength of blood affinities, of the special providence of God, of the strength and rewards of faith, of the nature and power of prayer—a story that has ever had a beauty supernatural and a pathos elsewhere unequalled, appeared still more beautiful when I here read it again.

I tried to picture the two and a half millions of Hebrews taking up their line of march towards the Red Sea, and Pharaoh worried almost to death by Moses, a friend, could he but have seen it, after burying his first born, gathering his armies, it may be from the very necropolis, to pursue the malcontents and force them to return, the safe passage of the latter and the final catastrophe that overwhelmed the haughty monarch and his hosts.

We reached Ismail, on the Canal, forty-seven miles from Port Said, where we stayed all night, in one of the prettiest towns on earth. The streets are as straight as an arrow, well shaded, macadamised and intersected by street car lines. The inhabitants are French and Arabs, and number three or four thousand.

The next morning was so stormy that we could not go aboard the steamer, because the canal here passes through lake Timsah, five miles in length, and the waves were so violent we could not come near enough in small boats to board her, and we had to walk three miles to pier No. 6, at the north-west end of the lake. There were many weakly ladies in the company, some of whom could not obtain conveyances and who had to walk also, and were of course exhausted. They were under the supervision of tourists' agents and held an indignation meeting that evening, after reaching Port Said, severely censuring Cook & Son for allowing them to suffer such inconveniences and also for detaining them a day too long at Port Said.

Port Said is three hours, by steamer, from Ismail, on the Suez Canal, cut all the way through the desert. It was so very windy that the air was filled with sand, and one could not see over a hundred yards. Dredges worked by steam are engaged lifting sand from the bottom of the canal by a number of large buckets fastened to an endless belt or chain. These buckets pass over a large spout, inclining downwards from the dredge and reaching a hundred feet or more from the canal. Into this spout the buckets empty their load of sand and water and it flows far off on the shore, and thus the canal is kept navigable. It is seventy-two feet wide at the base, at the narrowest place, and widening out to two and three hundred feet where the banks are low. The water is twenty-six feet deep.

The day we spent at Port Said is never to be forgotten. It was the Sabbath. Our steamer was appointed to sail that day, but could not load her cargo, though the sailors labored hard all day. The passengers went in a body to the office and tried to force the officers into measures, but all in vain. It was late in the afternoon Monday before she sailed. We were all shocked at seeing them load the boat on Sunday, but protested against having to rest ourselves. I remarked to Mr. M., it seems as if the Lord meant to make us rest to-day any-way, and though we went with the multitude, (shall I say to do evil?) amongst whom were four or five clergymen beside, we were glad of the delay. Our rule was not to travel on Sundays. All sorts of people live here—Arabs of course, (the country is full of *them*) Germans, English, but more French; the Arabs seem to take to the French and *vice versa*, besides the French followed De Lesseps, the canal builder, here and remained. No standard of morality is required, hence the most shocking scenes are common. Sailors of every nationality continually coming and going find a populace ever ready to commingle on the lowest moral stratum and pander to the most vicious tastes.

We inquired for a church, but none could be found. There is a large square where a band plays Sunday afternoon, and thousands are coming and going all the time. This is the only place where we saw Caucasians and Arabs intermarried. There were hundreds of rag-a-muffins parading the streets. Little girls from five to ten years of age with dresses that touched the ground wearing bustles large as water-buckets, and sporting beaux, presented a sight altogether novel to us, and extremely ridiculous. Men were dressed in female attire, and perhaps females were dressed as men. Whites were blacked, and the band and soldiers burlesqued by reckless boys, with all manner of squeaking instruments, and sticks for swords and guns—wearing false faces, &c. Thus the French holiday takes the place of the Christian Sabbath of rest and worship, and as a further consequence gambling hells and other ruinous institutions occupy where churches should have been built and Sunday schools carried on.

An Arab boy persisted in an effort to black my shoes, against all protestations, though I told him he should not, with all possible earnestness and emphasis, until, seeing escape from him was impossible, I told him I would not pay him. He followed, however, occasionally getting a stroke at them until he thought them polished sufficiently to justify a claim for pay. He then began to beg; I was unconcerned for a long while, wishing to see how long he would hold out; he probably would have stayed until night had not a stranger standing by slapped him over, or had I not left.

But to have any fair estimate of Port Said one must see it. On the greatest thoroughfare of the world it has caught up many of the worst of travellers' habits. It would be a great strategic point for missionary operations.

The great iron-clads of France, England and Turkey, that lie in waiting there continually for any safety their commerce may demand, teach us that we too, as a church or churches, should occupy and defend interests dearer than all else.

At last the *Venus* is ready to sail to Joppa and with regret we cast a last look upon old Egypt, wonderful in rivers and ruins, people and pyramids, an atmosphere translucent, a desert more awful if not sublime than mountains or ocean, a sky in a peculiar sense "inlaid with patens of bright gold," and gardens as fertile as Eden.

"Egypt, to which Abraham, the father of the faithful went when the famine was sore in his land; to which Joseph was sold; and to which the sons of Jacob went as their great-grand father, Abraham, had done before, because there was corn in Egypt; and to which pious Jacob followed captive Benjamin to receive an imperial welcome from long lost Joseph; Egypt where the children of Israel were in bondage four hundred years. Egypt, birthplace of Moses, whose life voyage began on the Nile, in an ark of bulrushes; scene of most wonderful displays of Jehovah's power, when river and air, sea and sky trembled with horror as an earthly potentate refused to obey the Infinites' command, "Let my people go"; whence he brought them out with a high hand and an outstretched arm; Egypt, which in the long history of Israel till the coming of the Son of Man was so intimately associated for good or for evil with God's chosen people that Dean Stanley calls it "the mother country" of Palestine, and which at last was a refuge for the Saviour of the world when "He came unto His own, and His own received Him not.' Egypt, farewell."—*Observations Abroad*.

CHAPTER XIV.

THE OLDEST SEAPORT.

Standing with fifty or sixty other passengers on deck of the steamship Venus, of the Austrian Lloyd Line, on March the 5th, the first gray streaks of dawn revealed to us the lowlying country of Philistia to the southeast and the ashy colored range of Judean hills stretching away to Mt. Carmel in the north and to Hebron in the south. What feelings of mingled joy and thankfulness filled each heart in anticipation of what lay before us. We were so soon now to make our way across those mountains to that city of all earthly ones most dear to Jew and Christian, and only second in sacredness to the Mussulman.

I was profoundly grateful that the fond hopes of many years were so soon to find full fruition; that I should have the privilege of visiting the land made sacred by the footsteps of the Son of God and some of the places once so dear to him; that my feet should press the soil once trodden by him as he toiled and taught.

With reverence new we hail this giant among the continents—oldest yet least understood—holding half of the human race; birthplace of races, religions, superstitions. Here "tenacious Judaism, progressive and spiritual Christianity;" indomitable, insolent Mohametanism, Budhism, Confucianism and other isms began.

If God ever spake to man in the vocabulary of earth, to tell of an infinite love and a glorious destiny, and

JOPPA OR JOFFA.

how to attain unto the fullest measure of life for time and eternity, it was beneath yon skies into which we look, under which we soon shall stand. No marvel if excitement thrills in every face, in every act.

We are not of the majority who at this season rough seas deny a landing. The fear we all had of not being able to land, was dispelled, and increased our pleasure at seeing our ship drop anchor in the oldest and worst of seaports—whence Jonah sailed when he had such a bad landing, and whither the wood that went into Solomon's temple was shipped. Our crew was a medley of Americans, Britons, French, Germans, Italians, Russians, Turks, Arabs, Copts and Ethiopians—Christians, Jews and Mohammedans—Tourists, Pilgrims, Scientists, Preachers, Teachers, Doctors and Merchants.

At sunrise the ship's great heart ceases to beat at Joppa. Her coming was anticipated, as evidenced by a score of boats manned by athletic Arabs hurrying over the swelling sea in their eagerness to secure customers. Some of them fly red flags with the names of H. Gaze & Co., Thos. Cook & Son, and Rolla Floyd, in letters of white. These have come out for those tourists who may be traveling under their auspices.

Rolla Floyd, with whom we stopped, is a Yankee by birth, but confines himself to Palestine, while the names of the other two are seen around the world. Both have headquarters in London, and are very necessary to those tourists who prefer to pay others for fighting their way through Italians, Arabs, Chinese and Japs, and for immunity from the responsibilities and security against the contingencies incident upon travel in strange lands.

From our ship about half a mile from shore, we watch the waves rushing in by the classic rocks, to one of which mythology says the beautiful Andromeda, on account of Juno's jealousy, was chained, and rescued by Perseus, becoming afterwards his bride. After death she was translated to heaven, where she still occupies a place in the constellation with her mother Cassiope. They wash the shore at the very base of the house of Simon the tanner, where Peter lodged and saw the wonderful sheet let down from heaven, containing "all manner of four-footed beasts and wild beasts, and creeping things and fowls of the air," revealing to his then too narrow mind the wideness of God's mercy in the Gospel dispensation, which is as the "wideness of the sea," and marvellously enlarging his idea of a preacher's mission. On the top of which, or one in its place, I afterward went myself; and in order to be sure of standing where Peter did, if he did, went all over it. From this standpoint one sees the "great sea" stretch far away north, west and south. Peter's eye no doubt swept that horizon in meditation, and watched the restless tides that beat upon that rocky shore, typifying the human hordes that had swept over Judea's hills and plains before and since the days of Noah.

> "Monarchs of Palestine, and Kings of Tyre,
> And the brave Maccabee have all been here;
> And Cestius, with his Roman plunderers;
> And Saladin and Baldwin, and the host
> Of fierce crusaders, from the British north,
> And shook their swords above thee, and their blood
> Flowed down like water to thine ancient sea."

So we will go ashore. We will land here whence Jonah sailed, on a firmer footing than he found on quitting his bark. We wish to tread the soil of the Holy Land.

I am in the Holy Land! What revelations await my

journey through it! Sweet were the optimistic dreams of her inspired seers. Shall the sweet waters of Cherith brook or Siloe's "that flowed fast by the oracle of God," or skies of marvelous softness, or the hills made sacred by the presence and frequent discourses of our Lord cause me to experience a kindred enlargement and make me still more hopeful of the strife?

I am going to "walk about Zion and go round about her, tell the towers thereof, mark well her bulwarks, consider her palaces, that I may return and tell it to the generation following." Will I feel as the Psalmist did? And if I do not, nor witness the sights so dear to him, nor feel the confidence in the supremacy and final universal racial triumph of Israel that her prophets did, conclude that these leaders in happy, sanguine hours were only overwhelmed with self-gratulation at their own providential election and dazed by hopes impossible of realization, shall I doubt the stability of the Divine government that for the present seems to be taking small cognizance of the chosen race?

Has fancy woven a web now to be unraveled? Has imagination reveled in a vista to fade when entered like the mirage? Shall the reverence and divine poesy that have ever clustered about the names of Judea, Jerusalem, Hebron, Galilee and Nazareth be dispelled? Shall the halo that has ever encircled the Holy Land, cutting it off from all others, vanish into thin air and leave it to be merged into the vast community of countries, and so make me loser of the inheritance of all my Christian life, until I shall regret the knowledge that increases my sorrow and the wealth that is worse than poverty? Shall I discover some of the "mistakes of Moses?" And see how that after all he did not lead the Israelites hither?

Shall I see that much blindness* and natural environment conduce to ocular delusion? And find facts favorable to doubting if not denying the probability of miracle? Especially that greatest of miracles the resurrection from the dead? Which stands out before the hopes of millions like a colossal tower, where they can shelter when the storms of life beat tempestuously about them and floods of adversity threaten to engulf them—whose wholesome shade protects them when solstitial suns dry up all the flowers that bloom along their path and wither all the green branches of earthly prospects—a tower pointing heavenward, around whose spiral stair hope ascends, till the din of earthly strife dies out below and the child of sorrow has all his tears and fears dispelled?

But "we shall see what we shall see." I will gain what I may from the land as well as from the Book; and if not in this mountain, nor yet in Jerusalem the true worshipers worship the Father, some dormant sentiment may be awakened, some active power intensified. I may learn from the lilies of the field; the thorny, stony, rich ground, the faithful shepherd, with ever imperilled‡ flock†. I will note the barren and fruitful fig tree; the fisherman and his nets; the ever waiting penny-a-day laborers; the fountain open in time of drouth. I will read the words of the Book, as nearly

---

*Three per cent. of the population are blind, and twenty per cent. have injured eyes. Because of the scarcity of water they seldom, if ever, wash. I never saw a washpan or basin in an Arab bazaar while among them, and the same customs are followed to a large extent as in the Savior's time, I think. I judge it was their custom not to use much water generally. They also wear turbans or hats without brims, and the sun is very hot. No doubt for these reasons there was about as much blindness then as now

‡We saw a boy drive a fox from his flock one day about noon. He ran towards us and turned down the hill and hid under the rocks, where "the foxes have holes," in sight of Jerusalem.

†At night the flocks are put into pens made of stone, over which it is difficult or impossible for foxes and jackals to climb. Sometimes they are put in large caves under the hillside, and the shepherd sleeps in the cave's mouth.

as I may where they were spoken, and study from all possible standpoints the ways of God to man. and from my treasury thus replenished, bring to my Master's service as much as I may, things new and old.

CHAPTER XV.

FROM JOPPA TO JERUSALEM.

The last chapter relates our emotions on entering Palestine. We halt a day at Joppa to visit Simon the tanner's house referred to in Acts, chapter 10, and the fine orange groves, of which there are many producing about 8,000,000 a year valued at about one *metterlich* (1 cent) each. Probably no larger or sweeter are grown anywhere. Self-indulgence, freed from domestic economy expands in the stingy traveler, we freely tested Joppa oranges and pronounce them first class.

There are two good mission schools and a hospital in Christian hands which we visited. Miss Arnott has given her fortune and her life to teaching young Arab girls how to become Christian wives and mothers. We can testify to the efficiency of her efforts from exhibitions of her pupils on the occasion of our visit.

Rev. J. R. Long has a male school under his control.

Miss Bessie Mangan succeeded in founding what is known as the Mildmay Hospital, where hundreds have been nursed and thousands treated, including Jews, Moslems, Greeks, Latins and Maronites. We noted the politeness and attention of the deaconesses, the contentedness of the patients and the promise of the whole institution as an agent for our Lord and for poor humanity.

The road from Joppa to Jerusalem is almost a perfect road. It passes Ramleh, the home of Joseph of Arimathea (?) Bareh or Gibeah, the Valley of Ajalon, where

Joshua commanded the sun and moon to stand still until he vanquished the Philistines. Ajalon belonged to Dan, Josh. 19:42. We stopped to dine at Latrum about half way to Jerusalem: It is traditionally held to be the home of the penitent thief, who was said to be named Disma and a robber of travelers. *Latro* is Latin for robber and no doubt Latrum was the home of this or some other robber. Abou Josch or Kirjath-jearim is about nine miles from Jerusalem. Here the Ark of God rested 20 years. The name signifies city of woods; it is in a semi-circular cove of the hills, somewhat like an amphitheatre. I felt strange emotions as I read I Chron. 13:5: "David gathered all Israel together from Shihor of Egypt even unto the entering of Hemath. to bring the ark of God from Kirjath-jearim." and Ps. 132:6—8:

"Lo, we heard of it at Ephratah; we found it in the fields of the wood.

We will go into his tabernacles; we will worship at his footstool.

Arise, O Lord. into thy rest; thou, and the Ark of thy strength."

What a multitude of people, all rejoicing with their king as they move along towards Jerusalem.

Perhaps the procession was many miles long. Suddenly they pause at the front. What is the matter? A man falls dead. Uzza, ignorant of the command of God, showing the sole manner of carrying the ark, when he thought to save it from falling from the cart, is struck dead for his rashness, and unutterable confusion ensues. David is chagrined; everybody disappointed and afraid to meddle further, and ignorant of the plainest direction, they leave the Ark at the home of Obed Edom, where it stayed for three months, in which time David and the priests read up a little, and had better success in moving it. The next place of interest is Kalomeh, near which it is claimed John the Baptist was born, and southwest of which is a Valley, *Wady es Sumpt*, in which tradition says David slew Goliath. In another hour we reach Jerusalem and stop at the Jerusalem hotel, about five minutes walk from the Joppa gate and the tower of David.

WEDNESDAY EVENING, March 6th.

Rev. C. D. Merrill, a Presbyterian minister of California, with whom I had traveled through Egypt, and myself contracted with Isa (Esau) Lobat to take us to Jericho, Jordan, the Dead Sea, Marsaba and Bethlehem, returning to Jerusalem the third day, for one hundred and fifty francs, about thirty dollars. We set out after 12 o'clock lunch the next day. A good donkey and donkey boy carried provisions, and a guard with a belt full of cartridges and a fine breechloading rifle represented the Ottoman empire protecting her guests. We had good horses shod with an oval piece of sheet-iron, without heels or toes, so shaped as to present to the road a convex surface, a rocker, four very large nails on each side held them on, thus all their horses are shod.

We go out of Jerusalem on the north side, and under the hill now supposed to be the hill Calvary, by the place where tradition says Stephen was stoned, cross the Valley of Jehoshaphat, pass the garden of Gethsemane and near to Absalom's pillar (tomb) up the south side of Olivet, through the Jewish cemetery, where one could walk over ten or twenty acres on tombs without touching the ground, over the spot where, it is thought, Jesus wept over the city, by two large stone columns supposed to be the remnant of the house of Simon the Leper. Then to Bethany on the east side of the hill, where a little house built of limestone is shown as the house of Mary and Martha, now kept for *backsheesh*. We came in an hour to the Apostles' fountain, and in two hours to an inn or khan, where it is claimed the good Samaritan deposited the unfortunate traveler and two pence for his support. We are going down to Jericho over the remains of the old Roman road over which, no doubt, Herod once could ride in a chariot, though it does not look as if it were ever good enough for that. We meet "robbers" (?) every mile or so. About the middle of the afternoon we reach the ravine that contains the brook Cherith, where Elisha lived in troublous times. And the word of the Lord came unto him, saying: "Get thee hence, and turn thee eastward, and hide thyself by the brook Cherith, that *is* before Jordan. And it shall be, *that* thou shalt drink of the brook; and I have commanded the ravens to feed thee there. So he went and did accordingunto the word of the Lord: for he went and dwelt by the brook Cherith, that *is* before Jordan. And the ravens brought him bread and flesh in the morning, and bread and flesh in the evening; and he drank of the brook"; the sides of the gorge often show perpendicular faces many hundred feet high. Isa said the Greeks had built a church on the supposed site of Elisha's repose. We reined up our horses and could hear the brook leaping over cataracts, going down to Jericho too. Herod the Great conducted this stream through an aqueduct to the imperial city of Jericho. Portions of this aqueduct still remain, though Jericho abides under the curse of Joshua till to-day; not a house remains. About sunset, having descended nearly four thousand feet since noon, we crossed Cherith, paused and drank of its sweet, limpid waters, rode two miles farther to Elisha's Fountain, whose waters, bitter no more, are very warm, say 80° Fah. We went about a mile farther through fragrant thorny shrubbery growing on the banks of the stream from Elijah's Fountain, and said to yield the fruit from which is made "balm of Gilead," and rest at the Russian Hospice on the site of ancient Gilgal. We retire amid the howls of jackals and the miserable music and dancing of the Bedouins who

"Vex with mirth the drowsy ear of night,"

to the delight of another party of tourists near by. We rise early next morning, ride across the plain to Jordan, by the same way, perhaps, the spies went when Rahab sent them off, to the place where Jesus was baptized possibly. Multitudes of pilgrims come here every year to be baptized. Here the Israelites entered the promised land, while the waters of Jordan stood on a heap, here Jordan was parted again when Elijah passed over to be carried to heaven in a chariot of fire. On the way we saw two women grinding corn or wheat in a mill.

The Jordan was muddy, rapid, deep, and about two hundred feet wide. We cut some pipe stems and canes and proceeded to the Dead Sea. I did not notice anything specially differing from other lakes of water, except its very bitter saltness, almost as strong to the taste as potash. It is in the midst of sterility. Some parties went bathing in it, but we did not, as it leaves a gum upon one's cuticle, which is very unpleasant unless one bathes afterwards in fresh water, which we did not have. We had provided bottles and filled them with water here, and bathed the hands and face.

WOMEN "GRINDING AT THE MILL."

The great depression of this funnel-shaped basin under a Meridian sun, (1292 feet below the Mediterranean sea) made it so warm that we had to take off our coats, but the same afternoon, having left the valley, we were in a hail and rain storm up in the mountains that gave us severe colds.

The face of the hill country is covered with beautiful flowers in the greatest variety. I am not botanist enough to name them, but enjoyed their fragrance and beauty no less on that account. Thousands of bees carry off to the rocks that crown every hill the nectar from their cups, and herds of cows, sheep and goats browse through them to their hearts' content. It is still a land flowing with milk and honey.

We noticed a great many piles of stone by the wayside, our guide said they were "Moslem prayers," offered up in sight of a mosque or *wely* (tomb); often twenty stones made an irregular pillar, each stone representing an act of worship.

A caravan of sixty donkeys laden with about four or five bushels of wheat each, and about twenty drivers, passed us going to Bethlehem to market. These patient little animals never stumble, even on the most rugged hill-side in the most tortuous path, even with a burden as heavy as his own weight upon his back. The "latter rain" was falling, and our guide said that the rain that day would depress the price of wheat half a franc, or ten cents, for, said he, "this rain will about insure a good crop." We spent the night in the Church of St. Saba. It is in the fastnesses of the rocks on one side of the gorge (Kedron) several hundred feet deep. St. Saba is said to have lived in a cave, which is shown here, with a lion, the austere life of an old monk. His friends and followers continued to build around the little nucleus until at last a most wonderful structure built of hewn stones and polished stones, stands there to shelter a score of lazy, greasy Greek Priests, who live on bread and olives. No woman is ever supposed to pass within the gates. When we reached the iron portal of the castle, heavy showers were driven by a north-west wind. We carried a permit from the Patriarch of Jerusalem, which gained admission for us, after waiting an incredibly long time in the merciless rain. Dr. Thompson thus describes his first visit to this castle or convent:

"We entered through a low iron door, turned round through a second door, then down again by winding stairs, across queer courts and along dark passages, until we reached at length our rooms, hanging between cliffs that towered to the stars, or seemed to, and yawning gulfs which darkness made bottomless and dreadful. I was struck dumb with astonishment. It was a transition sudden and unexpected, from the wild mountain to the yet wilder, more vague and mysterious scenes of Oriental enchantment. Light gleamed out fitfully from hanging rocks and doubtful caverns. Winding stairs, with balustrade and iron rail, ran right up the perpendicular cliffs into rock chambers, where the solitary monk was drowsily muttering his midnight prayers. It was long after that hour before sleep visited my eyes, and then my dreams were of Arabs, and frightful chasms, and enchanted castles."

One of the tenants showed us about the labyrinth. There is a chapel built and dedicated to St. Nicholas, one to St. Saba and St. John and the Virgin Mary. In the court-yard is St. Saba's octagonal mausoleum. They showed us, also, a room full of skulls—fourteen thousand human skulls—slain by the Persian King Chosroes II, when he stormed and took this stronghold A. D. 616.

They show, growing by the walls, a palm tree that

has miraculous power in certain cases, they say. We bought beads, canes and porcupine quills of them and departed to Bethlehem.

We go through the borders of the fields of the shepherds, reaching the city about noon.

On the spot where it is claimed and conceded our Lord was born is a Christian church, the oldest in the world, in part. A silver star marks the place, and this inscription in latin is around the star, "Here Jesus Christ was born of the Virgin Mary," and a marble manger, the place where they laid him, is near by.

Above these, four rows of lamps of silver and gold burn night and day—one row for each of the four denominations of Christians (Greeks, Catholics, Copts and Armenians) to which this church belongs. They all have chapels in the church, and all worship there every Sabbath and occasionally on week days. I witnessed a funeral conducted by the Coptic Christians. It was one of six children that had died with measles that day. The little corpse was laid on the cold marble floor. The Priest and friends were standing in a circle around it, performing the last offices due its mortal remains.

We went through the chapel of Joseph, where it is said the angel appeared to Joseph and advised him to go into Egypt.

St. Jerome's chamber is shown here, and he is represented with a lion in a stained glass window. Here he studied and translated the Vulgate.

"All about us were memorials of the Gospel history, and various altars—one devoted to the Magi, another to the shepherds and another to JOSEPH—on the spot where they had adored the

Holy Child, or received divine commands. Taking all the circumstances into the account, and comparing the little that can be said against the authenticity of this site with the very powerful consideration in its favor, I relinquished myself to the reverential emotions which the belief that I was in the very spot where the infant Saviour lay would naturally inspire in the heart of a Christian."—*Observations Abroad.*

In Bethlehem Boaz lived, and near by Ruth gleaned. Here David was brought up. Here is the "well by the gate," whose water he longed for, and poured out when he might have enjoyed it, because it was "the blood of the men that went in jeopardy of their lives." The people are brighter as in all the towns, and nearly all are Christians, nominally. They call their town Beit Lahm—that is, city of bread. It is well named, for their fields are very fertile and their olive orchards seldom fail. It is well named further, because it gave to the world Him who is the "bread of life" for the world. It is also claimed that the flock over which the shepherds were keeping watch was the one from which sacrifices were obtained.

"And there were in the same country shepherds abiding in the field, keeping watch over their flock by night; and, lo, the angel of the Lord came upon them, and the glory of the Lord shone round about them, and they were sore afraid. And the angel said unto them, fear not, for behold I bring you good tidings of great joy, which shall be to all people, for unto you is born this day in the city of David a Saviour, which is Christ the Lord, and this shall be a sign unto you; ye shall find the babe wrapped in swaddling clothes, lying in a manger. And suddenly there was with the angel a multitude of the heavenly host praising God and saying: Glory to God in the highest, and on earth peace, good will toward men. And it came to pass, as the angels were gone away from them into heaven, the shepherds said one to another, let us now go even unto Bethlehem and see this thing which is come to pass which the Lord hath made known to us. And they came with haste and found Mary and Joseph and the child lying in a manger."—*Luke* 2: 8-15.

Spending a few hours here, we proceeded to Jerusalem through a heavy shower of the "latter rain," passing on the way the tomb of Rachel, where Jacob buried her when Benjamin was born, "near to Ephratah, the same is Bethlehem." We go through the plains of Rephaim, where David "fetched a compass and came upon the Philistines, over against the mulberry trees," passing the "well of the star," and in sight of the "valley of Roses" on the way. We reach Jerusalem before night on the third day, having visited Jericho, Jordan, the Dead Sea and Bethlehem, and traveled about sixty miles.

*   *   *   *   *   *   *   *   *   *

The following Monday we went to Hebron, eighteen miles south of Jerusalem, passing Solomon's pools about half way between the two cities. One of these is 582 feet long, 210 feet wide and 50 feet deep; the other two are a little smaller. These supply the city with water through aqueducts made of stone and mortar.

*   *   *   *   *   *   *   *   *   *

By noon we reached Hebron. Here we saw grape vines doubtless similar to those that flourished in the days of Caleb and Joshua. Hebron, one of the oldest cities on earth, ranking with Damascus in antiquity, is blessed with splendid fountains. We had come up to look at the parcel of ground that Abraham bought of the sons of Heth " for a possession of a burying-place," and which contains the ashes of Abraham, Isaac and Jacob and their wives. There they buried Abraham and Sarah his wife, there they buried Isaac and Rebekah his wife; and there I buried Leah.

This place is as sacred to the Mahometans as to Christians—in fact they claim to be the true children of Abraham—the title of the Hebrews being only second, while Christians have no inheritance in him. So sacred is the place that they do not venture to disturb the repose of those distinguished sleepers. Nothing short of a mandatory order from the Sultan can turn the key that conceals from common mortals this most revered crypt. We were shown a hole in the wall into which they told us we could thrust our hands and touch the stone under which lie the ashes of heroes who led the race—who made the Bible, largely; who, without precedents, exemplars or formulæ, gave rules for mankind in the mere record of their experiences. Not being allowed to do more than walk around the walls protecting these men and women, we take our Bible and read Gen. 23 and Gen. 50. We tried to imagine the mighty hosts that came up from Egypt with the corpse of Jacob embalmed. Great man in life, "Prince of God"—worthy of the blood that flows in thy veins, and no less great in death! Sleep on—who knows but thy embalmed body may yet be found and attest anew the records dear to us as life itself.

We went up the valley from Hebron about a mile to see a very old oak called "Abraham's Oak." It is in the plains of Mamre and the only oak about there, and if an oak can live four thousand years, may-be this is the one under which Abraham sat when the angels passed down to destroy Sodom. If the *sequaia gigantea* in the Mariposa Grove are five thousand years old, as is claimed, may be this oak is four thousand. Dr. Thompson says: "It is a *baluta*, (evergreen oak) 26 feet in girth, and its thick branches extend over an area ninety feet in diameter." We stood on the enchanted ground where Abraham pleaded for the godless city of Sodom, and whose faith in a faithless people arrested his pleadings too soon.

We bought some of the acorns that grew on the oak, and photographs of it, repaired to our carriage and returned to Jerusalem.

CHAPTER XVI.

MT. CALVARY.

There is, and probably will forever be, dispute about locating the site of Calvary. Two places lay claims to it. One is a hill northeast of the Damascus gate, above a cave called Jeremiah's grotto, many scholars accept this as the true site. Several assert that they were the first to establish the claims of this place, but it is called in Jerusalem, Gordon's Theory. The place is covered with Mohammedan graves. One's first impression when shown this hill is that it answers to the description in the Gospels, and being considerably beyond the city limits and still bare, as if providentially left so, the conviction is deepened. We append below some facts and suggestions confirmatory of this theory by the Rev. Selah Merrill, D. D. LL. D.: (formerly Consul.)

" It is known that under the Convent of the Sisters of Zion which is near the Castle of Antonia, but on the opposite side of "Via Dolorosa," there is six or eight feet below the level of the street, some remarkably well preserved ancient pavement, which hundreds of travellers have visited and admired.

From certain indications we are led to believe that this pavement was connected with an ancient street that ran in nearly a direct line from Antonia northwards to the city wall.

The most important military route of Palestine at the time of Christ was that which connected Caesarea-on-the-Sea with Jerusalem, which it approached from the north.

At the point where the line of the street first mentioned, supposing such a street to have existed, touched the city wall, we find an old gate, closed at present, but bearing the significant name of "Herod's Gate."

If the line of this street be extended beyond this so-called "Herod's Gate," to the northwest, we shall find along it definite traces of an old Roman road. This we find to be identical with the great military road which connected Jerusalem with Caesarea.

It is perfectly natural to suppose that the place of the public execution of criminals would be somewhere on the line of the road. Between the castle and the fatal spot soldiers who guarded the criminals could move to and fro unobstructed.

A little after this road leaves the wall at the point marked as "Herod's Gate" we find on the left hand a hill remarkable in form, noticeable from its position, and with which are connected some traditions respecting the execution and burial of criminals.

Again, we find the name of St. Stephen connected with the western slope of this hill; here is the traditional place of his martyrdom; here a church was erected to his memory, which existed for nearly eight hundred years, and of which remains have been unearthed during five years past.

It is not unnatural to suppose that St. Stephen was executed at the place of the public execution of criminals. The theory that our Lord was executed at the same place has the most valid reasons in its support.

There is current among the Jews in Jerusalem a tradition that this hill was the place of stoning the "Beth Has-Sekilah" mentioned in the Mishna. Likewise another tradition that this hill was the place, or connected with the place, of burial of those who had been publicly executed. The origin of these traditions I do not know, nor do I pretend to estimate the value of them. That they exist at all is curious and—I should say—a significant fact, whether they are worth little or much.

In like manner I do not know the origin of the name "Herod's Gate," or why it should not have been called "Solomon's Gate," or "David's Gate." But the fact that this name is found in this particular locality is significant, when taken in connection with the other circumstances that are grouped around it.

In recent times or since it has been safe to build outside the walls, say within the last twenty years, the principal residences have been erected on the west of the city, because the Jaffa road leads off in that direction. At present, however, they are being extended also in the northwest quarter; but in the time of our Lord private houses or villas, surrounded by gardens and hedges, were on the north of the town because on that side there was not only the great thoroughfare leading to Damascus, but also that leading to Caesarea, which was then the main seaport to Palestine. The numerous ancient cisterns, now mostly in ruins, that are found in all the open region northwest of Jerusalem show that that quarter has been thickly inhabited.

If Joseph of Arimathea, who was a wealthy man, had a private garden near the city, we may suppose with reason that it was located in this direction. The statement in John xix. 41, "in the place where He was crucified there was a garden; and in the garden a new tomb, wherein was never man yet laid," seems to be very explicit. If, on the other hand, we press these words literally, and on the other insist that our Lord was crucified in the place of the public execution of criminals, we make this place and the garden of Joseph of Arimathea to have been identical. The question arises whether a man of position and wealth would have a private garden in such a place? But there is no real objection to supposing that the hill-top, which was easily accessible from the roman military road, might have been devoted to the purpose of execution, and at the same time the ground about it to the very foot of its slopes, to have been occupied by private gardens might have surrounded the hill on the southwestern and northwestern sides, and joined the Roman road on the north.

The Roman road which we have described as leading to Antonia through or near "Herod's Gate" skirted this hill at the foot of its eastern and northeastern slopes. Some miles farther north this road divided, one branch going north to Nablous or Shechem, and the other past Beth Horon to Antipatris and Cæsarea-on-the-Sea. Along this road Paul, strongly guarded, was taken a prisoner to Cæsarea. With what emotions did the prisoner, as he left the city and passed this Golgotha hill, look up to the spot where the Master had died upon the cross!

In the absence of a suitable diagram I will place before the reader a very large capital letter Y, which shall be inverted, and the extremities of its arms shall touch the wall of the city at the points A and B.

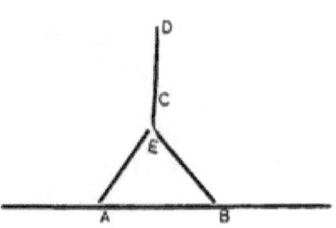

A will represent the present Damascus Gate, and *B* the one now closed called "Herod's Gate." *A C D* will represent the present Damascus or Nablous road, while *B C D* extended pretty directly would touch the Castle of Antonia. *E* represents the Golgotha hill, in which the Grotto of Jeremiah is shown. The bottom of the Y, or *D*, will be understood to be towards the north.

This figure is not correct, inasmuch as the lines *B C* and *A C* meet really at a considerable distance from the city wall; but it was designed to give only a general idea of the place we have been considering, and this purpose it serves sufficiently well.

There is in the western face of this hill a large tomb, before the mouth of which the earth, during past ages, has accumulated to a depth of six or eight feet. It is a peculiar tomb, and has suffered somewhat in the lapse of time, but from what remains of it one would say that it was Christian rather than Jewish in its construction. This point I do not attempt to decide absolutely, but even if it could be shown to be certainly of Christian origin it would only show that the slopes of this hill at a very early period, were thought to be desirable as a place of burial, and hence we may suppose that, at a still earlier period, they were occupied by Jewish tombs.

Very near this point, still in the western slope of this hill, there have been opened during the present summer some very remarkable Christian tombs, supposed to be those that were built by the Empress Eudocia.

My object in what I have now written was merely to group, in a way different from what had ever been done before, and likewise in a more complete manner, certain facts and suggestions which appear to me to be very reasonable in connection with this most important question. Very few points in the topography of ancient Jerusalem can be settled beyond dispute; but with reference to the site of Calvary I will close by repeating what I have already said, namely, that the strong probabilities are in favor of regarding the hill above Jeremiah's Grotto as the place of the crucifixion of our Lord."

The discoveries make by Helena, mother of Constantine, or said to have been made by her,* satisfy the Roman Catholics and Greek Catholics, the Copts and Armenians, that where the church of the Holy Sepulchre is (which is within the present city walls and near the center of the city) is the true site. The various stations occupied by the friends of the Saviour on the occasion of his death, are all marked by a chapel or stone, differing from the rest of the pavement of the floor, in color, shape or elevation. Within the church is a stone called the Unction Stone; on this spot they claim He was laid to be annointed for his burial. Pilgrims from Russia and other lands, numbering now about 2,000, kneel and kiss this stone, with a dozen others in the church, one marking the spot where He appeared to Mary Magdalene, another where John and Jesus' mother were standing when He said, "mother, behold thy son, and son behold thy mother." Then there is shown the Holy Sepulchre; millions have kissed the stones of it. It is divided into two rooms, an ante-room or "chapel of the angel," and the sepulchre proper. From the first, one passes through a stone wall about four feet thick, through an arched door not over three feet high and about two feet wide. Inside, the sepulchre is about five by seven feet; one half is devoted to a marble couch, on which it is claimed the Lord lay. The end farthest from the door is held by a Greek priest who will sell you a candle on Sunday or on any other day, for one or two metterlichs (2 cents). There is standing and kneeling room by the place occupied by the dead for about four. We went there

---
* First paragraph, chapter 17.

several times and always found it crowded. The pilgrims will approach it upon their knees, bending down every few feet to kiss the floor. The Archbishop of the Greek church pretends to have a candle miraculously lighted from heaven in this ante-room once every year. He enters, closes the door, and after awhile thrusts his lighted candle through a hole in the side, from which others light theirs, and then light up the sacred places in the church which they hasten to visit, extinguishing the candle before it is half consumed, carrying the remnant home to be interred with their bones.

The holy sepulchre is built entirely of marble, and is twenty-six feet long, about eighteen broad, and a little over twenty feet high, and four sets of lamps of gold and silver light it up day and night—one for each of the four sects that perform service within the church. It is not claimed that our Lord lay in this very tomb, but only that this is built upon the identical spot where the "Lord lay."

To the right of the main entrance and about fifteen feet above the floor there is a large rock, round about and above which is a chapel, say twenty feet square, (I speak from memory). The stone rises about two feet above the floor and is perhaps fifteen feet wide. It has three holes in it and it is said that in them were placed the crosses of Christ and of the two thieves. To the right of the centre one there is a large cleft in the rock. This they say was made when the rocks were rent.

Then one is shown the stock and pillar to which the Savior was chained, and the one on which he sat, and immediately underneath the cross, Adam's grave is shown; for they say it was needful that his blood should fall on Adam's head. When this tomb was pointed out to Mark Twain, he said he "wept, because he was a blood relation of Adam."

The foolish traditions connected with these sacred spots, rob them of that solemnity that belongs to them, and with the irreconcilable course followed by the various religious sects of Christendom here and now is the greatest hindrance to Gospel work amongst these heathen.

The Christian religion in its worst forms is far superior to the best types of Paganism; but what we wish to do is to make them see the same. And these same Mohammedans have to stand guard with musket and sword, not at the door of the above church, but within it, by the tomb of Christ. I was crowded from my place one Sabbath to make room for Turkish soldiers during worship, almost within arms length of the Sepulchre, and a few years ago, many were killed. Owing to suffocation an effort was made to escape from the building, and the soldiers mistook the rush for an attack upon them, and began fighting, so the greatest melee imaginable ensued, and three or four hundred perished; most however, were run over and trampled to death. The same thing has occurred since our visit, except that it was a real fight originating in bigotry.

The guards are kept because the church is the joint property of four denominations, Greeks, Catholics, Armenians and Copts, each of which wants more than the rest will allow. There is worship in the various chapels of the church every day.

CHAPTER XVII.

IN AND ABOUT JERUSALEM.

March 12.—We went first to the Holy Sepulchre already spoken of above; see two tombs near by the Holy Sepulchre, one of them called the tomb of Nicodemus, the other that of Joseph of Arimathea, they are vaults cut out of the rock on which the church is built. There is a chapel in a cave in the church, in which the Catholics say Helena found the three crosses on which Jesus and the two thieves were crucified, and so knew this to be the true Calvary; the other locality has been described in the preceding chapter.

On Mt. Zion we visited the Armenian cathedral, where St. James was beheaded, containing his tomb. The priest showed us about the splendid pile very graciously, and sprinkled rose water over us when we departed.

We passed out of the city through Zion's gate, to a mosque containing David's tomb, and the so-called coenaculum or upper room where Jesus took the last supper with his disciples. The upper room, about forty feet long and thirty wide, is on the first floor about eight feet above ground.

Near by is shown the house of Caiaphas and a stone pillar on which it is claimed the cock sat that crowed as the Lord predicted when Peter so vehemently declared his allegiance. Here the stone that was rolled away from the sepulchre by an angel is shown in an Armenian chapel. Near by are the Armenian and English cemeteries. From this point we have very fine views of the pools of Gihon on the southwest of Hinnom and Hill of Evil Council on the south. Zion is now plowed as a field. Jer. 26:18. Mic. 3:12.

In the afternoon we went to Mt. Moriah. There were several of us, and they required twenty francs admission fees. Only within the last 37 years could Christians enter the TEMPLE AREA at all, and Jews are still excluded or exclude themselves, some say, to avoid stepping on the Holy of Holies, the location of which cannot be identified. Once inside of the walls the Jews had a limit, where Gentiles had to pause on pain of death; now they are forbidden to pass the threshold leading to the grounds; so every Friday they repair to the outside and weep over their glory departed. We saw many of them the day we visited the "Wailing Place," and a sadder sight we have seldom if ever seen. We could not refrain from tears, as they read the old Testament books, and mourned responsively. As these Jews have come here to die, that they may be buried near the Holy City, oppressed by the sins of their past lives, a sense of their national calamities, the contempt of Christian and Mohammedan superiors, and in many cases by extreme poverty, their woe-begone appearance is well calculated to call out our profound sympathies.

We copy the following account of the Wailing Place, and the sad history connected with it, as well as the habits of the Jews who visit it now, from *By-paths of Bible Knowledge*, No. III, by Rev. James King, A. M.:

THE WAILING PLACE.

"Proceeding northward of Barclay's Gate, we come to an interesting section of the wall known as The Jews' Wailing Place, where the Jews assemble every Friday afternoon. It is a small quadrangular area, roughly paved with large square stones, situated between low houses and the Sanctuary wall. It is further hemmed in by walls on the north and south sides, and the area itself is only of small dimensions, being about a hundred feet in length and fifteen in breadth. The Temple wall above ground at this spot is about sixty feet high, and the lower courses of visible masonry are for the most part made up of magnificent stones, venerable from their high antiquity and from the fact that they are veritable remains of the old Jewish Temple. For many generations, at least once a week the Jews have been permitted to approach the precincts of their Temple, and it is a touching sight to see them manifest affection to the venerable wall, while they kiss the very stones and bathe them with their tears.

"The Psalmist's words were verily fulfilled: 'Thy servants take pleasure in her stones, and favor the dust thereof.' Kneeling before the vestiges of their desolate and dishonored sanctuary, the Jews still raise the wail of lamentation: 'God, the heathen are come into Thine inheritance, Thy holy Temple have they defiled, they have laid Jerusalem on heaps. . . . We are become a reproach to our neighbors, a scorn and derision to them that are round about us. How long, Lord? Wilt Thou be angry forever? Shall Thy jealousy burn like fire?'

"Outside Barclay's Gate, and close to the south end of the Wailing Place, Sir Charles Warren sank a shaft, and had to dig through rubbish to the enormous depth of about eighty feet below the colossal lintel, before he came to the foundation of the Haram wall. Beneath the surface are twenty-two courses of excellent masonry, each course being from three to four feet in height. The lowest course is let into the rock, and each course is set back about half an inch as it rises. The drafting of the stones is very finely executed, and for delicate finish will compare favorably with drafted masonry in any other part of the Temple enclosure.

"During a recent visit to Jerusalem, after an examination of this part of the wall, the author took up his position at the south end of the paved area, and watched the appearance and movements of the increasing crowd. Nearest to him stood a row of women clad in robes of spotless white. Their eyes were bedimmed with weeping, and tears streamed down their cheeks as they sobbed aloud with irrepressible emotion. Next to the women stood a group of Pharisees—Jews from Poland and Germany. These are known by the name of Ashkenazim, because they came from Ashkenaz—the name given to Germany by the Rabbins. For the most part the Ashkenazim are small in stature and fragile in form; but their supercilious looks indicate the same self-sufficient pride that characterised the Pharisees of old. The old hoary-headed men generally wore velvet caps edged with fur; long love-locks or ringlets were dangling on their thin cheeks, and their outer robes presented a striking contrast of gaudy colors.

"Beyond stood a group of Spanish Jews, of more polished appearance and dignified bearing. They are called Sephardim, because, according to the Rabbins, Spain is Sepharad. Besides these, there are Jews from almost every quarter of the world, who had wandered to Jerusalem that they might die in the city of their fathers and be buried in the Valley of Jehosaphat under the shadow of the Temple Hill. The worshipers gradually increased in number until the crowd thronging the pavement could not be fewer than two hundred. It was an affecting scene to notice their earnestness; some thrust their hands between the joints of the stones and pushed into the crevices as far as possible little slips of paper on which were written, in the Hebrew tongue, short petitions addressed to Jehovah. Some even prayed with their mouths thrust into gaps, where the weather-beaten stones were worn away at the joints. The explanation given of this strange proceeding is that it arises from a desire on the part of the worshippers that their prayers may rise from holy ground, and, ascending like the morning and evening incense, may, through the sacred wall, rise to the God of Abraham.

"The congregation at the Wailing Place is one of the most solemn gatherings left to the Jewish Church, and, as the writer gazed at the motley concourse, he experienced a feeling of sorrow that the remnants of the chosen race should be heartlessly thrust outside the sad enclosure of their father's holy Temple by men of alien race and an alien creed. Many of the elders, seated on the ground with their backs against the wall on the west side of the area and with their faces turned towards the Eternal House, read out of their well-thumbed Hebrew book passages from the prophetic writings, such as 'Be not wroth very sore, O Lord; neither remember iniquity forever; behold, see, we beseech Thee, we are all Thy people. Thy holy cities are a wilderness, Zion is a wilderness, Jerusalem a desolation. Our holy and our beautiful house, where our fathers praised Thee, is burned up with fire, and all our pleasant things are laid waste. Wilt Thou refrain Thyself for these things, O Lord? Wilt Thou hold Thy peace, and afflict us very sore?'"

About four o'clock a Rabbi stood up, facing the Sanctuary wall, and, resting his book against the stone, read aloud from the Jewish lamentation service a kind of litany. After each petition the assembly responded in a peculiar buzzing tone, rocking their bodies to and fro, after the manner of their fathers. The following litany of eight petitions is often rehearsed:

The Rabbin reads aloud—	All the people respond—
For the place that lies desolate:	We sit in solitude and mourn.
For the place that is destroyed:	We sit in solitude and mourn.
For the walls that are overthrown:	We sit in solitude and mourn.
For our majesty that is departed:	We sit in solitude and mourn.
For our great men who lie dead:	We sit in solitude and mourn,
For the precious stones that are buried:	We sit in solitude and mourn.
For the priests who have stumbled:	We sit in solitude and mourn.
For our kings who have despised Him:	We sit in solitude and mourn.

Another litany, written after the manner of an antiphonal psalm, is often repeated. It consists of five petitions offered up on behalf of Zion; and, in response to each petition, the assembly offer up a petition for Jerusalem:

The Rabbin prays thus—	The people answer—
We pray Thee have mercy on Zion;	Gather the children of Jerusalem.
Haste! haste! Redeemer of Zion;	Speak to the heart of Jerusalem.
May beauty and majesty surround Zion;	Ah! turn Thyself mercifully to Jerusalem.
May the kingdom soon return to Zion;	Comfort those who mourn over Jerusalem.
May peace and joy abide with Zion;	And the Branch of Jesse spring up at Jerusalem.

The following is an account of a visit to the Wailing Place by Dr. Frankl, a Jew, who visited the Holy City:

"The Jews have a firman from the Sultan, which, in return for a small tax, ensures them the right of entrance to the Wailing Place for all time to come. The road conducted us to several streets, till, entering a narrow, crooked lane, we reached the wall, which has been often described. There can be no doubt but the lower part of it is a real memorial of the days of Solomon, which, in the language of Flavius Josephus, is immovable for all time. Its cyclopic proportions produce the conviction that it will last as long as the strong places of the earth. Before we reached the wall we heard a sort of howling melody—a passionate shrieking—a heart-rending wailing, like a chorus, from which the words came sounding forth, 'How long yet, O God?' Several hundred of Jews, in Turkish and Polish costumes, were assembled, and, with their faces turned towards the wall, were bending and bowing as they offered up the evening prayer. He who led their devotions was a young man in a Polish *talar* who seemed to be worn out with passion and disease. The words were those of the well known Mincha prayer, but drawled, torn, shrieked and mumbled in such a way that the piercing sound resembled rather the raging frenzy of chained madmen, or the roaring of a cataract, than the worship of rational beings. At a considerable distance from the men stood about a hundred women, all in long white robes, the folds of which covered the head and the whole figure, like white doves, which, weary of flight, had perched upon the ruins. When it was their turn to offer up the usual passages of the prayer they joined the men's tumultuous chorus and raised their arms aloft, with their white robes looking like wings with which they were about to soar aloft into the open sky; and then they struck their foreheads on the square stones of the wall of the Temple. Meanwhile, if the leader of their prayers grew weary, and leaned his head against the wall in silent tears for a moment, there was a death-like silence. I happened to be near him, and I could mark the sincerity of his agitated soul. He gave a rapid glance at me, and, without stopping short in his prayer, said to me, 'Mokam Kodesh,' *i. e.,* 'Holy place,' and pointed to my covered feet. My guide had forgotten to inform me that I must take off my shoes.

I now did so, and was drawn into the vortex of raging sorrow and lamentation.

"The Jewish Sabbath begins on Friday evening at sunset; therefore, when the sun is sinking low in the western sky, the worshippers at the Wailing place sometimes chant in Hebrew a plaintive hymn known as the Wailing Song. The melody is thought to date from the time of Ezra, and, consequently, is accounted to be amongst the oldest pieces of music extant. The following is a translation of the hymn:

> He is great, He is good,
> He'll build His Temple speedily.
> In great haste, in great haste,
> In our own day speedily.
> Lord, build—Lord, build,
> Build Thy Temple speedily.
>
> He will save, He will save,
> He'll save His Israel speedily.
> At this time now, O Lord,
> In our own day speedily.
> Lord, save—Lord, save,
> Save Thine Israel speedily.
>
> Lord bring back, Lord bring back,
> Bring back Thy people speedily;
> O restore to their land,
> To their Salem speedily.
> Bring back to Thee, bring back to Thee,
> To their Savior, speedily.

"How long the Jews have assembled for lamentation at the Wailing Place cannot be determined with certainty, although there is historical evidence to prove that they have assembled to mourn over their lost glory and desolate Temple since the time of the Apostles. After the merciless destruction of Jerusalem by Titus, in 70 A. D., the priestly families fled to Tiberias, on the shores of the sea of Galilee; and the great men of the Jewish nation found homes in Egypt, Cyprus, and other places, while only the poor and the officiating priests remained in the Holy City. Slowly Jerusalem rose from her ashes, and for sixty years enjoyed such peace as comes after the maddening din of warfare.

"During that period the Jews bewailed their downfall, and nobody interfered with the poor inhabitants of the city. At length, after sixty years' freedom from accursed warfare, a mighty insurrection arose among the Jews against the oppres-

JEWS' WAILING PLACE.

sive yoke of Rome. The insurgents were headed by Bar Cochaba, the Son of a Star, the last and greatest of the false Messiahs After three years of warfare and butchery, Bar Cochaba, with sword in hand, fell down slain on the walls of Beth-er, near Bethlehem, and forthwith the domination of the Romans was restored. The Emperor Hadrian, filled with wrath at the insurrection, again destroyed Jerusalem, and drove the Jews from their hallowed city. He fixed a Roman colony on Zion, built a heathen temple on Moriah, on the site of the sacred edifice of the Jews, and dedicated it to Capitoline Jupiter. When the colony had increased in size he bestowed upon the new city the name of Ælia Capitolina, combining with his own family title of Ælius the name of Jupiter of the Capitol, the guardian deity of the colony. Christians and pagans were permitted to reside there, but the Jews were forbidden to enter the city on pain of death; and this stern decree remained in force in the days of Tertullian, about a century afterwards. About the middle of the fourth century, however, the Jews were permitted to dwell in the neighborhood, and once a year—on the anniversary of the capture of Jerusalem—they were allowed to enter the Temple enclosure that they might approach the *lapis pertusus*, or perforated stone, and anoint it with oil. 'There,' says an ancient writer, 'they make lamentations with groans, and rend their garments, and so retire.' "

"Jerome, the eminent Latin Father, who founded a convent at Bethlehem, and for thirty years led an ascetic life in the Holy Land, when commenting, about 400 A.D., on Zephaniah i. 14, 'The mighty man shall cry there bitterly,' draws a vivid picture of the wretched crowds of Jews who in his day assembled at the Wailing Place, by the west wall of the Temple, to bemoan the loss of their ancestral greatness, On the ninth of the month Ab, might be seen the aged and decrepit of both sexes, with tattered garments and dishevelled hair, who met to weep over the downfall of Jerusalem, and purchased permission of the soldiery to prolong their lamentations (*et mies mercedem postulat ut illis flere plus liceat.*) The perforated stone, called *lapis pertusus*, is probably the Sakhra or sacred rock of Moriah, originally the threshing-floor of Araunah the Jebusite, and now covered with the elegant sanctuary called Kabbet es-Sakhra or Dome of the Rock.

After the Moslem occupation of Jerusalem in the seventh century, the *lapis pertusus*, or sacred rock of Moriah, was invested with a sanctity second only to the Kaaba of Mecca. This sanctity was afterwards extended to the whole of the top of Moriah, and, consequently, the heretic Jews were driven outside the Temple's enclosure. In course of time, however, they approached the outer walls, and there continued to celebrate their lamentation service. Thus for above twelve centuries have the Jews assembled outside the walls of their ancient Temple; but it would be difficult, with our present knowledge, to prove that the present Wailing Place has been the identical spot of lamentation throughout the many generations that have lived and died since the Moslem occupation of Jerusalem under Khalif Omar in 637 A. D."

I neither saw nor heard anything to favor the supposition that the Jews are rapidly returning to Palestine. I think that the beneficence of Sir Moses Montifiore, and of the Rothschilds, the former having built tenement houses in abundance, nearly or quite rent free; the latter building hospitals, induced many poor Jews from all over the world to return to their historic and sacred city; and this movement in connection with certain prophecies of scripture, gave rise to the belief. The following however throws light on the subject from a more recent observer:

CHARLOTTE, N. C., Jan. 19, 1891.—Dr. A. W. Miller, pastor of the First Presbyterian church, of this city, has received a letter from Dr. Ben. Oliel in charge of a mission established in Jerusalem by Dr. Miller, for the conversion of Jews, which says that eighty thousand Jews had reached there from Russia since December 1st. The letter says Russia had even attempted to annoy the Jews in Jerusalem.

There must be an error in the figures. There are no transportation facilities adequate to such results. This immigration is chiefly from Russia, no doubt, and is due to persecution.

CHAPTER XVIII.

AROUND, ABOVE, BENEATH AND IN JERUSALEM—MT. MORIAH—GETHSEMANE.

The temple area is bounded by a wall fifteen hundred feet long on the east, nine hundred and twenty-seven on the south, sixteen hundred feet on the west, and one thousand on the north, and covers thirty-five acres; it is above Ophel, a hill between the Tyropœon Valley and the Valley of Jehoshaphat; it is now nearly level, for Solomon built walls and pillars on the top of which he placed arches, supporting a platform, on the top of which he built other pillars and continued the circumscribing walls to a very great height, still another opinion places this masonry in the age of Justinian, when in 529 A.D., he built a church on Temple Hill to the Virgin Mary.

The walls are, mostly, now, under ground, but the same platform built by King Solomon, as some think, remains, and the subterranean caves made by covering over these pillars are called Solomon's stables, and the pillars have holes for rings, in which no doubt the halters were tied. If they were not used by King Solomon for stables, they were by the Knights Templar. A little to the west of the center of the temple area is the Mosque of Omar, on the site of Solomon's Temple. It is an elevated platform of stone fifteen feet higher than the surrounding area. Julian, the apostate, attempted to rebuild the Temple to prove that Christ was a false prophet; but while excavating, balls and flames of fire issued from the ground, consuming the workmen. It was attempted again, afterward, with similar results.

"After the conquest of the country by the Mohammedans, one of the first acts of Calif Omar was to build a splendid Mosque, known as the 'Dome of the Rock,' on the site of Jehovah's Temple. This edifice, afterward beautified by Calif Abdel Marwan, still crowns the summit of Moriah, and the place is regarded by the Moslems as only second to Mecca in point of interest, as Mohammed is said to have ascended to Heaven from here. The Mosque is an octagonal building, five hundred and thirty-six feet in circumference, surmounted with a graceful dome supported by twelve exquisite antique marble and porphyry columns. Covering, as it does, simply this naked rock so sacred in its associations to Jew, Christian and Mohammedan, nothing could be more appropriate or grand. It is much finer than St. Sophia at Constantinople, or St. Marks at Venice; has no rival for grace or sanctity, and its peculiar shape is the only reason it has not been more extensively copied; but as a shrine for the 'Rock of Ages' it is perfectly beautiful, and when the sunshine streams through its fifty-six gorgeous windows, its golden mosaics seem to kindle up with a divine fire, rendering the spot truly glorious. The building is encased on the outside with encaustic tiling and colored marble; within it is golden arabesque mosaic, very rich, with passages from the Koran everywhere inserted in the walls. And, what is remarkable, no reference is made in the inscription to David, Solomon, or Mohammed, but the name of 'Jesus, the Son of Mary,' is mentioned four times. Is this prophetic of its becoming some day a Christian church?

"The profound repose and death-like silence of this Temple is in keeping with the sacredness of the place, for here alone, in all the earth, was the only living and true God worshipped throughout long ages! When Greece was ignorant of God, and Rome had 'changed the glory of the Incorruptible into an image made like to corruptible man,' the descendants of Abraham on this mount and in this place still preserved the writings of Moses, and the worship of the one true and only God. It was here Solomon erected his beautiful Temple; here through long centuries the daily sacrifice was offered, and God manifested himself to his people in the mysterious Shekinah as nowhere else on the earth. Here first were sung those stirring psalms of David, which ever since have been ascending like incense from earth to Heaven. Toward this spot God's people in every age and in every land have turned their faces when they prayed; and it was here the Great Teacher himself taught his disciples, wrought his miracles, and near by, on Calvary, a spur of the same mountain, as the 'Lamb of God,' was sacrificed for the sins of the world. Surely, 'This is none other but the house of God and the gate of Heaven.' " *

The rock beneath this gorgeous dome is the one on which Josephus says Abraham built an altar for the sacrifice of Isaac. Through the rock there is a hole about twenty inches in diameter, used, no doubt, for conveying the remains of sacrifices and the ashes to some subterranean sewer or passage emptying into the valley of Jehoshaphat, but the Mohammedans say that Mahomet went from this place to Heaven, passing through the rock (there is a cave under the rock, his praying place) making this hole. He sprang up from the rock, and they pretend to show one of his tracks on the rock. They say the rock started to follow him, but Gabriel flew from Heaven and caught the stone, checking it in mid air. He left the print of his hand upon it, which is shown you, and they pretend that the rock has been miraculously suspended there ever since, having no visible support. They also say that from the east wall of the Temple area to Mt. Olivet a bridge will be built as narraw as a razor's edge; Christ will sit at one end and Mahomet at the other; every mortal will have to cross over it; the righteous alone will succeed; the wicked will fall off and perish in the valley of Jehoshaphat, over which the

---
*Dr. De Hass in "Buried Cities Recovered."

bridge is built. The Rabbis could equal the Arabs in imaginary creations. Speaking of Og, King of Bashan, they say: "The soles of his feet were 40 miles long, and the waters of the Deluge only reached to his ankles. He was ante-diluvian, but escaping became Eliezer of Damascus, Abraham's servant. Abraham was only 74 times the size of ordinary men. Scolding Og one day, Og trembled until a double tooth fell out. Abraham made himself an ivory bedstead of it, on which he ever afterwards slept." "Moses, who was ten ells high, once attacked Og—by this time King of Bashan. He seized an ax ten ells long, jumped ten ells high, and struck Og on the—ankle. The blow finally killed him; for Rabbi Jochanan says: 'I have been a grave-digger, and once when I was chasing a roe it fled into a shin-bone. I ran after it for three miles, but could neither overtake it nor see any end to the bone, so I returned and was told that it was the shin bone of Og, King of Bashan.' "—*Thompson.*

Near the Mosque of Omar is the Mosque El Aksa, built for a Christian church. In this, contrary to reason, for it occurred in the Temple, they show where the angel appeared to Zechariah, where Mary lodged, and a cradle (a marble one) in which Christ lay during his stay on the occasion of his circumcision. This is in a cave under the temple area and is possibly true. The print of his feet where he stood on the occasion of arguing with the doctors and lawyers, is pointed out.

We wandered about the hallowed spot until nearly sundown, went through the Via Doloroso by the churches of the Flagellation, Ecce Homo and by Pilate's Gate. We went to see Robinson's arch the same afternoon; this is the remainder of a ruined bridge once crossing from Mt. Moriah to Mt. Zion, over Tyropeon valley; it was more than three hundred feet long, fifty-one wide, and eighty high. On it Titus parleyed with the Jews before striking the final blow, A. D. 70.

One day Mr. M. and I walked around the city about a mile beyond the walls, taking in eight high hills. We passed a cemetery from which a melancholy and monotonous bugle sounded for hours. In our conjectures about the occasion of such a, to us, unique procedure, we finally concluded some soldier was dead and these were expressions of military grief. (as such they would have been fitting.) We stood and watched the manœuvres of the camp some hundreds of yards away in Gihon valley; we decided this time they were about to inter some noted charger, as certainly they were handling a dead horse, whereupon we thought the solo still more appropriate; but the horse was disposed of and our musician still made the welkin ring. Subsequent inquiry revealed to us that he was a mile from the city, in obedience to a delicate sense of the fitness of things, to practice. I thought at once of Dr. Talmage's remark that an embryo cornetist might get to heaven, but it would be hard for his neighbors to do so. Did the city fathers of Jerusalem see no chance unless they ostracised for the time their band recruits?

We took one day to do the hills around Jerusalem and one the valleys. We start down Gihon, called Hinnom, below the lower pool of Gihon, and pass four most pitiable looking lepers, some of whom have lost fingers, some toes, some the voice, except a dry husky whisper. A good house has been provided for them, and support, about one mile south-west of the city, but they prefer to

sit by the way-side and beg. We go down Hinnom to
En Rogel, in Jehoshaphat valley; here is a pool of most
filthy looking water, but used; here David's friends,
Jonathan and Ahimaaz, came for news when he fled
from Absalom—2 Sam., 17:17. Here Adonijah made a
feast with a view of gathering adherents and seizing the
Kingdom when David was about to die. Joab, the great
captain, was in his party to his own ruin. We then go
up through the King's gardens, which are luxurious and
fruitful enough, watered, as they are, from the pool of
Siloam, to deserve the name. We pause at Siloe's brook
to see the daughters of Siloam come over for water and
do their washing. It is no longer a "shady rill," nor an
inspirer of lofty song, except to the blind indeed. We
ascend to Gethsemane, enclosed by a wall of stone about
seven or eight feet high; it covers about one-third of an
acre, contains eight large olive trees, possibly the same
under which the disciples slept when He was withdrawn
from them, about a stone's cast, to pray. It is in the
possession of the Franciscan order of the Latin church,
and kept by a kind and courteous gardener, who gave
us, unsolicited, small bouquets, for which he refused
backsheesh! He also refused to increase the size of them
for pay. We tried to call up the scenes of that doleful
night, when our best friend "trod the wine-press alone,"
"and of the people there was none with Him." Hard
by is a cave called the "Grotto of the Agony," into which
the Savior retired to pray. The Latins have a church
there now and in it a beautiful statuette representing the
agony and the angel strengthening Him. "And he was
withdrawn from them about a stone's cast, and kneeled
down, and prayed, saying, Father, if thou be willing,
remove this cup from me: nevertheless, not my will,

but thine, be done. And there appeared an angel unto him from heaven, strengthening him. And being in an agony he prayed more earnestly: and his sweat was as it were great drops of blood falling down to the ground." *Luke* 22: 41-44. My heart swelled with gratitude that already such an inheritance had fallen to me by His sufferings and death, and that these good things are but the earnest of what awaits us beyond.

Before leaving Jerusalem we went into the subterranean quarries, where King Solomon got stone for building the city, the Temple and the Walls of Jerusalem. One can wander here for hours over new ground all the time, see how the stone was cut from the living rock and severed by wooden wedges. Here are tons on tons of chips, where the stones were trimmed before going into the wall. Thompson says:

"We found water trickling down in several places, and in one there was a small natural pool full to the brim. This trickling water has covered many parts with crystalline incrustations, pure and white; in others stalactites hang from the roof, and stalagmites have grown up from the floor. The entire rock is remarkably white, and though not very hard, will take a polish quite sufficient for architectural beauty.

"The general directions of these excavations is south-east, and about parallel with the valley which descends from the Damascus Gate. I suspect that they extend down to the Temple area, and also that it was in these caverns that many of the Jews retired when Titus took the Temple, as we read in Josephus. The whole city might be stowed away in them; and it is my opinion that a great part of the very white stone of the temple must have been taken from these subterranean quarries."

We also went to see the models of the Temples of Solomon and Herod and the Mosque of Omar, by Mr. Shick, who has been present at all modern excavations about the city, who has read all the books that have been written on the subject, and who probably knows more about Jerusalem—ancient and modern—than any other living man on earth. This model was thirty years in building and is a perfect piece of workmanship. He offers to sell the whole for $3,000, which is cheap. We bought photos of this model, and in London I had them put on glass for use in a stereopticon.

We went to Mt. Olivet and ascended the tower there, from which one has a splendid view. To the east, four thousand feet below and eighteen miles away we can clearly see the Dead Sea and the Jordan valley for fifty or sixty miles; beyond, the mountains of Moab. On the west Jerusalem lies on the slopes of the hills rising from the valley of Jehoshaphat, while to the south fruitful fields stretch out in pleasing panorama towards Bethlehem. North we see many small towns, which no doubt were large cities in David's day. We are near the place, possibly on the very spot, on which the disciples and friends of our Lord gathered that memorable day to see their Lord ascend. The Russians have a Greek Catholic church here—a very fine one—called the Church of the Ascension.

The country contains many convents of the Roman and Greek Catholic churches, built at enormous cost, but they are dead, not embalmed, not buried, that were better, they are putrid cadavers, a stench in Mohammedan nostrils.

There is a good Protestant work going on in the city and community. I have formed the acquaintance of several native Christians, some Christian Hebrews, all Protestant, and their type of piety is very satisfactory, so far as one can judge on short acquaintance.

MOUNT OF OLIVES.

The Church of England has a resident bishop and several priests here, an elegant church, a good school, a good Bible depository and two olive wood factories in which they work Christian Jews. I worshipped with them on two Sabbaths and about twenty-five young Jews from twelve to 17 years old made the music, and several grown Jews were in the congregation. I conversed with some of them and rejoiced to see a devotion to Christianity equal to the opposition they had once shown.

One of the priests whom I met handed me the following, which I copy to show the character of the only Protestant missionary work going on in the Holy City:

THE LONDON SOCIETY FOR PROMOTING CHRISTIANITY AMONGST THE JEWS.

JERUSALEM MISSION.

The following are the various means used for bringing the Gospel to bear upon the Jews in this city:

1. CHRIST CHURCH.

In the Hebrew Church on Mount Zion there is a daily Hebrew Service at 7 o'clock in the morning. Also a daily English Service at 9 o'clock.

Sunday services at 10 a. m. and 7:30 p. m. in English.

German Service at 3:30 p. m.

2. SCHOOLS.

The Boys' School, where 42 Jewish boys are boarded and clothed, and a large number partly fed.

3. THE JEWESSES' INSTITUTION.

In this Institution 32 Jewish girls are boarded and clothed, and many day scholars are taught and partly fed. In both Schools, Christianity is distinctly taught.

4. THE ENQUIRERS' HOME.

Here Jewish Inquirers are provided with shelter while their sincerity is tested, as well as their Industry.

5. THE HOUSE OF INDUSTRY.

This is a home for young Converts and tested Enquirers where they are taught Trades and provided with work.

6. THE HOSPITAL.

Here the sick Jews are treated for various complaints; twenty-six beds being provided for them. Also large numbers of Out-Patients are attended to both at the Hospital and in their Homes.

7. THE BOOK-STORE.

Bibles in various languages, and other useful books are sold and given away.

8. THE BOOKBINDING AND PRINTING SHOP.
9. THE CARPENTER'S SHOP.
10. THE SHOEMAKER'S SHOP.

By such methods and works carried on by voluntary subscriptions the Society seeks to spread the knowledge of the Gospel among that people from whom the Church received the truth at the first.

Travelers interested in Christian work are invited to inspect the various parts of the work carried on in Jerusalem.

A conference of Jews and Christians recently held in Chicago, sent a memorial to President Harrison, March 5, 1891, asking his diplomatic aid in an effort to secure for Jews, especially Russian Jews, peaceful possession of homes in Palestine.

CHAPTER XIX.

TRAVELING IN PALESTINE.

Many readers would like to know how the tour of Palestine is made. From Joppa to Jerusalem, Bethlehem and Hebron one can go on wheels; the rest of the country must be visited on horseback, except from Haifa to Tiberias and I believe there is a road from Joppa to Nablous and there is a good road from Beirut to Damascus, 72 miles.

Tourists either camp in tents or lodge in hospices of the Latin and Greek churches, finding hotels only in the larger towns. We chose the second, as being both more economical and affording a better opportunity to study the customs and character of the people now living here.

We made arrangements with Mr. Floyd, a contractor, to take us from Jerusalem to Beirut. The cost of the trip varies according to the size of the party and the amount of baggage, from five to fifteen dollars per day, and takes, by Damascus eighteen to twenty days, and by Tyre and Sidon twelve days.

Both routes are the same as far north as Nazareth Cana and Tiberias, where those going by Damascus go East of the Jordan, while those going up the coast go westward to Mt. Carmel, and Haifa. The road passes Bethel, Shiloh, Plains of Ephraim, Mts. Gerizim and Ebal, Sychar, Jacob's Well, Samaria, Jenin, ("En Gannim" Fountain of Gardens)—the Kishon rises in this city; the plain of Esdraelon, Gideon's Fountain, Gilboa, Shunem, Nain, Endor, Mt. Tabor, Sea of Galilee, Cana, Nazareth, Mt. Carmel, Acre or Akka, Ain or Ez-Zib, where Hyrcanus had his ears cut off and Herod's brother knocked out his brains against a wall to escape indignity, Tyre, Sidon, Sarepta and many other cities of doubtful identity. I will relate some incidents of the journey farther on.

I will give one day from our itinerary. A dragoman, well acquainted with the country, takes charge of the party. He informs us the previous evening at what hour we are to start, and promptly calls us at the appointed time. Our baggage ready, while we take breakfast, it is put on the mules. Breakfast is bread, butter, eggs, cold meats and coffee. This done, with pencil, paper and notebooks and such protections as we need against bad weather, we go out for the day's ride. If the donkey boys have not done strapping on the baggage, it is interesting to watch them fasten half a dozen valises, trunks and bundles of different sizes and shapes so well balanced on a horse, mule or donkey that it will not fall off all day, up and down the mountains, nor gall the beast. I have seen a horse fall flat with his load on the smooth stones of Tyre and not affect the load on his back, but rise and go right on as if nothing had happened. They quarrel a great deal in everything they do —these Arabs, they never seem to understand each other, so that often in tying a rope or fixing a rein, they will talk as if about to fight the whole time—though I believe they seldom do fight. Everything ready we mount our horses for the morning ride.

The first day out from Jerusalem is over a very rough road, being a portion of the old Roman road from Cæsarea, it has greatly deteriorated. We have just turned our backs upon the once more growing city, when two gentlemen in black waterproofs ride into our path; a glance suffices to show they have traveled considerably, and only a minute is required to learn they are Drs. Brancroft, Principal of Phillips Academy, Andover, and Buckley, editor of *The Christian Advocate* (New York.) The former on his second or third trip abroad, the latter on his fourth; the conversation turns from one pleasant topic to another. I learned from Dr. Buckley the sad news of Bishop McTyeire's death.

We go North-west by the tombs of the Kings and the hill Scopus; about one and a half miles out the dragoman says, turn your horses now and look at Jerusalem for the last time. We turn and look; within the walls the city seems to be young; without she appears to be but the work of yesterday.

As we take this last look we remember the Salem (peace) of Melchizedek, the Jebus, strong hold of the Jebusites, and how David came and took it for Israel and made it the capital city of his realm, and how disobedient Israel had to surrender it to Shishak of Egypt, and how this was but the beginning of a long list of sorrows whose anticipations well nigh broke the heart of Jeremiah, and whose realizations were but the fulfillment of the words of Moses, Deut. 28th, and of many of his successors, especially of the man like unto him whom the Lord God should raise up unto Israel. We think of Titus' hosts encamped just here to the left on Scopus, of that final shock when all was lost, even to the holy temple itself, of the brave and the wise Josephus, cool in the hour when

"Death rode upon the sulphury siroc,
Red battle stamped his foot and nations felt the shock."

And not only nations, but the world. Poor, fanatical, ritualistic, starving Jews, your house now desolate, is not even left you; vainly hoping to the very end for a Saviour, the Messias, had he returned indeed, it would have been to be again rejected, and hither wandered the poor, deluded crusader, urged by fanaticism, ambition and revenge at a cost of millions of lives and billions of gold to take the holy Sepulcher from Moslem hands with barbarous butchery; to be surrendered again to Islam under Saladin.

Just over the city walls rises the magnificent dome of the mosque of Omar on the site of Solomon's Temple, to the left, the Mosque El Aksa, beyond, the tomb of David on Mt. Zion, to the right the Tower of David, the splendid double-domed church of the Holy Sepulchre, and to the right of the walled part the Russian Hospice worth hundreds of thousands of dollars. To the left and visible enough is Mt. Scopus and Mt. Olivet, at whose base is Gethsemane, beyond is Siloam, beneath which flows "Siloe's shady rill" "fast by the oracle of God." Just over the Eastern wall is the "hill of Evil counsel." The minarets, domes, towers and cathedrals all are photographed indelibly on memory's page; with a deep sigh we bid the City of David farewell. What a history of voluptuous splendor, of religious solemnities, of ignominious captivities, of more than melancholy tragedies, she has known! What future awaits her, who can tell!

We turn our horses' heads towards the North, grateful for that mercy that has brought us here and so greatly increased life's richness. We soon reach Shafat, called Nob, where David fled and fed in trouble, I. Sam. 21. Tradition says this is the birth place of the prophet

JERUSALEM FROM THE SOUTH SIDE OF OLIVET.

Joel. Nothing now remains except ruins, with a few poor houses, and it stands about one hundred yards from the road. We next and soon come to Ramah, the home of that Levite who was so unfortunate at Gibeah of Saul, Judges 19. Saul's seven sons were hanged near here at Gibeah; Jer. 31:15, also immortalizes this place, though now not one Jew lives here, and only a few wretched Arabs. Over very stony (old ruined Roman) roads about 11 o'clock we pass on our right Beeroth, where it is claimed Joseph and Mary turned back to look for Jesus, when lost at 12 years of age. The day has become exceedingly cold and windy. We have reached Bethel by 12 M., and ride down into an old reservoir and eat on the ground, pic-nic fashion, behind the wall of the reservoir. While the dragoman and cook arrange for lunch we read up the history of Bethel and find that this is where Abraham built an altar to God, that here Jacob took some of these stones, possibly the one I sit on was one of them, to make a pillow to rest on as he fled from Beersheba to Padanaram, and had that wonderful dream, seeming to see the angels of God ascending and descending on a ladder, and though the ancients called it Luz at the first, it has been called Bethel ever since. Here he built an altar and annointed it with oil and called it " El-Bethel, because there God appeared unto him, when he fled from the face of his brother." Here he vowed. Here Rebekah's nurse died and was buried. Near here the two she-bears slew forty and two children for mocking Elisha, the prophet of God. Here Jeroboam set up a golden calf and sought to turn away the people from God; and on one occasion, stretching out his hand to smite God's prophet, it was withered, and restored again in answer to the prophet's prayer. Just across a ravine and in full view is Ai, which has a history following Jericho's overthrow. Josh. 7 tells us that the host of Joshua were routed because of Achan's covetousness at Jericho in stealing a wedge of gold, two hundred sheckels of silver and a goodly Babylonish garment, and could not prevail until after Achan's execution.

Lunch over, we mount our steeds and make towards Jifna, where we are to lodge for the night.

We pass no places, these two hours now recognized as connected with sacred history, though no doubt could these stones speak they would rehearse sad stories of blood and tears. We observe on the way steep hills terraced to the top, and estimating the time and labor required to do the work of terracing according to American standards of valuation much of this land costs two thousand dollars per acre, and fifty to one hundred dollars per acre annually to keep it in repairs. But humanity is very cheap, and time is not money, as with us.

There is a great variety of climate, not much in soil. The Jordan valley and along the coast of the Mediterranean is very warm now; the hills are temperate and pleasant while the mountain tops are colder, and Lebanon and Hermon covered with snow. Nearly all the soil is red, some spots of grey land are seen, and a few belts of black ground in Galilee, but all is productive to an amazing degree. Some of the hills and mountains seem at a little distance to be destitute of any soil, and to be only made of rocks, yet here the herds of sheep and goats find pasturage. There is no more beautiful land perhaps anywhere than the plains of Jezreel and all the panorama seen on all the sides of Mt. Tabor, from the top, and all the country from Mt. Tabor to the sea of Galilee is excellent for farming and not very hilly.

But turning from the agricultural to the political condition of this country I have observed that it is, if not fully ripe, nearly so for a change, if I may not say revolution. One typical American to every one hundred inhabitants here would bring about a revolution in, I think I may say, five years at the farthest, but it is coming any way, only Moslemism stays it, but the claims of humanity are asserting themselves steadily. The English, French, Germans and Russians are all fully apprised of the coming smash, and each fully awake to a sense of the possible gain it may result in to each. Each watches all the rest with Arguslike vigilance; each is putting as many men in position in every salient point as possible.

At Beirut there is a post office for the English, one for the Austrians, one for the French, etc., and enough men of these three nations, i. e., of either of them, to do the most important civil service of Syria, which they expect to do some of these days.

CHAPTER XX.

NORTH OF JERUSALEM.

The second day out from Jerusalem was very rainy, and we needed the Arab *abais* (a kind of overcoat used by Bedawins) we had bought in Jerusalem, which were good waterproofs.

We passed through Hora-Meiyeh or Robbers' Glen, where we met a caravan of about forty camels, with as many drivers; their cargo was wheat, which was set on the ground while the camels were grazing. There is an excellent spring in this glen at which we got a good draught. Our road wound up the ravine, while on either hand the hillsides were terraced to the top, with no less than one hundred stone walls, some of them ten and twelve feet high. On these terraces wheat or lentils are sown, or fig or olive trees planted.

We reached the site of ancient Shiloh about noon, where we lunched in an old ruined church. We saw the desolation spoken of by Jeremiah 7: 12-14 and 26: 6, and remembered that this was once Joshua's capitol, where he reared up the tabernacle.—Joshua 18. That here Eli lived and died, that here Hannah came and prayed and was heard and obtained the desire of her heart, and made yearly visits to bring her boy a little coat.

And as I read this history, and considered the happy results I thought how beautiful to give our children to God in infancy and rear them for his service.

We ride during the afternoon through the fertile plains of Ephraim and Mukhna, reaching Jacob's well just before night. It too is walled in and a gate kept for backsheesh, but the gate-keeper was absent, and we climbed up some other way, i. e., over the wall. A church was once built over the well, but it has gone to destruction, leaving only broken columns projecting here and there from the debris. A large stone, like a mill-stone, covers the shaft; this stone has a hole drilled through it about two feet in diameter. It was very deep but dry. We longed for a draught from its depths. Since our visit the Russian government have bought it from the Turks and will give it all needed improvements. We sat on that well's mouth and looked over the fields two months later in the year than when our Lord said: "Say not ye, There are yet four months, and then cometh harvest?" Just out there a few hundred paces is a tomb called Joseph's tomb in the parcel of ground that Jacob gave to his son Joseph, where they buried him, and the bones of Joseph, which the children of Israel brought up out of Egypt, burying them in Shechem, in a parcel of ground which Jacob bought of the sons of Hamor the father of Shechem for a hundred pieces of silver; and it became the inheritance of the children of Joseph.—Joshua 24: 32. We look up at Mt. Ebal and Gerizim, called mountains of Cursing and Blessing.—Josh. 8: 33.

I copy from my Diary the following, written the evening we were there: "Our Lord must have been here in winter, but at any season the scene is inspiring. Already the place was old and full of history, beneath him was Jacob's well before him the parcel of ground he had bought and lost in unequal conquest and retaken with his "sword and bow," in the midst of it was Joseph's tomb, above him the Mountains of Blessing and Cursing, around him a people dead to their privileges and duties, and void of any knowledge of the truth.

No place on earth was better suited to reflection on the remote and romantic past, the serious and pregnant present, the sad foreboding future. Oh, Son of God, I am riding by where thou walkedst and wast weary with the journey, resting thy tired head, it may be, that night on some of these stones, because the Jews and Samaritans have no dealings with one another. I go up to Shechem, whither, perhaps, thou couldst not, and find a good home. I have enough of all but thy spirit. Thou carriedst all our woes. Thou art worthy to be crowned Lord of all. Be my portion forever, and lift me, a constant beneficiary of thy grace, to a higher plane of living.

We ride between Ebal and Gerizim to Sychar of old, called now Nablous. It is a city of 13,000 inhabitants and contains the remnant of the old stock of Samaritans (about one hundred and fifty) whose chief or high priest, Jacob Shalaby, we saw at Jaffa. They still worship in Mt. Gerizim as directed.—Ex. 12. I saw the old Pentateuch manuscript in their possession, which they claim to be twenty-six hundred years old. It is parchment and rolls on two cylinders from one of which it unrolls as it rolls upon the other, it is about twenty-four inches wide, and very dingy as one would expect. The Turks have a garrison here. There are signs of great poverty. The curse of leprosy abides and abounds. There is a steam wheat mill and a soap factory or two, though none of the inhabitants appear to have ever used any of the soap. We spent the night with Mr. Fulcher, a missionary, who was so busy trying to right some altercation (I think) that had arisen that we had little conversation with him.

He remarked, in answer to some questions, he was only sowing seed now.

The next morning we rode down a stream on a splendid road that went to Jaffa. On the banks of this creek that emptied its water into the Mediterranean, grow the richest vegetation, the finest olive trees, and most luxuriant gardens. We also passed about a dozen flouring mills run by water power. No dams were built across the stream but a long race carried the water until a fall of twenty feet could be secured, then in an aqueduct made of stone the water is carried to the centrifugal wheel which is the only power we saw used in Palestine. We saw one turned by concussion in Syra. I dismounted and entered one of these; the stones were about three feet in diameter, the upper one was about six inches thick, without a hoop, while the flour, unbolted, ran out in a depressed place on the floor. The miller was standing barefooted in the grist; two or three donkeys and as many dogs were standing around near enough to begin a meal the moment the guard (the miller) should leave his charge.

We leave the good road and take a bridle path to Samaria, the old capitol of Samaria, two hours distant. A hundred columns, monoliths, some *in situ*, marking the course of the vast colonnade three fourths of a mile long, some scattered over the fields tell of a magnificence and splendor worthy of the Roman that whilom ruled this ruined realm.

"Sixteen columns on the topmost terrace are still thought to mark the site of Baals temple which Jehu demolished—2 Kings, 10."—*Land and Book*. But all that is left of the ancient palatial and colonnade splendor are some rows of stone pillars, twenty feet in height, three feet in diameter, and still retaining some of the polished surface which glistened in beauty two thousand years ago. The situation of Samaria is remarkable. It is on a lofty hill, with a ring of still loftier hills surrounding it. A valley ring and a mountain ring are its double engirdling of beauty and strength. The sides of the central hill, upon which sat the capitol of Israel, slope down to the valley, and bear remains of buildings and terraces. On the northern side, and near the base of the hill, are several rows of massive stone pillars. The situation alone gives us a fair idea of what it used to be in attractiveness and natural strength. After looking at it I did not marvel that it took the Assyrians three years to secure its capture.

It was in this city that was begun the idolatry that proved the ruin of Israel. Here Elijah came and preached to Ahab and Jezebel. Naaman, with his chariots and gold and his leprosy, visited this city, seeking relief. Elisha lived in the neighborhood, and afterward in the city itself, as the scripture tells us that he was there during a certain siege. It was here that occurred several scenes that have always peculiarly and powerfully impressed me. It was on one of these mountains before us that Elisha's servant saw the horseman and chariots of the heavenly army. On the walls here walked the king in hitherto concealed suffering of mind, until the wind blew aside his cloak and the tortured body was revealed. Across that valley sped the lepers in the moonlight to the vacant camp of the besiegers. Over those hills in the distance swept the strange sound that affrightened a whole army and put them to flight; and underneath the walls of this place Elisha led an army blinded by the power of God, and then transformed them all into the lasting friends of Israel by kind treatment—good piece of gospel let down into Old Testament times. Here Philip preached the gospel with great success, and here Piter withstood Simon the Sorcerer."—*Carradine.*

We leave this desolate city and pass through charming landscapes ; far away on every hand, nestled under the hills, are towns that look pretty in the distance, a circumstance that always helps a Mohammedan town. We passed through one—Jeb-a—where the children came out and cried after us " go on," "leave here!" "you are infidels!" " you will all go to hell!" " God will not give you long life!" "you are Nazarenes," &c. We met another large caravan of Damascus merchants going down to Joppa or Egypt. We pass Sânûr on a high hill and the last fortress to yield to Ibrahim Pasha when he overran this country, Dothan, where Joseph's brethren were feeding their flocks when he visited them and met such unkind return for his beneficence, and where Benhadad sought Elisha, and his men were stricken with blindness—2 Kings, 6. We stop for the night at Jenin, on the boundary of the plain of Esdraelon. It is a well watered town containing about four thousand inhabitants. There is no hotel there and we lodged with an Arab. They gave us the principal room in the house. The floor was covered with matting for a carpet. Some real fine paintings were on the wall; and they gave us an excellent dinner of soup, pigeons, sheep and vegetables, including plenty of lettuce, which has no substitute nor rival in the world, as they grow it and prepare it.

While we were eating, however, our dragoman and the Arabs in the yard had some bitter words. I think it was about our stopping in the town, as they used the word Christian and Nazarene a good deal. He would not tell us the cause, which confirmed my conviction that I had conjectured aright. He left them and came in and closed the door, not, however, until they had thrown a stone or two. I made bodily protection a matter of special prayer that evening. A Christian missionary (Catholic) had been driven from the town, and where Catholics can't retain a hold, it is not the place to be careless in. We found a body of soldiers in a few yards of our dwelling next morning, and to them, under God's good providence, we may have owed our safety.

The Arabs failing to kill us the fleas tried. Mr. M., who was tender and afforded good pasturage, remarked that one could stand two or three hundred fleas, but when they came by baskets full and bushels, the supply was beyond the demand, reminding one of the boarder at school who said he did not mind hash for sixty or seventy meals, but when it became a regular thing he got tired of it. We survived them, however, and arose next morning to pursue our way over *the* battle-field of the world—the Plains of Jezreel. It is ravishingly beautiful as a tract of country, and possessed of a history that will ever claim a share of the research and study of the historian and antiquarian. Thothmes III, before the Exodus of the Israelites from Egypt, and Necho fought here. Here fell Ahab and Ahaziah, Jehoram and Jezebel, Sisera and Saul. The following is our diary for that day, March 21:

"Leaving our dwelling at 7 o'clock we go out by a very large crystal fountain, source of Kishon, pass a large Khan, full of Arab travelers, the Pasha's to the right and a mosque to the left, and in two minutes are on the plain. Jenin is full of gardens, cactus and palm-trees. Twenty miles or less to our left is Mt. Carmel; on each side the *fellahs* (farmers) are weeding the wheat and barley; the air is vocal with the songs of birds, and misty clouds, just enough to temper the rays of the ascending sun, are flitting about. Soon we descry Mt. Hermon, covered with snow, far to the north, Mt. Tabor to the north-east, and Gilboa to the south-east. We are in the midst of the plain, every acre of which has drunk the blood of fallen warriors. It is well cultivated for Arab farmers, and very fruitful, but the poor *fellah* is robbed by the government of all except the scantiest support; to be tardy in paying tax is a crime severely punished. The collectors go in pairs, often in squads of four and six, armed with swords and repeating rifles. They levy on olive trees and collect for them before they bloom. Arabs have taken the sword and literally perish by the sword in the hand of the tax-gatherer. We come in two hours to Jezreel, home of Jezebel, Ahab, and Naboth, of Jehu, Jehoram and Gideon. Jezreel is on a hill, the first of the Gilboa range from the west. The houses are all built of mud.

We pass Fuleh, scene of the battle of Mt. Tabor, 1799, where Kheber, with fifteen hundred French soldiers fought twenty-five thousand Turks for six hours, when Napoleon came up with six hundred more and routed them. Here at hand is the part of the plain where Gideon, with his three hundred that lapped vanquished the Philistines by night. There they in turn triumphed over Saul the day after he had gone over yon hill to consult the witch whose cave is in Endor, just behind.

One or two miles to the east are the "high places"—1 Sam. 29; 2 Sam. 1: 19-27. And sparkling in the sunlight to our right are the waters of Gideon's fountain, where his thirsty troops lapped water as a dog—Judg. 7: 6. Before we are done taking in these things our horses have walked into Shunem, scene of Elisha's labors, where lived that woman with such correct ideas of taste and political economy as to have her husband build a room to their house for the preacher. If any would learn how she was paid many fold let him read 2 Kings, 4: 8-37. Mt. Carmel, to which she made her servant drive the donkey in a trot, without stopping, is in sight about fifteen miles west. Shunem is surrounded by a wall of living cactus, through which no living animal much larger than a rat could pass.

A mile beyond the town we pass a Bedouin encampment; they are flaying a sheep of the species called "fat-tail." The tail is about the ordinary length of a sheep's tail, but except the bone and skin is a solid lump of fat weighing sometimes forty pounds, and is used by the natives for butter!

We dine at Nain in a Catholic church, or rather in a room joining the church. Here was performed the miracle recorded in Luke 7: 12-15: "Now when he came nigh to the gate of the city, behold, there was a dead man carried out, the only son of his mother, and she was a widow: and much people of the city was with her. And when the Lord saw her he had compassion on her, and said unto her, weep not. And he came and touched the bier: and they that bare *him* stood still. And he said, Young man, I say unto thee, Arise. And he that was dead sat up, and began to speak. And he delivered him to his mother." It is now a miserable Arab village, about three miles from Endor, whither we go to look into the cave visited by Saul the night preceding his death. The cave is there; so are others; so we looked into it and some others also; a large one is shown as the real scene of the dialogue—1 Sam. 28: 11-19. A surly Turk was sitting in the cave when we visited it. He had a sword, but did not speak nor strike. Here we saw many bee-gums on the roofs of the mud houses, and quantities of bees very busy carrying honey into gums made of mud. It is two hours ride from this place to the top of Mt. Tabor, where we go to spend the night.

CHAPTER XXI.

MT. TABOR, SEA OF GALILEE, NAZARETH.

While some doubt shades the title of Tabor to the honor of the scene of our Lord's transfiguration, we gave it the benefit of our sanction, and tried to feel that near by us somewhere that august event occurred.

Napoleon had been here, we cared not for that, Alexander perhaps, the Crusaders, Barak and Deborah and even Melchizedek. Each had engaged in conflicts affecting the destiny of nations, to greater or less extent, but not for any nor all of these would we have gone thither. We hoped to come if possible where the Son of Mary was made so glorious before His Brethren's eyes.

We went up a zig-zag road through a thin forest of low scrubby oaks, the summit is nearly level and elliptical in shape, being about five hundred yards long by three hundred wide. Old walls and fortifications scattered in confused masses cover the entire top. It is about eighteen hundred feet high, standing alone in the plain.

From a certain point both the Mediterranean and Sea of Galilee are visible, the country of Bashan and most of central Palestine and all of the Plain of Esdraelon. Nazareth fifteen miles across the plains among the hills may be plainly seen.

A great educator from Massachusetts asked me, if I had to obliterate from memory all that I had seen in the

Holy Land with a single exception which particular thing or place would I retain? Finding it difficult to decide he quickened my thought by mentioning Esdraelon.

The Russians or Greeks and Latins both have churches here, and priests but no worshipers. We spent the night with the latter, cut a nice walking stick or two, some pen-holders, and read up such history as we had in the Bible and guide-books relating to Mt. Tabor.

Next morning we rode across the plains passing a fair of which a missionary testifies:

" The noise is incessant, and at a distance sounds like that "of many waters." Every man is crying his wares at the top of his voice, chickens cackle and squall, donkeys bray and fight, and the dogs bark. Every living thing adds somewhat to the many-toned and prodigious uproar. It is now a miscellaneous comedy in full operation where every actor does his best, and is supremely gratified at his own performance.

The people find many reasons for sustaining these antiquated and very curious gatherings. Every man, woman, and child has inherited the *itch* for trading, and, of course, all classes meet at this grand *bourse* to talk over the state of the markets, from the price of a cucumber to that of a $5,000 horse from the Hauran. They meet to talk of the news. These fairs are the daily newspaper, and there is one for every day within a circuit of forty miles. They are the *exchange* and *forwarding office*, corresponding to our markets, fairs, conventions, picnics, excursions, etc."

Millions of bees gathered sweets from nature's prodigal gardens, through which also shepherd boys tended hundreds of sheep, and goats with ears a foot in length, making them equally as conspicuous as the fat-tail sheep. About noon our dragoman, who rode in front of us reined up his horse and turned him around, saying BACKSHEESH! by which he meant I have led you to a sight worth plenty of money, and so he had. In one minute more we paused at the top of a hill that descended suddenly for a thousand feet; under the hill lay the city of Tiberias in the margin of the sea of the same name. The sea of Galilee is thirteen miles long by seven wide, greatest diameters, and 666 feet below the level of the Mediterranean. Its surface was pretty smooth, except here and there it appeared to be the play-place of just the tiniest zephyrs which would go in every direction, never staying long enough nor yet hastening strong enough to more than betray their presence and make a picture as by one magic touch.

> "The winds with wonder whist,
> Smoothly the waters kissed."

The lake is girt about by a plain in places one or two miles wide. We walk down this dreadful hill, take dinner, get a boat and go to Tel-Hum or Capernaum, now desolate; go through the ruins over-run with weeds, stand on the foundation of an old church supposed to be the one built by that Roman who wished Jesus to heal his servant—Luke 7:3-5, and the synagogue in which Jesus often preached. I looked over the desolate place and thought of his reproofs, when this was his home. Here he called Peter, James and John;—here he delivered that most remarkable discourse—John 6.

It is a never-to-be-forgotten object lesson one learns in wandering amongst these cities once so populous, once so blessed, now so forsaken.

We return by Bethsaida (fish town). Nothing remains of it but a mill. We gathered some shells for far-away friends, saw our boatmen catch a nice draught of fishes, and returned through the darkness. The jackals screamed and howled on the shore. We were under a clear sky and gazed up at the

"stars that shine nightly on blue Galilee."

The wind arose and we talked of the night that followed the miracle of feeding the five thousand when the disciples were in such evil plight. We read all the references to the Sea of Galilee, and the Gospels became, in a sense, new to us.

Next morning I went out and took a bath in the pellucid lake, picked up a smooth stone, rode down to see the Sulphur Spring, where baths may be had in a well fitted bathroom free of charge. They are said to be very potent in curing rheumatism. The temperature of these springs is 128° Fah, and when we visited them the rooms were so filled with sulphurous vapor that one could hardly breathe in them.

Our next objective point is Nazareth. We pass, on the way, the Mount of the Beatitudes, by which the Crusaders fought their last battle and were vanquished by the Moslems under Saladin, A. D. 1187. We reach Cana about noon and take lunch in a pomegranate garden, Drs. Burkley and Bancroft ride by, going towards Tiberias. We all wish to see the jars which held the wine made of water by Jesus, at the wedding, but the Greeks and Catholics have possession of them (if they exist at all) and are quarreling about whose they are, and we were debarred the privilege. Going over the same road Jesus so often traveled from Nazareth to Capernaum, we reached Nazareth Saturday afternoon about 3 o'clock and stayed until Monday morning.

We took a guide and went to the precipitous place over which the wicked Jews purposed throwing Jesus, called the Hill of Precipitation. "And all they in the synagogue, when they heard these things, were filled with wrath, and rose up, and thrust him out of the city, and led him unto the brow of the hill whereon their city was built, that they might cast him down headlong. But he, passing through the midst of them, went his way." —Luke 4:28–30. I attended the Episcopal Mission church in the forenoon and looked through their splendid Female College in the afternoon, where about 80 or 100 girls are being educated and Christianized. They also have seven other schools in the country around, superintended by Miss Edith Gaze Brown. These girls are to become wives and mothers some of these days, and that of the best people of the country. They are sowing good seed in a fruitful field. I should say that this mission belongs to the "Ladies' Evangelical Society in the East," whose headquaters are in London. They repeat Psalms, and sing from "Gospel Hymns" in Sunday School and also use the International Lessons. The tourists spending Sabbath in Nazareth were invited to tea in the college Sabbath evening and addresses were made by several clergymen.

In Nazareth one is shown Joseph's house, work-shop, Church of the Annunciation, and a stone over which a church is built, on which it is claimed Jesus ate with his disciples before and after his resurrection, though the evidence to establish the truth of these claims is not very satisfactory.

We ascended the hill to the Wely Sem'an, (tomb of Simeon) above the town. We can see Acre and the Sea; beyond Esdraelon and the intervening hills, the plain of Sharon. While enjoying this sumptuous panoramic feast three young men came up, one of whom was nearly blind, (20 per cent. of these people have injured eyes.) He told me he would give me a hundred dollars to cure his eyes; a more impossible task was never presented. I thought of my weakness, and at the same time of the power of Him whose boyhood was spent in the city below and on these hills and plains, who undertook just such a case while he lived, and whose power was not shortened because He had moved His dwelling place. I preached unto him Jesus. He was a Christian. They drew a Bible on me to know on what I based my belief that Jesus would heal his eyes. I told him to read John 14: 13-14. He said he would pray for eye-sight, and I promised to pray for him.

They left me and went off to an olive tree, under which they sat down to read the book they had and ponder no doubt upon the liberal construction they had just heard put upon its announcements. As I looked at them I thought of the boyhood of Jesus, who must often have climbed these hills to gaze at the snow-covered mountains in the north, the luxuriant plain below and the great sea beyond. Yes, all these, so delightful to me, were all familiar to Him. He must often have lingered here till twilight softened the scene and darkness shut out all but His own thoughts upon human life, man's folly and his danger, his possible attainment and the effort he purposed putting forth to rescue us; His conflict with evil and error, His rejection and death, that life might become a more stupendous reality to man, and immortality might be brought to light.

CHAPTER XXII.

MT. CARMEL AND THE COASTS OF TYRE AND SIDON.

Leaving Nazareth we reach Haifa under Mt. Carmel in six hours, passing on the way several small towns, some among the hills built of stone, some on the plain, of mud. We met between thirty and forty women, with large copper basins filled with milk, holding five or six gallons each, going to Nazareth. Several men were with them, but they rode donkeys, never deigning to touch the loads carried by their wives, mothers and sisters. That is the custom here; the women are on a level with the donkeys, as laborers. We find a good hotel, dine, and spend the afternoon going through the German colony, which is a model in its way. It is a cosmos in miniature. Next morning I went with our muleteer to the top of Mt. Carmel. The Catholics have a church over the cave in which Elijah hid, when Ahab sought his life. Near by is the cave in which Obadiah is said to have hid the fifty prophets—1 Kings 28: 13. Napoleon used this church for a hospital when he besieged Acre, twelve miles across or around the bay, in 1799.

Haifa is a seaport. Most of the inhabitants are Christians and Germans. They seem very thrifty, and came here to have religious liberty as our pilgrim fore-fathers came to America. I do not understand their creed, however, even after hearing it explained. The government is macadamizing a road from this place to Tiberias by Nazareth and Cana. From this point telegraph wires run to Jerusalem, Shechem, Tiberias, Nazareth, Beirut.

There are many nice orange groves and vineyards here, and much wheat is shipped hence to France and Spain. In the afternoon of next day we rode around the bay, crossed the Kishon, "that ancient River Kishon," on whose banks Elijah slew the prophets of Baal—1 Kings, 18: 40. It is a small stream, barely large enough to turn a mill at this season, though large enough to sweep away companies of soldiers under Sisera's retreat.

We stopped for the night in Acre, called also Ptolemais and St. John d'Acre. It is the "Key of Palestine," has been besieged and burnt often. Its history goes back to the Egyptian kings, centuries B. C., and it figured largely in the crusades. Its present population is 5,000, of whom 700 are Christians, the remainder Mohametans.

A German preacher, named Bitzer, joined us here and traveled with us the rest of the way.

I and Isa (our dragoman) took a boat and went out to the steamer on which Mr. M. was going to Beirut, to see how he was getting on. There were about twenty Arab boats laden with wheat, destined to some distant market. While we were on the steamer all business was suspended and the greatest possible uproar began. I thought one of the wheat boats was sinking, but the confusion increased to such an extent I concluded the steamer was going down. The Arabs (about one hundred of them) were all talking at once; some of them were frantic and gesticulated like madmen. I could not understand a word they said, but knew that something awful had happened or was about to happen, so I told Isa to let us be going. He laughed, and told me the occasion of the excitement, as follows: One of the crew had smiled at a Mussulman who was praying on the deck of the boat, (a very common thing), the Arab had seen him; and wanted him punished by the officers of the ship, and all the rest were in sympathy with the aggrieved devotee.

In the twelfth century more than ten times the present population were killed here during a single siege. In the thirteenth century Khalit-Ibn-Khalaem, Sultan of Egypt, besieged and captured it in thirty-three days and slew 25,000 Christians, many of whom (ladies) cut their own noses off to escape more barbarous treatment. Many remnants of the crusaders may still be seen, notably the old church of St. John, and a hospital. We drank from a fountain of brackish water, said to have wrought miraculous cures. But the greatest honor the place has ever known is recorded in Acts xxi: 7.

Leaving Acre next morning we saw many people gathered on the outside of the city gate. They were both from the town and country, the former had come out to buy the vegetables, the latter had brought to sell, which were auctioned off by the donkey load without unloading the beast. The following articles were selling at different stations as we passed: Onions, carrots, potatoes, lettuce and other salads, oranges lemons, milk and curds. They are sold outside the gate to avoid taxation.

A splendid aqueduct brings water from the mountains to the town. We ride by this about ten miles. Our road now lies to the north and passes through rich plains in which are groves of oranges and lemons. We dine at Khan de Rhauna on fresh fish, which they catch in a large circular net by wading out into the surf until the fish comes in sight when the net which has been slightly twisted is thrown like a lasso, and having a leadline sinks down rapidly around the fish, the leadline is pulled up then to a focus by a draw string, a hole is left in the top just large enough to take out the fish.

We pass over White Cape, where the road is cut around the cliff five hundred feet above the water and a stumbling or misstep of the horse would precipitate the rider into the sea. This is the old Roman road leading from Caesarea to Antioch. We descend into the plains filled with old wells and stone troughs, and walls, and steps, remnants of Hiram's Tyre, which was nineteen miles in circumference. We pass near by Hiram's tomb and ride into Tyre and to the house of Abdul Malak (Servant of the Angel). There are ruins here that would tempt the archaeologist and antiquarian to linger many a day.

The wharf is built of polished columns of stone that once supported domes of palaces and temples "of perfect beauty." Massive pillars of red granite, monoliths, a section of which looks like a heart cut of stone, and twenty-five feet long by four in diameter, and smaller pieces lie scattered all about, marking the tracks of the destroyers, which Ezekiel, chaps. xxvii-xxviii, said would come this way. Tyre was built 2350 B. C., and with her parent, Sidon, taught navigation to the world, and colonized Carthage. Earthquakes, fire, the sea and war have all exhausted their resources upon Tyre. Tyre and Sidon were given to Asher in the division of Canaan but they never got possession of them. The Israelites were feeders to them and they were necessary to the Israelites, possibly until they became so amalgamated, especially in religion, as to have all things in common, peaceably. A huge mound stands by the way just before reaching Tyre; on this it is said once stood the temple of Hercules.

From Tyre to Sidon we cross the Leontes River, called here Nahr-el-Kasineiyeh, on a beautiful stone bridge supported by a single arch sixty feet wide, the ruined city of Ornithopolis, the Cave-temple of Astarte, Sarepta, now in ruins, and a house of white stone on the site of the house of the widow that fed Elijah.—1 Kings, 17: 9-16. Every inch of this ground has been employed in making the history of our race, and imagination re-peoples it, rebuilds its cities, with streets full of business and romping children, its temples resounding with Astarte's praise, repaints its battle scenes of holocaust and captive's clanking chains, feels again the earthquake's shock, and trembles at the terrible vengeance of the Almighty angered.

"Therefore, thus saith the Lord God; Behold, I am against thee, O Tyrus, and will cause many nations to come up against thee as the sea causeth her waves to come up. And they shall destroy the walls of Tyrus, and break down her towers; . . . . and they shall lay thy stones and thy timber and thy dust in the midst of the water. And I will cause the noise of thy songs to cease: and the sound of thy harps shall be no more heard. And I will make thee like the top of a rock; thou shalt be a place to spread nets upon; thou shalt be built no more: for I the Lord have spoken it, saith the Lord God."—Ezk. 26.

We stop at a good hotel at Sidon, kept by an Arab. The parlor, saloon, and bed-rooms are on the second floor, while some shops face the street on the lower story. The whole building surrounds an open court about fifty feet square, where the horses and donkeys are kept. The latter kept up a constant braying which prevents one from becoming lonesome.

The saloon accommodates from one to two hundred guests. It is fitted up with tables for billiards, cards, backgammon, checkers, &c., &c., for all the city Arabs gamble and smoke all day and often till midnight.

Our dragoman had been cross and negligent the day we reached Sidon; I had seemed displeased. That evening after supper he came into my room and begged my pardon, took my hand, put it to his forehead and kissed it, and took it several times to repeat his professed submission to my will. I tried to think him sincere, forgave him, and dismissed him seemingly satisfied.

Sidon is a very ancient city and was so named probably in consequence of its having been a fishery. (*Saida* means fish). It was built by the grandson of Noah, and invented the art of navigation, carpentry, sculpture, making glass, stone cutting, casting iron, &c.—Josephus, b. 1: 6.

The present population numbers about 12,000, of whom 2,500 are christians, 300 are Jews. Nearly all of these, however, belong to the Greek and Latin churches; but there is a Protestant school doing a good work, under the patronage of the church of England.

The road from Sidon to Beirut is the roughest we have traveled over, though the French soldiers made a splendid road here only a few scores of years ago, but it is ruined now. Every two or three miles on all the important roads of Palestine and Syria there is a little stone house built, called a guard house. We were glad to see that traveling had got to be very safe, as indicated by the absence of the guards from most of these.

We pass over the battle ground of Ptolemy and Antiochus the Great, fought 218 B. C., and where tradition says the whale left Jonah, and where the Nahr-El-Danûr flows cool and deep from Mt. Lebanon. There are many silk factories along the road and thousands of acres of the plains and hillsides are devoted to the culture of mulberry trees for the manufacture of silk. We leave to our right the perishing home of the eccentric lady Stanhope, who died as she had lived in self-imposed exile, "unwept, unhonored" and unloved.

We pass through a belt of deep red sand for three or four miles between walls made of this sand when wet, about four or five feet high, through groves of pine trees, owned by the government and used for telegraph poles. They are trimmed up and are as thick as pines can grow, even in North Carolina. We pass the customs officers and at 4 P. M. on the twelfth day after leaving Jerusalem; stop at the Hotel del' Universe, kept by a native Syrian, and never found a better, nor cheaper one in all our travels.

CHAPTER XXIII.

BEIRUT.

Our first thought on reaching Beirut was one of relief at having terminated a journey perilous on account of the treachery of the people one must associate with and depend upon, and the excessive heat of the climate along the coast. We were mindful of the good providence of God that had shielded us hourly through the worst dangers we would brave. Grateful letters awaited us at the post office, and newspapers from home. After dinner our dragoman, muleteers and donkey boy came to my room to bid me farewell and receive *backsheesh*. These fellows will appear to be nearly heartbroken at parting with the traveler, but if disappointed in the quantity of backsheesh expected, will go off pouting and it is said, sometimes not even say good-bye at all.

We had a written contract to the effect (specified) that all backsheesh was to be paid by our *cicerone ;* nevertheless he, with all the rest, seemed to have lost sight of that, and wanted all possible perquisites.

Next morning I went to see Mr. M. at the Hospital of the Knights of St. John, where he had gone the day previous to our arrival, and though blessed with the best medical attention to be found anywhere his convalescence was so slow as to require him to stay about two weeks. I remained with him four days, and bade him adieu with a sad heart, for in the seven weeks in which we had been constantly together, our attachment for each other and dependence upon one another, had grown to be like that of two brothers. Now our journey lay apart, and both were once more alone at the farthest point from home.

The following is an extract from a letter written since his return home: "After you left Beirut I had to remain about ten days, for Dr. Post would not let me go for a week after I was up and about the garden. Dr. Post told me he and Dr. Dight had a consultation every morning over my case, for they did not understand it; concluded it was malaria in the main. . . . . Well, it was a grand trip, was it not? Who could picture old Egypt as it is? Or ever get a just view of the Holy Land as we saw it? Or imagine Pompeii or Rome? It is all like a dream, but when I fix my thought on any one part of it, it becomes all clear as a picture."

Beirut is a city of over one hundred thousand inhabitants, most of whom are Arabs and Turks, but there are many French, Germans, Greeks and Italians also, and some English. The English, French and Austrians each have a post office, as well as the Turks, and I believe the Italians as well. It is the principal seaport of Syria, and carries on a large wholesale trade with Damascus and the inland towns farther in the interior. There are several factories here making silk goods, soap, nargilehs, glass goods, shoes, sandals, copper-ware and hard-ware generally. The city is taking on an European air to a considerable extent.

I went one day to Nahr-El-Kelb, (Dog River) which is a sight well worth the time and trouble to see. It flows from the Lebanon mountains and is cold. From this stream Beirut is supplied with drinking water, driven about six or seven miles through pipes, by a steam engine. The Nahr-El-Kelb flows through a canon whose sides are nearly perpendicular and about five or six hundred feet high. The rock forming the sides of this canon is limestone, and several places have been cut smooth for receiving inscriptions and reliefs. One of these, life size, represents Salmanezer, another Rameses the Great, cut in relief. There are also inscriptions in relief to Marcus Aurelius and Napoleon III. A stone bridge, centuries old, spans the stream about a quarter of a mile from the beach; over this bridge mules were carrying sugar cane on their backs, and I judged there was a sugar factory near by from the vast amounts hauled. Two large bundles weighing three or four hundred pounds are balanced on the mules' backs and they go without a driver to the proper destination.

The highway is a continuation of the old Roman road to Antioch, and is in good condition, being macadamized; it passes through mulberry groves all the way around the sandy beach of St. George's bay.

This entire population is Christian, even for many miles in the interior. And so bigoted are they that they will not only not hear any other sect, but will not allow others to plant a school or church among them; they are Catholics chiefly; some, however, belong to the Greek church. They are as violent as the Latins in their hostility to Protestanism. Dr. Jessup had in hand the case of a missionary at Sidon who had been arrested on the charge of murder; everything was being done by the Catholics that could be to secure his execution. It was my privilege to contribute to a fund being raised to secure his release. The wounds our Lord has received in the house of his friends have checked the onward march of his kingdom more than all the infidelity, rationalism, agnosticism, and all other forms of skepticism together.

It was my privilege to visit the various institutions doing work directly for Christ in Beirut, and I copy from statictics and statements placed in my hands by our Missionaries a concise history and outline of their labors.

The following is an extract from a letter written by myself to the RALEIGH CHRISTIAN ADVOCATE, from Beirut:

"I thought I would write you about the wonderful work of missions here in Beirut, but I have found to my hand a summary, by the dauntless Dr. Strong, to the correctness of which I wish to bear testimony. I had the pleasure of visiting their college for young men, and through the courtesy of the President, Dr. Bliss, of acquainting myself somewhat with their equipments and methods. It is nearly, if I may not say, quite an ideal college. They have about two hundred pupils, who show real culture in manner and conversation. The College is well equipped, located and managed. I may say the same of Miss Thompson's school, except as to numbers; she has only 50 or 60 I think. Their hospital is all one could desire. They have a large printing establishment, through which I looked, and it keeps many hands busy. I called on Dr. Van Dyck, who remarked in answer to my interrogations regarding the history, present status and outlook of missionary labors in Syria and among the Mohammedans, that already there was crystallizing energy sufficient to cast a system or polity for local church government. This fact furnishes very practical evidence in support of the claims of Christian Missions."

Dr. Strong says: "Beirut, in Syria, is called the 'crown-jewel of modern missions.' It was taken from the bed of Moslem degradation, cut and set by the deliberate planning of a handful of American Christians. As late as 1826 Beirut was a straggling, decaying Mohammedan town, without so much as a carriage-way through it, a wheeled vehicle, or a pane of window glass in it. The missionaries who came to it were persecuted by the authorities and mobbed by the populace. Some were driven to the Lebanons; others fled to Malta. There they matured their plans, chimerical to all but the eye of faith. They projected Christian empire for Syria, not the gathering of a few converts. Schools, colleges, printing-houses, Western culture in science, art and religion, were all included in their plan. They returned to Beirut bringing a hand-press and a font of Arabic type.

Night after night a light gleamed from a little tower above the mission building—a prophetic light seen out on the Mediterranean—where Eli Smith, and, after he was gone, the still living Dr. Van Dyck labored in translating the Bible into Arabic. When, in 1865, Dr. Van Dyck flung down the stairway the last sheet of 'copy' to the compositor, it marked an era of importance to Syria and Asia Minor, to Egypt and Turkey, and all the scattered Arabic-speaking peoples, greater than any accession or deposition of Sultans or Khedives. There is nothing more eloquent than the face of the venerable translator, in which can be read the making of the grandest history of the Orient. The dream of the exiles has been accomplished. Beirut is to-day a Christian city, with more influence upon the adjacent lands than had the Berytus of old, on whose ruins it has risen. Stately churches, hospitals, a female seminary, a college, whose graduates are scattered over Syria, Egypt and wherever the Arab roams; a theological seminary, a common-school system, and three steam presses, throwing off nearly half a million pages of reading matter a day; a Bible-house, whose products are found in India, China, Ethiopia, and at the sources of the Nile; these are the facets of that 'crown jewel' which the missionaries have cut with their sanctified enterprise."

The following condensed report explains itself:

PLACES OF EVANGELICAL WORSHIP IN BEIRUT,

Together with brief statistics of Evangelical Work in the city, and of the American Mission in Syria.

I.
WORSHIP AND PREACHING IN THE ENGLISH LANGUAGE.

1. American Mission Church.
2. Church of England Service.
3. Chapel of Syrian Protestant Church.
4. British Syrian Schools.

II.
WORSHIP AND PREACHING IN THE GERMAN AND FRENCH.

1. Chapel of Prussian Deaconesses.

WORSHIP AND PREACHING IN ARABIC.

1. American Mission Church.
2. Syrian Protestant College.
3. Eastern Chapel.
4. Musaitebeh Chapel.
5. Orphan House of the Prussian Deaconesses.
6. Hospital of the Knights of St. John.
7. Moslem School of Miss Taylor.
8. Six Arabic Sunday Schools.
9. Six Classes during the week for Bible Instruction to Women.

IV.
EVANGELICAL CHRISTIAN WORK AND EDUCATIONAL INSTITUTIONS.

1. American Presbyterian Mission, American Bible Society. British and Foreign Bible Society. London Religious Tract Society.
2. Theological Seminary of the American Mission.
3. Syrian Protestant College.
4. American Female Seminary.
5. British Syrian Schools—One Boarding School and seven Day Schools.
6. Church of Scotland Mission to the Jews.
7. Prussian Deaconesses Orphan House and Boarding School for Girls.
8. Miss Taylor's St. George's Moslem School for Girls.
9. German Boys' School.

10. Day School of Syrian Protestants, and three other day Schools.
11. Blind Schools for Men and Women.

V.

THE PRESS.

Rev. Samuel Jessup, Manager.
Mr. W. R. Glockler, Supt.
The Arabic Press of the American Mission printed in 1885:
Total pages... 27,981,600
Of which Scriptures.. 17,378,600
Vols. of Scriptures distributed during 1885.............. 23,576
Total No. of distinct books on the Press Catalogue.... 368
Total pages printed from the first............................311,742,044

VI.

STATIONS OF THE AMERICAN PRESBYTERIAN MISSION IN SYRIA.

1. Beirut.—Rev. C. V. A. Van Dyck, M.D., D.D.; Rev. W. W. Eddy, D.D.; Rev. H. H. Jessup, D.D.; Rev. J. S. Dennis, D. D.; Rev. S. Jessup, and their wives. Miss E. D. Everett, Miss E. A. Thomson, Miss A. S. Barber, of the Female Seminary.

Theological Seminary.—Instruction given by members of Beirut Station.

Syrian Protestant College.—Rev. D. Bliss, D.D., President; Rev. J. Wortabet, M.D.; Rev. G. E. Post, M.A., M.D.; Rev. Harvey Porter, B.A.; Thos. M. Kay, M.D.; Charles F. Dight, M. D.; John C. Fisher, M.A., M.D.; Samuel P. Glover, M.D.; Robert H. West, M.A.; Frank E. Hoskins, B.A.; Louis F. Giroux, B.A.; Mr. Yuhanna Dakhil, Sheikh Khalil Ul-Yazigil, Frank S. Woodruff, B.A.; Robert H. Beattie, B.A.; Henry M. Hulbert, M.A.; Yusuf Aftimus, B.A.; Daud Salim, B.A.; Mr. Francis Richa.

    Medical Students 31
    Collegiate Department.............................. 61
    Preparatory Department........................... 75

    Total..167
Total Pupils in American Mission Schools in Syria........... 5,665
Of whom Girls.. 3,736
Total Number Members in Syrian Native Churches......... 1,301
Sabbath School Scholars.. 3,804
Contributions of Native Churches $6,451

2. Abeih and Suk el Ghurb.—Rev. Wm. Bird and wife; Miss Emily Bird; Rev. T. S. Pond and wife.
3. Sidon.—Rev. W. K. Eddy and wife; Rev. Geo. A. Ford. Female Seminary.—Miss H. M. Eddy, Miss R. Brown, Miss C. Brown.
4. Tripoli.—Rev. O. J. Hardin and wife; Rev. F. W. March and wife; Ira Harris, M.D., and wife. Female Seminary.—Miss H. La Grange, Miss M. C. Holmes.
5. Zahleh.—Rev. G. F. Dale, Jr.; Rev. W. M. Greenlee, and their wives.
6. Total American Missionaries, Men....................... 14 } 38
  "   "   "   Women.......... .... 24 }
  Native Pastors.. 3 }
  Total Native Syrian Preachers .... 35 } 189
  Teachers and others... 151 }

VII.

ST. JOHN'S HOSPITAL FOR 1888.

Indoor patients... 491
Patients treated in Polyclinique...... 8,390
Total days of treatment..11,953

SEA OF GALILEE.

CHAPTER XXIV.

THE LAND, THE PEOPLE, THE MAN.

When we consider the geographical position of Palestine, the topography, climate, and vegetable productions of the country, and the peculiar history and characteristics of the Hebrew people, we see a remarkable fitness in the land and the people to entitle them to that choice made by God in using them to carry out his purpose concerning the race of mankind in their development. Geikie says the land is peculiarly adapted to qualify its inhabitants to write a book for all men, on account of the cosmopolitan character of its vegetable growth. "The teachings and illustrations of our Lord would have been out of place in any other country except this. *They could not have been uttered anywhere else.*"—*Thompson.*

But what is still more significant is the character of the Israelites. The call of Abraham from Ur of the Chaldees has no counterpart in the history of any other family. The announcements made to him, from time to time, were new, mysterious, wonderful, and as far removed from him in their ultimate designs as the steamer that carries the international mails is from the secrets that slumber in its mammoth hold.

Palestine has been on the highway of the nations from time immemorial. Asia Minor, Assyria, Persia, and all the north and east passed that way to Egypt, Abyssinia, Ethiopia and all places in Africa and *vice versa,* whether their mission was one of hostility, of commerce, of investigation or emigration; thus making it one of the strategic points most valuabe in impinging against the citizenship of the world. The characteristics of Abraham and his posterity were such as God would teach to other peoples.

1. *In the first place, Abraham had faith in God.* He believed God meant well towards man; that all he *did* was for man's good; that he had a great concern for man. He believed this with such an intensity that he was ready to co-operate with God in any plan, to undertake any task imposed upon him by God, so that he obtained the honorable titles "Friend of God," "Father of the Faithful."

This same peculiarity is exhibited in his children, Isaac, Jacob, Joseph, and others whose names are recorded in Hebrews xi.

2. *Domestic affection* is peculiar to the Hebrews. While God has given parental love to the lower animals even, it is a remarkable fact that fallen human nature descends below the brute world in many respects; and the nations of the east show an aversion to their children, especially female children, that is not paralleled among the lower animals, so far as I know. At this time there are places where a little money would purchase a car load of children from their parents, and many female babes are strangled at birth. But the Israelites loved their children. Witness Jacob when he thought Joseph torn by wild beasts, and when Benjamin was required ere they could obtain more bread. "All these things are against me;" said he, "you will bring down my gray hairs with sorrow to the grave," or Joseph when he saw Benjamin—Gen. 45—or David

weeping over a would-be parricide until his heart seemed broken.*

Take the following from the *Nashville Advocate*, of February 14, 1891.

"We can still learn salutary lessons of the Jewish people as well as of the Jewish Scriptures. Filial respect is one of the most important elements in character, of which these times is sadly deficient. It still lives in that ancient people. A correspondent of the New York *World* draws this delightful picture of filial reverence:

" 'There is nothing in the world of pleasure and recreation to compare with the beautiful devotion that is paid the old Hebrew people by their children and grandchildren at the various summer resorts. A rude remark is never made in their hearing, nor a disrespectful word uttered to aged mother or father. The gentle yielding of easy chairs, the offering of choice things to eat and drink, the last consideration of self where there is a drive or sail for a limited number, and the graceful anticipation of creature comforts, are attributes of the children to which the filial respect of the youthful Christian is not approachable.' A lesson much needed among Christians."

3. They were a very *sentimental* people, and carried their sentiment into their religion. Other nations built temples in honor of their gods and sacrificed in them, and feared and revered their divinities, but nowhere is it said they loved them. Their worship was of the head— it never reached their hearts. Hebrews had conceptions of a being with sentiment. Jacob wrestled and agonized in prayer until he prevailed. The Psalmist said, "my heart and my flesh crieth out for the living God." And their sentimental nature is seen to-day by the way they repair weekly to the outside of the Sanctuary wall, and weep as near the site of their once glorious temple as possible, and the further fact that every Jew buried in a

---
* Every one loves his children, but the Hebrews love them more tenderly than other people.—EBERS, *Uarda*.

foreign land wishes the "holy sand," or some of Palestine's soil sprinkled upon his grave, and the Talmud says they think that in some mysterious manner the pious dead will make their way under ground to Mt. Olivet, just above Jehoshaphat and appear on that ground at the resurrection.

4. The Jew was *conservative*. This fitted him for receiving the sacred oracles, the written and oral law. No better evidence need be adduced than the facts that they have kept the Pentateuch intact, or not materially altered through the greatest imaginable vicissitudes, the rising and falling of empires, the birth and death of many nations, the extremes of climate, exaltation persecution such as no other people has known; all have been too weak to more than barely modify the habits of this people. The Samaritans, of Jewish origin partly, (about one hundred and fifty remain at Sychar,) still retain a Pentateuch manuscript said to be twenty-six hundred years old, and it is about the same as ours, and they still worship in the mountain of Gerizim, as the woman of Sychar said to Jesus, and as they were directed by Moses—Exodus 12.

5. Once more, the Hebrew was *aggressive*, or rather had the faculty of impressing his faith upon other people, as Joseph in Egypt, whom we cannot think of having a higher office at first than that of a donkey-boy, who nevertheless made such progress as to stand beside Pharaoh, all the time taking care of his religion, and saying that it was in consequence of his God that he did well. He preached God the GOOD to the King, and with success, for he obtained favor for his (alien) people until another Pharaoh was on the throne who "knew not Joseph."

Daniel, a captive lad, did the same, became prime minister to four or five of the world's greatest monarchs, and made Nebuchadnezzar say there is no God but Daniel's God. "Now I, Nebuchadnezzar, praise and extol and honor the King of heaven, all whose works are truth, and His ways judgment; and those that walk in pride He is able to abase."

Likewise did Esther and Mordecai and Ezra and Nehemiah.

Endowed thus, with powers and peculiarities on which to base individual and national prosperity and development, (the home is the bulwark of civilization and stable government, but the home is built on *Domestic* affection,) God put this nation in contact with the people of the earth at opportune times and in wise ways, making such occasions reciprocally serviceable, mutually elevating, developing and diffusing light and knowledge until other nations, besides, might be put in charge of the mission which only one at first could undertake.*

We owe the Jew a debt. We obtained from him what is best in us, at least the fertilizing of the germs of it; if not the nature, a knowledge of the first principles. We believe for his excellence he was chosen. His excellent qualities were made prominent by the favor of God, and his testimony is not nearly at an end. Let him be kindly considered, for it is as George Eliot has said, "The well-being of Israel is the well-being of the church."

Traveling the length and breadth of this land, if there has been any change whatever in my religious views it has been to intensify my faith in the inspiration of Scripture and the divinity of Jesus Christ. When we consider the narrow limits of Palestine, the arduous

---
*For I know him, that he will command his children and his household after him.

toil necessary to production, and no resources whatever besides those of agriculture and the feeding of flocks; and when we consider that the Canaanites and other tribes filled the country and occupied cities with high walls, and that a nation which had for centuries been in bondage, and showed its capacity and disposition for war in the conduct of ten of the twelve spies sent to investigate, and the conduct of the camp on hearing their report: "And they brought up an evil report of the land which they had searched unto the children of Israel, saying, The land through which we have gone to search it, *is* a land that eateth up the inhabitants thereof; and all the people that we saw in it *are* men of a great stature. And there we saw the giants, the sons of Anak, *which come* of the giants; and we were in our own sight as grasshoppers, and so we were in their sight. And all the congregation lifted up their voice and cried; and the people wept that night. And all the children of Israel murmured against Moses and against Aaron: and the whole congregation said unto them, Would God that we had died in the land of Egypt! or would God we had died in this wilderness! And wherefore hath the LORD brought us unto this land, to fall by the sword, that our wives and our children should be a prey? were it not better for us to return into Egypt? And they said one to another, Let us make a captain, and let us return into Egypt."—*Num.* 13: 32—14: 4, when we consider, too, little time was occupied in taking enough land for their use and cities enough for their comfortable dwelling; and when we read the law guaranteeing peace and prosperity, and the conditions forfeiting the divine favor in Deut. 28, etc., and study the history of the Jews, we see a proof of the divine hand through all.

When we consider, again, these narrow limits, and contrast the products of this shepherd people in the world of thought and morals, with those of surrounding nations, the conclusion is they were under the divine guidance. There are the Ganges, the Euphrates and the Nile flowing through lands of incalculable wealth. There are Greece, Rome, and all the rest. From them arose Ninevah, Babylon, Thebes, Cheops, the Acropolis, Parthenon and Colosseum. They have given us warriors, statesmen, historians, poets, painters, sculptors and architects, showing that there was not an indigenous genius here, for many other lands have equalled this in ordinary and extraordinary talent. But this little section has done more than ony other one, or all others, for it alone inherited ability to give to man an ultimate ethical code; and if we judge by the standard given by its supreme law giver: That the servant of all is greatest of all, then is it entitled to the first place.

The Philosophers have all had a sameness about their sayings, but the heroes of Scripture had uncommon and unique experiences and gave utterance to equally uncommon thoughts. Abraham, Job, Moses, David, Elijah and Daniel were not as the other great men of the earth. They were in many respects similar to one another; but unlike the heroes of poetry, history and biography of other lands.

Abraham, Isaac and Jacob stand out alone before the world as moral pioneers, marking a highway of faith and obedience, not yet improved upon, and in studying these men we must do so remembering that they were without the written word and examples since recorded. "These all died in the faith, not having received the promises, but having seen them afar off, and were persuaded of them, and embraced them."

But once more; when we remember that this people, with such noble sires, proved unworthy sons, lost their liberty and became subject to pagan masters, from one of the meanest of their towns, of the poorest parents, gave to the world a man of pure lips, of pure habits, of great knowledge and wisdom, yet having never learned, totally unselfish amidst the most selfish, possessed of miraculous power, fearless amidst hosts of enemies, defiant of accumulated ecclesiastical and traditional energy and prestige, of wealth, or other forces, arresting in their progress storms, devils and diseases, going about doing good gratuitously amid the most mercenary, and choosing the most ignoble men to take up and carry forward his work where he left it off, until it should fill the earth; who put greater premium on suffering as a means to secure adherents than on temporal gratifications; in fact, a man doing all things in a manner different from all other men, against all men's natural propensities, yet making them say "he hath done all things well;" when we study his life in his land, his time and his people, when we consider how unfavorable his antecedents, and his environments from every human standpoint, and the sublimity, purity, simplicity and universal sweep of his teachings, and that his biographer said "the common (!) people heard him gladly," and who himself said for eternal record, "If a man compel thee to go a mile with him, go with him two," and "if he sue thee at the law and take away thy cloak, let him have thy coat also"—a man who, without reading history, political or moral science, yet announced instinctively the foundation principles on which alone pure and substantial civil and social institutions can permanently be based; whose foundations need not to be widened nor narrowed, and "other foundation can no man lay:" "Heaven and earth shall pass away, but my word shall not pass away;" when we consider all these things and stand before this cosmopolitan character speaking to every nation and every man, whose words need no altering forever, but only to be obeyed, we bow down before him and say with Nicodemus, "Thou art a teacher come from God," and with the centurion, "surely this man was the son of God," and with Peter, who knew him best of all, "Thou art the Christ of God."

Two years after writing the above "The Land and the Book" fell into my hands. As it so forcibly and fully speaks on this subject I copy what forty years of sojourn amongst that people enabled the learned author to testify with accuracy. He says:

"Jesus grew up from his youth to manhood amongst a people intensely *mercenary*. This vice corrupted and debased every relation of life. We can fill up the outlines of his picture from the every-day life and manners of the people about us. Every body trades, speculates, cheats. The shepherd boy on the mountains talks about *piastres* from morning to night; so does the muleteer on the road, the farmer in the field, the artisan in his shop, the merchant in his magazine, the pasha in his palace, the Kady in the hall of judgment, the mullah in the mosque, the monk, the priest, the bishop—money, money, money! the desire of every heart, the theme of every discourse, the end of every aim. Everything too, is bought and sold. Each prayer has its price, every sin a tariff. Nothing for nothing, but every thing for money. Now our Lord was an *Oriental*, and grew up among just such a people; but who can or dare say there is the faintest shadow of this mercenary spirit in his character? With uncontrolled power to possess all, he owned nothing. He had no place to be born in but another man's stable, no closet to pray in but the wilderness, no place to die but on the cross of an enemy, and no grave but one lent by a friend. At his death he had absolutely nothing to bequeath to his mother. He was as free from the mercenary spirit as though he belonged to a world where the very idea of property was unknown. And this total abstinence from all ownership was not of necessity, but of choice; and I say there is nothing like it, nothing that approaches it in the history of universal man. It stands out perfectly and divinely original.

"Jesus was the founder of a new religion. Milton makes the Devil say to Jesus: 'If at great things thou would'st arrive, get riches first; get wealth, and treasure heap.' And this temptation no man under such circumstances ever did or could resist. But Christ from the first took his position above the human race, and to the end retained it without an effort. He divorces his Gospel from any alloy of earth. Money, property, and all they represent and control, have nothing to do with membership in his society, with citizenship in his Kingdom. Not only is the idea not human, it is every whit contrary to what is human. He could not have borrowed it, for he was surrounded by those who were not able to comprehend the idea—no, not even the apostles, until after the day of Pentecost. As to the multitude, they sought Jesus, not because they saw the miracles and were convinced, but because they ate and were filled. And so it always has been and is now in this same country. . . .

. . . . . He *knew* that the multitude followed him for the loaves and fishes; that they sought to make him King that they might revel in ease, luxury and power; that they crowded around him to be healed as people do now around our physicians; that one called him *master* to obtain a decision in his favor against his brother in regard to the estate, as many join the missionaries the better to press their claims in court. . .

. . . According to the parable, some will even claim admittance into heaven because they had eaten and drank in his presence, and still more absurd, because he had *taught in their streets*. Now, however ridiculous such pretensions may appear to men in the Western World, I have had applications for *money* in this country, urged earnestly, and even angrily, for precisely the same reasons. Our Lord founded the parable, *even to its external drapery and costume*, not on fancy, but on unexaggerated fact."

CHAPTER XXV.

AMONG THE GRECIAN ISLES.

"Where burning Sappho loved and sung—
"Where Venus rose and Phœbus sprung,"
We sailed, the Grecian Isles among.

From Beirut we embarked on the VESTA, of the Austrian Lloyd Line. On account of cargo, we were delayed thirty hours, and it is dark ere the rattle of loading machinery ceases and the thud of the propeller begins. All night we go one hundred and fifty-six miles over a rough sea ere we reach Cyprus, our first landing place. As we stay here four hours, there is an opportunity and a proposition to go ashore. We are half a mile from Larnika, the principal town of the island, and land in small row boats. Cyprus derives its name from *Kupros*, a plant that grows here and makes a reddish and yellowish dye, with which the women throughout the East color their nails. Once the island was covered with forests, but these have all disappeared. Once large copper mines were worked, and from Homer to Alexander and later, they excelled in the manufacture of brazen armor. It is said the metal copper derives its name from *Aes Cuprium*—euphonized or anglicized into copper.

The King of Larnika, called Chittim in the Scriptures—presented Alexander the Great with a sword, so we are told by the historians. Cyprus produces wheat, barley, cotton, silk, madder, oil, wine, caroobs (the husks of the prodigal son) and salt. But locusts are said to eat up and destroy nearly half the products of the farmer commonly.

General di Cesnola, who was consul here for several years, made very important discoveries at many of the ancient city sites, all of which are fully detailed in his book. We saw one place which he had honey-combed, finding only an ancient cistern containing a few relics of a remote age.

About the only thing worth visiting at Larnika is the Church of St. Lazarus, (Greek.) You are shown the spot where he died, after coming from Palestine, and where he is buried (?). There is a painting of him in the church, also of his resurrection, in which a bystander is holding his nose to shut out the scent of the corpse. Our young readers of Mythology will remember that it was here the goddess Venus rose from the foam of the sea, and a yearly festival is still held, in which all go out on the water in boats; it is believed to be on the anniversary of Venus' birth from the sea, and so celebrated. Anciently young men specially sought wives on these festival occasions; no doubt many do still.

Ezek. 27: 6 represents these islands as making box and cedar wood fabrics, inlaid with ivory. They have maintained this habit to the present time, although ivory has given place to mother of pearl, which is probably meant by the prophet, for when we reached Rhodes, the next point at which we anchored, the natives came on board with large baskets full of boxes for tobacco, matches, card cases, etc., with books and birds, and canes of olive and lemon wood, some of them containing at least fifty pieces of mother of pearl, manufactured by the state prisoners, and selling very cheap.

We all bought several articles apiece. The most popular article of any seemed to be a bird. It was made so that the wings open and shut on hinges, and the back with the wings open on another hinge, showing a jewel case in the body. As they hurried from the boat one of these birds was dropped from the basket in which they were carried. I and a Greek Priest were the first parties on deck next morning, and he found it. I told him that the Captain would take it back to the owners when the vessel returned and it should be sent back to them. The thought of such a thing seemed strange to him. He said such things were never done thereabouts; and I judge he spake truly if he did not act honestly.

Very anciently there was a high state of civilization among the Rhodians, and they were very powerful in commerce and on the seas, and Strabo tells us that the city of Rhodes was more magnificent than either Rome or Alexandria, both of which he had visited. Rhodes (the island) furnished three of the cities that formed the Dorian Hexapolis. These three afterwards united to make the city of Rhodes, B. C. 409. 184 years later they erected the statue of Apollo, 105 feet high, which stood little over half a century as one of the wonders of the world. The Romans drew largely on their codes of civil laws, which were in advance of those of other contemporaneous nations. Some of our tourists heard a Greek relate that when a disturbance arose between the women of the island to break it up a reward was offered to the woman who could dive the deepest and stay under longest.

They were engaged in many of the wars that were waged on the various coasts of the Mediterranean. They very bravely fought to maintain their independence against the European masters from Greece and Italy. They submitted, however, to Alexander, but renounced the domination of his successors. It is painful now to see the degenerate race that occupy where once large wealth and learning were common; now there is a proscription on even the effort to learn to read; scarcely five per cent. of the people can write their names; nor is it vastly better in most of these classic islands. I might relate sad tales of fire and bloodshed in the history of several of the group forming the Grecian Archipelago, but the school boy can find them all in his history.

The next day after leaving Rhodes we came fairly into the Grecian Archipelago. From the deck one sees islands rise from the water, seeming to shut us in on all sides; now one rises suddenly from the sea and projects several hundred feet into the air; some rise into lofty mountains, one or two of which were covered on top with snow, while others stretch far away into undulating hills and plains. At sunrise we sight Kos, or Cos, far ahead; it seems that we will leave it to the right, when the ship turns North and we leave it to the left. Everybody wishes to see all they can of Kos, and are above, with glasses, taking in that part nearest the ship. Here Hippocrates was born, the great medical man, and some claim Apelles, the famous artist, who painted a portrait of Alexander the great, who would not suffer it done by any other artist. Kos, the capital, is a pretty seaport town.

Soon we come to Halicarnassus, the birth place of the great historian, Herodotus, of Dionysius, and Heraclitus, the poet, the principal city of the island of Caria. It was here that Artemesia, the Queen, 354 B. C., built the famous Mausoleum over her husband, Mausolus, that ranked as one of the seven wonders of the world. Causing his bones to be burned and powdered, she put the ashes thus made into water, which she drank until she had made herself to receive all that remained of her lamented lord. It was far off our line and we could only see it through glasses.

We next land at Leros, a town of 3,000 inhabitants, built in and on the steep sides of a ravine. From the sea back the houses rise like stairsteps. On one hill top, overhanging the city, are the remains of the old fortress, besieged so long in vain by the Turks; on another are about half a dozen windmills with giant-like arms, which look very lazy to one accustomed to seeing every thing done by steam power. We pass Patmos without stopping. Hither the proud Roman thought to exile and silence God's Apostle. But from this rock pulpit he preached so loud all nations shall hear him. Tradition points out the spot where the revelation was given. A monastery has been built near by, the location of which we could dimly see; the island was in view for several hours. Of course there was universal regret that we must be content with merely looking from the ship's deck, instead of traversing from side to side, and gathering at least a flower or a stone as a memento of a visit to the one island of all the seas most sacred by its associations to every Christian; but anxious as we were to stop, and glad as we would have been to linger, it was different with those who managed the ship. A famous writer then on board says:

"PATMOS is the embodiment of sternness and force; its altitude is that of a giant who had thrust himself up and out of the sea, and stood through the ages defying its power. As the plain of Bethlehem was pre-eminently adapted to the heavenly visitation and jubilant song of the shepherds, so this bleak barren rock is in harmony with the revelations of the absolute triumph of God over sin and of the Kingdom of Christ over all kingdoms, there given to JOHN.

"Nor is there any thing within or without the Bible more sublime than this:

"'I, JOHN, who also am your brother, and companion in tribulation, and in the kingdom and patience of JESUS CHRIST, was in the isle that is called PATMOS, for the word of GOD, and for the testimony of JESUS CHRIST.'"

About sunset we passed Scio, one of the many places that claim to be the birth place of Homer.

> "Seven cities boast the birth of Homer dead,
> Through which the living Homer begged his bread."

We pass many steamers and sail boats in these waters, indicating a vast amount of commerce. I have often wondered how ships could sail so much among these islands without shipwreck. The seas are deep to the very shores, however. They have erected light-houses where the danger is greatest, and lie to when it is very dark. Notwithstanding all this, the wonder of sailors' skill and good judgment and great success does not cease. And we lie down to sleep, feeling secure in their hands under the merciful protection of the Father of us all. We awake in the beautiful harbor of Smyrna.

CHAPTER XXVI.

SMYRNA AND EPHESUS.

We landed at Smyrna on Sunday morning, and as usual had the Turkish Custom-house Officers to pry into every little parcel in our baggage; this may commonly be avoided, however, by giving them *backsheesh*. If time is precious, or one has doubtful articles, liable to duty, or does not care to have a rough march through one's luggage, it pays to end the matter by giving a *franc*. If, on the contrary, one has plenty of time, nothing liable to duty, and wishes to see what a Turk can do in the matter of impudence and disregard for others' property or feelings, when he has an opportunity, one only has to give up his baggage and seem not to understand that he should pay any "thank money," and the officer will show him pretty soon. Smyrna has a population of 200,000 to 300,000, and with its suburbs extends ten or twelve miles around the bay.

It has the prettiest quay I have seen anywhere, and a row of buildings for two miles facing the sea, that for elegance would adorn any city. They are largely coffee houses, (Turks have no bar-rooms except for "infidels," that is, Christians,) with dwellings overhead, offices, hotels, and private mansions. The street, 100 feet wide and three feet above the water, inclines towards the bay just enough to carry off the rain, and is traversed the whole distance by a tram-way track, at the end of which is the railway to Aidin. Across the bay steam yachts or ferry-boats go flying every few minutes laden with passengers to and from some suburb, while a score of steamers of all the European nations load and unload their cargoes. It would be well not to leave the quay, for very little else is so charming; all the other streets are narrow and mostly very filthy. I remember to have seen dead dogs and cats and rats which were removed only by the slow process of decomposition. Nor were these sights the worst. I went through their fish market. It is a study for the Zoologist—shell fish, slick fish, scaly fish, red fish, black fish, abound. When there, it would appear that there was nothing in town but fish. It is largely so in the vegetable quarter. Then in the bazaars, all covered over with an arch-way, and divided up into stalls much like a livery stable, in each of which a Turk sits cross-legged. The way these Turks sit cross-legged and read the Koran during business hours is totally unlike any thing an American sees at home; oblivious to all but his book, till his goods are called for, then he shows the greatest anxiety to trade. Their bazaars have sections for certain kinds of goods, each consisting of many stores, calico merchants, silk merchants, tobacco nargeleh (or pipe) merchants, etc., with some good French and Jew stores.

The London *Daily News*, 1890, gives the following interesting facts and figures about Smyrna:

"According to Consul-General Holmwood's report the population numbers 210,850. But of this total only 52,000 are Mohammedans. The Mohammedans are largely outnumbered by the Greeks, who count 62,000, exclusive of 45,000 "Greek subjects." The railways are wholly under British management and have been constructed by British capital. The gas-lighting of Smyrna is the work of a British company; but—and here comes the irony of the situation—'the municipality of Smyrna is at present wholly composed of Ottoman subjects.' To sum up the position, Smyrna is, as far as population goes, a Greek city; as far as public works with their capital outlay are concerned, an English city; but as regards government, a Turkish city. The Turk is the incubus. As a commercial port Smyrna the Beautiful has several great advantages over Constantinople, but so long as the Turk blocks the way the vast development of which Smyrna is capable will be retarded. It is the same all over the Mediterranean and Black sea coasts. Wherever there is progress the Greek is at the bottom of it."

The population is heterogeneous, consisting of Turks, Greeks, French, British, Jews, etc. The Greeks are very much like the Jews in appearance. The houses, which are jammed together too close to allow of a yard or garden, or even a street wide enough for a vehicle, often are supplied on the upper or second story with a projecting balcony or box with glass windows on all sides, called *masharobeahs*, which are often latticed. In these the ladies sit to witness life on the streets below.

I attended services at the English church on Sunday, and at the Sailors' Bethel, called Smyrna Rest," Sunday night, when Dr. Buckley preached to a small band of sailors, and I gave a short talk and prayer.

Protestantism meets with the most violent opposition here, both from the Greeks and Mahometans. The American mission, however, has a good church and two good schools. I met one missionary, rather an aged man; he was hopeful of final results. One good thing in Smyrna attracted our notice—their observance of the Sabbath day. All shops were shut except restaurants and *cafes*. We also saw a policeman arrest a vender of green fruit (almonds I believe) as if they had some regard for the health of the people.

The English Church has in large letters above the pulpit the following:

"*Be thou faithful unto death and I will give thee a crown of life.*"

In the following is the only reference to Smyrna in the Bible, and that is by our Lord:

"I know thy works, and tribulation, and poverty, (but thou art rich) and *I know* the blasphemy of them which say they are Jews, and are not, but *are* the synagogue of Satan. Fear none of those things which thou shalt suffer: behold, the devil shall cast *some* of you into prison, that ye may be tried: and ye shall have tribulation ten days: be thou faithful unto death, and I will give thee a crown of life. He that hath an ear, let him hear what the spirit saith unto the churches: He that overcometh shall not be hurt of the second death."—*Rev.* 2: 9–11.

Smyrna contained one of the seven churches, whose site is still shown. It is a very ancient city, though many think the original city was some miles away. The present one was built or rebuilt by the order of Alexander the Great, in consequence of a vision he had on Mt. Pagus, by Antigones and Lysimachus, after his death. I went up on Mt. Pagus for the view. In ascending we passed the tomb of Polycarp, a disciple of John, and by some believed to have been the "angel of the church in Smyrna." On the summit or acropolis is an old fort in a fair state of preservation, though not dating prior to mediæval times; in this is said to be remains of the old church or mosque in which Polycarp preached. We are now about 500 or 600 feet above the sea, and behold a splendid panorama. The quiet city at our feet, beyond, the bay with every variety of boats, from the trim caik to the great ocean-going iron-clad, and far and near many a suburban village nestles between the mountains and the sea. Farther out are the islands of the Grecian Archipelago. Just here, on the mountain side, is the old theater, its proscenium all torn away to build garden walls or pave the streets, its shape scarcely discernible, where 2,000 years ago the tragedies of Sophocles and the Comedies of Aristophanes delighted the airy minds of the Greek populace, and where, nearly 1800 years ago, Polycarp was sacrificed to make a holiday sensation. When the Pro-consul said: "Blaspheme Christ and I will release you, he replied: "Eighty and six years I have served him, and he hath never wronged me; how then can I blaspheme my king who hath saved me." We look towards the interior; how splendid! There is the caravan bridge, and the cemeteries above which wave graceful cypresses; there are the country roads winding their tortuous way for many a mile until lost behind the hills, and the railways with trains hurrying on with western ideas for this sluggish people; in the background are the many mountains where nymphs and Goddesses were born, and the spirits of poesy and song emanated to immortalize their favorite offspring. It seemed as if there lingered still the enchantment known to nature's sons.

I descended to go to Ephesus, that I might see more of this inexhaustible and lovely country, so miserably managed under Moslem rule.

Our Consul said it would be only a waste of time and money to go to Ephesus—that all who went came back disappointed; but some people have a way of their own; such composed our party. At the station I met Rev. Mr. Mills, President of Earlham College. We two failed to telegraph for horses, which Drs. Buckley and Bancroft and Bishop Fowler were careful to do. But we were well, while several of their party were not. I recently received the following from Dr. Mills:

"MY DEAR SIR: Your letter recalls to my memory our exceedingly pleasant acquaintance in the East last spring.

"That journey to Ephesus and back, and our rambles in Athens! Ah, those were experiences worth living over a thousand times.

"I have just last week received three cases of Syrian objects, including a plow, yoke and goad, a mill, &c. &c.

"Yours, Fraternally,

J. J. MILLS."

The site of Ephesus is half a mile to a mile and a half from Ayasolook, the railway station, and forty-nine miles from Smyrna. It lay on all sides of the small mountain, Prion, and at the foot of a larger one, Mt. Coressus, separated by a valley about 500 feet wide. In this valley, and on the side of Prion next to Coressus, south, was one of their gymnasiums, the walls of which are still *in situ*, and near the gymnasium the Magnesian gate, through which on May 25th of each year processions bearing the image of Artemis came from the Temple of Diana along the *Via Sacra*, and at which they were met by Ephebi, or young men of the city, and so were led to the theater, and afterwards to the Corresian gate, whence they returned to the Temple, having passed through the main streets of the city, and entirely around Mt. Prion; it was by locating the gates and tracing the course of the streets leading from them that Wood (1869) discovered the long lost, and until then vainly sought temple of Diana. Philostratus says a covered way led from the Magnesian gate to the temple.

Going south from the Magnesian gate we pass the Basilica, of Roman production, the agora or wool market, the Odeon, or Lyric theater.

This is built on the South side of Prion, the natural incline of the hill serving for the elevation of the seats. The front is 153 feet in diameter, and it is estimated to have had a seating capacity of about 2300. Wood, who exhumed the buried city, found here the statue of Lucius Verus, now in the British Museum, and a life-size statue of the muse Erato, with a 7-stringed lyre and a pedestal at her side. All the interior of the Odeon was white marble, vast amounts of which are scattered all around; the door-posts and many seats are still in their original position. A little farther on towards the south we passed another market place, and still farther on the west side of the mountain is the great Theater, which is of so much interest because of its connection with the history of St. Paul. We walked about through the vast but wasted place, and while we endeavored to recall in imagination the ancient splendor of the pile and the excited people, who "rushed with one accord into the Theater," I took out my Bible and read the account of the excitement stirred up by Demetrius, who made silver shrines of the goddess and who brought great gains to the craftsmen making and selling the same—saying: "Sirs ye know that by this craft we have our wealth. Moreover ye see and hear that not alone at Ephesus, but almost throughout all Asia, this Paul hath persuaded and turned away much people, saying that they be no gods, which are made with hands: So that not only this our craft is in danger to be set at naught, but also that the temple of the great goddess Diana should be despised and her magnificence should be destroyed, whom all Asia and the world worshippeth. And when they heard *these sayings* they were full of wrath and cried out, saying, Great *is* Diana of the Ephesians. And the whole city was filled with confusion: and having caught Gaius and Aristarchus, men of Macedonia, Paul's companions in travel, they rushed with one accord into the theatre. And when Paul would have entered in unto the people, the disciples suffered him not. And certain of the chief of Asia, which were his friends, sent unto him, desring *him* that he would not adventure himself into the theatre. Some therefore cried one thing and some another: for the assembly was confused; and the more part knew not wherefore they were come together. And they drew Alexander out of the multitude, the Jews putting him forward. And Alexander beckoned with the hand, and would have made his defence unto the people. But when they knew that he was a Jew, all with one voice about the space of two hours cried out, Great *is* Diana of the Ephesians. And when the townclerk had appeased the people, he said, *Ye* men of Ephesus, what man is there that knoweth not how that the city of the Ephesians is a worshipper of the great goddess Diana, and of the *image* which fell down from Jupiter? Seeing then that these things cannot be spoken against, ye ought to be quiet, and to do nothing rashly. For ye have brought hither these men, which are neither robbers of churches, nor yet blasphemers of your goddess. Wherefore if Demetrius, and the craftsmen which are with him, have a matter against any man, the law is open, and there are deputies: let them implead one another. But if ye inquire any thing concerning other matters, it shall be determined in a lawful assembly. For we are in danger to be called in question for this day's uproar, there being no cause whereby we may give an account of this concourse. And when he had thus spoken he dismissed the assembly."—*Acts* 19: 25-41.

This theater is in the shape of a horse-shoe, and is 495 by 467 feet through the two greatest diameters. It is variously estimated to have held from 25,000 to 60,000 people. Like the Odeon, it is also on the hill side. The front and gates were of marble, carved into figures of exquisite beauty. This was repaired after the temple had been destroyed, as shown by many decrees passed and carved on the stones of the building, one of which gives citizenship to Agathocles in consequence of his giving the city 14,000 measures of corn. One is a decree of Hadrian, A. D. 120.

Evidently this theater, or some similar one, suggested the idea of the Colosseum to Vespasian. In front of the theater are the *Agora* and the great gymnasium, while a few miles west we look out upon the sea. On the north side of Prion is the Stadium of the Augustinian age, similar to that of Antioch, where Ben Hur, Aldebaran, Atair, Antares and Rigel made themselves to be sung by the women and children in the tents, because of victory over the insolent Roman. We try to find the seat where poor Simonides and Esther would have sat to look upon the exciting scene; to fix the place where the unfortunate Messala was crushed to the wall, and fill the great area, nearly one thousand feet long, with excited spectators.

The west end was adorned by an open columniated screen in tiers. The bases of some of the supporting columns are still to be seen. In front of the Stadium, to the west, is the Serapion, where offerings were made to Serapis. It is elevated about fifty feet above the race course of the Stadium and covers about two hundred and fifty square feet; in the center is a hewn rock foundation containing an altar, reached by four flights of steps and three piers for columns between each flight.

Passing out by where once stood the Corresian gate, a little north of the Stadium, the principal street led to the Temple of Diana or Artemis, about one mile north of Prion. On the east of Prion is the cave of the Seven Sleepers and many Christian tombs. We now cross the fertile plain and the Cayster, formerly much larger than at present, and come upon the site of one of the seven wonders of the world, until 1869 concealed from human eyes by twenty feet of siltings, the world-renowned Temple of Diana; the stoa or platform covered eight acres, and rested on a bed of charcoal, between layers of mortar, charcoal and skins. This served the double purpose of diminishing moisture about the base and danger of destruction by earthquakes. The temple was seven times destroyed, and rebuilt always upon the same foundation. The last but one, which Pliny says was 220 years in building, was burned by Herostratus, who had despaired of making a great name by fair means, and thought to immortalize himself as an iconoclast.

The city fell into the hands of Alexander the Great before the last temple was finished; the previous one was burnt on the night of his birth. He offered to complete it at his own expense if the Ephesian City Magnates would allow his picture to be placed in it, but they refused by the flattering but evasive reply that it was not fitting that one God should pay homage to another. We copy some of the dimensions of this wonderful structure. On the lowest step it measured 418 feet by 239 feet 4½ inches. The pavement of the peristyle was 9½ feet above the street and reached by 14 steps 19 inches wide in the tread. The temple itself was 342 feet 6½ inches by 163 feet 9½ inches, and was octastyle, i. e. with 8 columns in front, and dipteral, i. e. with two rows of columns on the sides. These were in rows of 20 each, one hundred columns in all (27 of them the gifts of Kings) of the Ionic order, measuring 6 feet ½ inch at the base and 8 ½ diameters in height, making them, base, capital and all, about 60 feet high. We saw great quantities of the ruins—many drums—of these columns scattered about. The parts of the Temple were called Pronaos, or porch in front, the vestibule, cella, or large chamber, at the end of which was the altar for sacrifices; beyond the altar was the statue of the goddess, then a room called Opisthodomos, the treasury, and the Posticum or porch on the rear, corresponding to the Pronaos on the front. (Some of these temples that we have visited are very suggestive of the human nature of the deities inhabiting them, notably that of Denderah.)

" Ephesus was the third capitol and starting point of christianity, Jerusalem and Antioch being the other two. Ephesus witnessed its full development and the final amalgamation of its inconsolidated elements in the work of John, the Apostle of Love. It lay one mile from the Icarian Sea, in the fair Asian meadow, where myriads of swan and other waterfowl disported themselves amid the windings of Cayster. Its buildings were in the delightful neighborhood of the Ortygian Groves. Its haven, once the most sheltered and commodious in the Mediterranean, had been silted up by mistakes in engineering, but was still thronged with vessels from every part of the civilized world. It lay at the meeting point of great roads from Sardis, Troas, Magnesia and Antioch, thus commanding access to the valleys of Hermus and Meander and the interior. Its seas and rivers were rich with fish; its air was salubrious; its position unrivalled; its population multifarious and immense. Its markets glittering with the produce of the world's art, were the Vanity Fair of Asia. They furnished to the exile of Patmos the local coloring of those pages of the Apocalypse in which he speaks of "the merchandise of gold, and silver, and precious stones, and of pearls, and fine linen, and purple, and silk, and scarlet, and all thyine wood, and all manner vessels of precious wood, and of brass, and iron, and marble, and cinnamon, and odors, and ointment, and francincense, and wine, and oil, and fine flour, and wheat, and beasts, and sheep, and horses, and chariots, and slaves, *and souls of men.*" Rev. 17: 12, 13.

And Ephesus was no less famous than it was vast and wealthy. Perhaps no region of the world has been the scene of so many memorable events in ancient history as the shores of Asia Minor. The whole coast was in all respects the home of the best Helenic culture, and Herodotus declares that it was the finest site for cities in the world of his day. It was from Lesbos and Smyrna and Ephesus and Halicarnassus that lyric and epic poetry and philosophy and history took their rise. It was here that Anacreon had sung the light songs which so thoroughly suited the light temperament of the Greek colonists in that luxurious air; here that Mimnermos had written his elegies; here that Thales had given the first impulse to philosophy; here that Anaximander and Anaximines had learned to interest themselves in those cosmogonic theories which shocked the simple beliefs of the Athenian burghers; here that the deepest of all Greek thinkers, "Heraclitus the Dark," had meditated on those truths which he uttered in language of such incomparable force; here that his friend Hermodorus had paid the penalty of virtue by being exiled from a city which felt that its vices were rebuked by his mere silent presence; here that Hipponax had infused into his satire such deadly venom; here that Parrhasius and Apelles had studied their immortal art. And it was still essentially a Greek city. . . . While the presence of a few noble Romans and their suites added to the gaiety and power of the city, it did not affect the prevailing Hellenic cast of its civilization, which was far more deeply imbued with Oriental than with Western influences. Such was the city in which St. Paul found a sphere of work unlike any in which he had hitherto labored. It was more Hellenic than Antioch, more Oriental than Corinth, more popular than Athens and more wealthy and more refined than Thessalonica, more sceptical and more superstitious than Ancyra or Pessinus. It was, with the exception of Rome, by far the most important scene of all his toils, and was destined in after years to become not only the first of the Seven Churches of Asia, but the seat of one of those great Œcumenical Councils which defined the faith of the Christian world.

The character of the Ephesians was then in very bad repute. It was the headquarters of many defunct superstitions, which owed their maintenance to the self-interest of various priestly bodies. South of the city was the olive and cypress grove of Leto, where the goddess brought forth her glorious "twin-born progeny." Here was the hill on which Hermes proclaimed their birth; here the Curetes protected their infancy from wild beasts; here Apollo took refuge from the wrath of Zeus after he had slain the Cyclopes; here Bacchus had conquered the Amazons during his progress through the East, or so argued Ephesian ambassadors before the Roman Senate when pleading for right of Asylum. Nor did they see that it was a right ruinous to the morals and well-being of the city. Legend told how, when the temple was finished Mithridates stood on its summit and declared that the right of asylum should extend around it as far as he could shoot an arrow, and it flew miraculously a furlong's distance.

The temple, which was the chief glory of the city, and one of the wonders of the world, stood in full view of the crowded haven, the temple was the most splendid ornament of this most splendid city of Asia. This temple—the eighth—had been rebuilt with ungrudging magnificence out of contributions furnished by all Asia—the very women contributing to it their jewels, as the Jewish women had done of old for the Tabernacle of the Wilderness. It gleamed far off with a star-like radiance. Its peristyle consisted of one hundred and twenty pillars of the Ionic order hewn out of Parian marble. Its doors of carved cypress-wood were surmounted by transoms so vast and solid that the aid of miracles was invoked to account for their elevation. The staircase that led to the roof was said to have been cut from a single vine of Cypress. Within were the masterpieces of Praxitiles, and Phidias, and Scopas, Polycletus. Paintings by the greatest of Greek artists, of which one—the likeness of Alexander the Great by Apelles—had been bought for a sum equal to $25,000 of modern money, adorned the inner walls. The roof of the temple itself was of cedar-wood, supported by columns of jasper on bases of Parian marble. On these pillars hung gifts of priceless value, the votive offerings of grateful superstition. At the end of it stood the great altar adorned by the bas-relief, behind which fell the vast folds of a purple curtain. Behind this curtain was the dark and awful adytum in which stood the most sacred idol of classic heathendom; and again behind the adytum was the room, which inviolable under divine protection, was regarded as the wealthiest and securest bank in the ancient world.

The image for which had been reared this incomparable shrine was so ancient that it shared with the Athene of the Acropolis, the Artemis of Tauris, the Demeter of Sicily, the Aphrodite of Paphos and the Cybele of Pessinus, the honor of being regarded as "an image that fell from heaven." She was represented on coins—which may have easily passed through the hands of Paul—as a figure, swathed like a mummy, covered with monstrous breasts, and holding in one hand a trident and in the other a club. The very ugliness and uncouthness of the idol added to the superstitious awe which it inspired. The Jewish feelings of St. Paul would have made him regard it as pollution to enter her temple; but he must have seen on coins and paintings and in direct copies the strange image of the great Artemis of the Ephesians, whose worship, like that of so many fairer and more human idols, his preaching would doom to swift oblivion."—*Farrar's Paul at Ephesus.*

The Goths set fire to this last temple, A. D. 226 and the world's great centers have gone on changing from place to place, until Ephesus, once so magnificent, has so well nigh perished as to be almost forgotten. Once Antony and Cleopatra lived here; once Alexander begged in vain for honors it might give; once here was the image that "all Asia and the world worshippeth" enthroned in "marble halls." Here Paul fought with beasts, because of the advantage he should gain by the resurrection of the dead. Here was one of the seven churches to whom John was commissioned to write and say: "I know thy works and thy labor and thy patience, nevertheless I have somewhat against thee, because thou hast left thy first love." Here was that band of brethren whom Paul "ceased not to warn day and night with tears, by the space of three years," and to whom he afterwards wrote from Rome, by Tychicus, his "most sublime" and "majestic" epistle, so full of encouragement, solicitous exhortation and prayer. Some think also from Ephesus was written the first epistle to Corinthians.

Alas, that all this greatness should perish—that these splendid monuments now should be inhabited only by bats, jackals and serpents—that these columns and gates should be put into mean and useless fences; yet so it is.

Still further to the north is an old Castle, built by the Knights of St. John in the 14th and 15th centuries; also a Mohammedan mosque, into which much of the material of the temple was worked. On this side are left standing a few of the pillars of the ancient aqueduct that supplied the city with water. On the tops of these, about 40 feet high, the storks build and rear their young. They were very numerous, tame as chickens, and dignified in appearance.

It was our good fortune to have the best guide procurable—Mr. Mills and I—one who was with with Wood in his excavations, 1863-1869, and knew how to guide fairly well. Quite satisfied with our visit, at 4 P. M. we took the cars for Smyrna. The scenery was very fine. To the north was Mt. Tmolus, covered with snow, and on both sides smaller members of the range covered with bright angelicas, and the low shrubbery with bursting buds and springing grasses. In one of these hills the myths say Artemis was born, but we did not try to visit her birth-place.

We ran upon a herd of several hundred horses grazing, but they were fearless of the locomotive. We passed many *fellahs* plowing with the same kind of plows used thousands of years ago. However, they break the land well, about one fourth of an acre per day. To-morrow we shall bid adieu to Asia and sail for Greece.

The question is often asked: "If Christianity is destined to predominate, why have Mussulmen sway in the countries where once Paul preached and Christian churches stood, which have gone to decay?" It may be said, in reply, that the religion of the Moslem is nearer to the truth than either the ancient Greek or Roman paganisms which prevailed in those countries referred to, and the true religion has more protection now in those places than it then had. Besides, the aggressive force of Christianity has been expended in other directions rather than at those places where it began to manifest itself. Perhaps few if any of those places have grown worse since Paul's day. Many of them have grown better. It is true, as Carlisle says in his Hero-worship: The good of the old is retained until it is absorbed by and recast in the new.

CHAPTER XXVII.

FROM ASIA TO GREECE.

"Immortal Greece—dear land of glorious lays,
Lo here the unknown God of thine unconscious praise."—*Keble*.

We left Smyrna for Athens on a stormy sea, that grew more boisterous every mile we advanced, and only three of our number were comfortable on deck, of whom I was one, and proud to think myself able to defy, at last, the Mediterranean's worst. We pass on the route the temple of Minerva Sunium, situated on a high, rocky promontory overlooking the sea. Out of sight of human dwellings, it is a magnificent ruin, standing, like "the lone Indian," a sentinel over the land whose glory has departed, and the seas where that glory was largely won. For an hour before reaching the harbor Athens was in view—not the city proper, but portions of it—and the Acropolis stood out in bold relief against the April sky. All glasses were brought into requisition. And we quote Archdeacon Farrar to portray the thoughts and feelings then filling our minds:

"ATHENS! with what a thrill of delight has many a modern traveler been filled as, for the first time, he stepped upon that classic land! As he approached the Acropolis what a throng of brilliant scenes has passed across his memory; what processions of grand and heroic and beautiful figures have swept across the stage of his imagination! As he treads upon Attic ground he is in 'the Holy Land of the Ideal;' he has reached the most sacred shrine of the 'fair humanities' of paganism. It was at Athens that the human form, sedulously trained, attained its most exquisite and winning beauty; there that human freedom put forth its most splendid power; there that human intellect displayed its utmost subtlety and grace; there that Art reached to its most consummate perfection; there that Poetry uttered alike its sweetest and sublimest strains; there that Philosophy attuned to the most perfect music of human expression its loftiest and deepest thoughts. Had it been possible for the world by its own wisdom to know God; had it been in the power of man to turn into bread the stones of the wilderness; had perfect happiness lain within the grasp of sense, or been among the rewards of culture; had it been granted to man's unaided power to win salvation by the gifts and power of his own nature, and to make for himself a new Paradise in lieu of that lost Eden before whose gate still waves the fiery sword of the Cherubim—then such ends would have been achieved at Athens in the day of her glory. No one who has been nurtured in the glorious lore of that gay and radiant city, and has owed some of his best training to the hours spent in reading the history and mastering the literature of its many noble sons, can ever visit it without deep emotions of gratitude, interest and love."

The topography of the sea and land required us to steam by the city in order to come into port. At 11 A. M. we reached Piraeus, the harbor of Athens, filled with the crafts of all nations. Four miles to the northeast is Athens with 75,000 inhabitants. Some of us go up in carriages, some on the cars.

The first impression made on the mind is relief at the vast improvement upon the populations of Egypt, Palestine and Asia Minor, in the dwellings, manners and clothing of the people. Business is conducted much as I had been used to at home; the streets were clean, the buildings tasteful, and life, energy and snap greeted us at every turn. I and President Mills hire a guide to conduct us to the sights of Athens of yore. We go first to the Temple of Theseus, who made himself immortal on the field of Marathon before the haughty Persian was vanquished there; to whom was ascribed the honor of uniting into one commonwealth the twelve States into which Cecrops divided Attica, after destroying the Minotaur of Minos, who required a tribute of fourteen youths and maidens to be sent every nine years from Athens for the monster to devour. The national hero of the Greeks, they erected this temple to receive his bones which Cimon brought from Scyros, B. C. 469, and it became a tomb, a temple and an asylum all in one, and while one of the earliest works of ancient Athens, it is the best preserved; 104x45 feet, having a peristyle of Doric columns, it served as a model for the advanced age and national prosperity that produced the Parthenon under Pericles, the first of Grecian statesmen, and Phidias, the first of *all* sculptors. We then went to the so-called prison of Socrates, where he is said to have drunk the fatal cup of hemlock. It is only traditional, and forever beyond the reach of certainty, but certainly every indication favors the tradition.

It is a cave, divided into two rooms, cut into the solid stone, the first cave or room faces the Acropolis, and is entered by a door of about ordinary size; the second one, in which the sage was confined, is entered from the first by a narrow door on the back side and near the right corner. We go next to Areopagus or Mars' Hill. It is reached by sixteen steps which though cut in the solid stone are nearly worn out, one or two being gone entirely. A few places cut smooth on the top point out, it is thought, where the accuser and accused stood in trials held here; the Council that met here was called the Upper Council, the one meeting in the valley being called the Council of Five Hundred. Its name is derived from the double name of Mars and Ares. He was tried on this hill, for the murder of Neptune's son, by the gods and the place has since been called Areopagus or Mars' Hill! It lies to the west of and one hundred feet below the Acropolis and is separated from it by a valley, which has largely been filled up by the accumulation of rubbish for many centuries. We regreted that we could not stay and attend the service to be held there the day after our departure. held there because of what is written in Acts 17:

Then Paul stood in the midst of Mars' hill, and said, *Ye* men of Athens, I perceive that in all things ye are too superstitious. For as I passed by, and beheld your devotions, I found an altar with this inscription, TO THE UNKNOWN GOD. Whom therefore ye ignorantly worship, him declare I unto you. God that made the world and all things therein, seeing that he is Lord of heaven and earth, dwelleth not in temples made with hands; neither is worshipped with men's hands, as though he needed anything, seeing he giveth to all life, and breath, and all things: and hath made of one blood all nations of men for to dwell on all the face of the earth, and hath determined the times before appointed, and the bounds of their habitation; that they should seek the Lord, if haply they might feel after him and find him, though he be not far from every one of us: for in him we live, and move and have our being; as certain also of your own poets have said, For we are also his offspring. Forasmuch then as we are the offspring of God, we ought not to think that the Godhead is like unto gold, or silver, or stone, graven by art and man's device. And the times of this ignorance God winked at; but now commandeth all men everywhere to repent: because he hath appointed a day in the which he will judge the world in righteousness by *that* man whom he hath ordained; *whereof* he hath given assurance unto all *men*, in that he hath raised him from the dead.

And when they heard of the resurrection of the dead some mocked: and others said, We will hear thee again of this *matter*. So Paul departed from among them. Howbeit certain men clave unto him, and believed: among the which *was* Dionysius the Areopagite, and a woman named Damaris, and others with them.

Vandalism has well nigh done its worst in Athens. Only think of demolishing the temples that were not only the pride and glory of Athens at her acme of greatness but the production of architectural genius unrivalled in any age, for material with which to shelter an ignoble race, too lazy to go to the quarries, or of taking the columns that formed the supports of the roof or architraves of the temples of Jove or Minerva, and use them for burning lime kilns, and we have a sample of what has been going on for centuries, and an answer to the question, why are there not more of the remains of ancient Athens? Renan, the sceptic, insinuates that the works of art in Athens perished because St Paul called them *idols*. He writes:

"Ah beautiful and chaste images; true gods and true goddesses, tremble! The mistakes of this ugly little Jew (St Paul) will be your death-warrant."

It was their death-warrant as gods, but only as gods.

"We have learned to see God in all that is refined and beautiful; whom his love has lifted up above the perils of an extinct paganism; whom His own word has taught to recognize sunbeams from the Fountain of Light in every grade of true art and every glow of poetic inspiration may thankfully admire the exquisite creations of ancient genius:—but had Paul done so, he could not have been the Paul that he was."—*Farrar.*

The thought occurs that only by searching for the divine are such productions obtained, only by uplift of soul and outstretching of his powers toward his God, do man's capacities fully develop in any sphere of life.

The second day we visited the Acropolis, the elevated rock upon which Cecrops began to build Athens 1550 B.

C. It is a nearly level area, about one thousand feet from east to west by half that distance from north to south. It was fancifully said to be the center of four concentric circles, viz.: Athens the city, Attica, Greece, the world.

It is entered only through the propylea, on the west, the finest ever built, executed under the direction of Pericles, and though much abused by the unappreciative rulers that have dominated Greece for many centuries, and the inevitable friction of rolling years, the mind easily rebuilds the abused but still graceful structure, and rejoices in contemplation of what it once was, while we

"Sigh for the touch of a vanished hand
And voices hushed in death forever."

We pass the great Propylea and stand on soil pressed by some of the greatest men of antiquity. Just to the right of the gate, Lord Byron is supposed to have sat as he wrote the following lines:

"Slow sinks, more lovely ere his race be run
Along Morea's hills, the setting sun;
Not, as in northern climes, obscurely bright,
But one unclouded blaze of living light!
O'er the hush'd deep the yellow beam he throws,
Gilds the green wave that trembles as it glows.
On old Aegina's rock, and Idra's isle,
The god of gladness sheds his parting smile,
O'er his own regions lingering, loves to shine,
Though there his altars are no more divine
Descending fast the mountain shadows kiss
Thy glorious gulf, unconquer'd Salamis!
Their azure arches through the long expanse
More deeply purpled meet his mellowing glance,
And tendered tints, along their summits driven,
Mark his gay course and own the hues of heaven
Till, darkly shaded from the land and deep,
Behind the Delphian cliff he sinks to sleep."

Here they concentrated their thoughts, their genius and wealth for the glory and protection of their nation.

THE ACROPOLIS OF ATHENS AS IT WAS.

On this area were to be found many temples erected in honor of their gods and goddesses, the chief of which was Minerva or Athena, in whose honor three images arose and the two grandest of their temples. The irregular Erectheum and the Parthenon both contained images of Jove's virgin daughter. The Parthenon, 228 feet long by 101 feet wide, which contained her statue, 39 feet high, the work of Phidias and made of ivory and gold, covered with gold ornaments to the amount of nearly half a million dollars, presented in its Doric columns, metopes and fretted frieze not only the best study of architecture, but the righest museum of sculpture and choicest collection of paintings in all the world: "dedicated to the national glory and the worship of the gods."

The Venitians bombarding the Turks in the 17th century, set fire to a powder magazine on the south side of the Parthenon, and well nigh demolished this temple. The columns on the west end present many indentations made by bombs and grape shot. May we not hope that a perpetual peace has settled upon the Acropolis at last?

The present King, George, has shown a praiseworthy disposition to exhume and preserve whatever relics still remain undiscovered. He has had a museum fitted up in the rear of the Parthenon for the reception of such relics as have been recently found, or may be, and had the ancient Stadium excavated a year or two since at his own expense.

We went through the museum and was distressed at the paucity of the remains that greeted our eyes. We visited the Acropolis on three successive days, with the same sense of admiration for the Greeks of the perishability of all earthly productions, though they may be marble or brass, of the truth of the poet's words that

"He builds too low who builds beneath the skies," and of the Scripture that saith "Except the Lord build the house they labor in vain who build it."

The atmosphere seemed to be charged with a sombre enchantment, and a solemn grandeur shrouded the sixteen remaining columns of the once magnificent temple of the Olympian Zeus, where century after century the patient destroyer has beat his silent vigils.

The Odeon, or Theatre of Herod, is still to be seen on the south side, below the Acropolis, and east of this the Theatre of Dionysius, with the seat of Dionysius, in which we sat. It is one piece of marble with rests like an arm chair, and his name is carved on the front of it in Greek. These theatres were for the enactment of tragedies, recitations of poems, etc. The seats were of stone or marble and were arranged in semi-circular receding tiers, one above another.

There was a pedagogue surrounded by about fifty or sixty young men and boys standing at the entrance of this theatre, and our guide said (for though I had read Greek at school, I could not understand a word he spoke), he was lecturing on the political history of Greece, and striving to arouse their patriotic impulses by speaking to them amid the ruins of better times. He would point to the Acropolis above, the theatre in front, the country or battle-fields in the distance, and was animated in his delivery and interesting to his audience. I was reminded of the old peripatetics of whom I read when a boy.

Other objects of which I may not speak at large but which we could not afford to slight, were the temple of Nike, or the Wingless Victory, at the threshold of the Acropolis, Tower of the Winds, Stadium, the Gate of

Hadrian, on the west side of which an inscription says: This is the city of Theseus." One on the east side says: This is the city of Hadrian, and not of Theseus. Hadrian built the city east of the Agora or market place, where St. Paul disputed "daily with them that met with him."

While we were in Athens an officer of the army died. The pall-bearers carried him through the streets in a coffin, the upper part of which was removed, exposing the profile of the corpse to persons on either side of the street.

CHAPTER XXVIII.

AMONGST SAVANTS.

The morning of April 12th was somewhat threatening; several watery looking clouds were floating through the skies not very high above the Capitol city of Greece. The train was due to leave the station for Peloponnesus at 7 o'clock. On the previous evening, seven of us met in the parlor of the Hotel D'Estrangers, where all were stopping except myself, I being at the Hotel of the Ionian Islands, two squares away, and arranged with a guide to visit Corinth by the early train. The distance was three hours, and we had six hours in which to do old Corinth and the Acro-Corinthus, which was the chief object of our visit.

Five of our company were preachers, four of these D. D's.; five were Americans; two were college Presidents; the two who were not ministers were Sunday school teachers.

Soon after starting we passed a hillock to the left, which our guide called the Academy of Socrates, a little farther on, to the right, the place where Plato's Academy was, or his garden which he inherited and in which he is said, by Diogenes, to have taught, as well as in the Academy. Near by our guide pointed out the birthplace of Miltiades and the plain in which the first cereals, given by the goddess Ceres for the rescue of her daughter, Proserpine, were planted. They chose a good place to begin at, as the soil is still very fertile after continued cultivation for more than twenty-five centuries. It is a dark red clay and had a fine crop of wheat or barley growing on it during our journey. There were a great many poppies in full bloom, mingled with the wheat, which, however, some of our company, better versed in Botany than myself, contended were not poppies, but anemones, or something else.

It is in the same locality in which the Greeks claim the first Olive tree was planted on earth; they still abound.

Our first stopping place was Eleusis, once powerful enough to contend with Athens for the sovereignty of Attica, and more ancient than Athens or even Ceres whom they worshipped, whose temple the Persians destroyed when they invaded Attica, but which was rebuilt by Ictines the architect of the Parthenon under Pericles, but to be again demolished by the German vandal Alaric, A. D. 395. Its shattered walls stand on a rocky knoll, about two minutes walk from the station, in the midst of a people who seem not only to have no pride at remembrance of the glory attained by their ancestors, but not even the remembrance of that glory or even conception of it; "no heritage of the past remains but monuments, decrepitude and corruption;"

"All except their sun is set."

The road winds around the bay of Eleusis, then the gulf of Ægina filled with small islands. We saw hundreds of birds floating on the surface seeming to be feeding on the small fishes just below the surface.

The hillsides are covered with worthless, scrubby pines, a few feet high, besides which we saw no timber at all. We passed over the Corinthian Isthmus where many centuries B. C. the Isthmian games were celebrated, through which many rulers vainly sought to cut a channel large enough for the passage of vessels. Among those wishing thus to unite the Saronic and Corinthian gulfs were three of the Cæsars and Alexander the Great, and previous to them Diodorus Poliorcetes, who abandoned his purpose because he found he would inundate the country on the Saronic gulf! However, the moderns have found out the error of Demetrius and will soon have the two seas flowing together, and Peloponnesus will be an island. The canal is cut through the stone most of the way, and is one or two hundred feet deep in several places, judging from what I could see from the cars as we crossed.

How strange to think, as we looked upon the rough ground between the two seas, almost five miles apart-that the Greeks used to draw their vessels from one to the other overland! However, that was previous to the days of ironclads and the Great Eastern. We stopped at Corinth Station, near to or within the old city limits, but about six miles from the citadel, Acro-Corinthus.

We took carriages and rode to a small village of half a dozen dwellings, passing on the route several places paved with smooth stones and circular in shape, about one hundred feet in diameter. It was probably on one of these that the "sweet Gallio" had his "judgment seat" when the Jews made "insurrection with one accord against Paul" saying, "This fellow persuadeth men to worship God contrary to the law." A matter of so small concern to him that he drove them from his presence and looked with indifference on, while they beat Sosthenes, their chief. To-day hundreds of millions could be enlisted in defense of Paul's attitude, then "no man stood by him." Gallio, the Roman Proconsul gave not a thought to the creed of Paul or of the other Hebrews.

Our carriages halted in a cluster of houses under some large sycamore trees, one of which extended its ample shade over us while we dined on a rude table, for the use of which we paid a drachma (20 cts.) We were soon besieged by antiquity venders, having "*genuine antiques*," tear bottles, cups, kylixes, &c.; which they said were once used by the ancient Corinthians, and which may have been several months old.

Near by where we ate, a few Doric columns, tied at the top by large stones, fragments of the old architrave, mark the site of the only remaining temple of the gods of Corinth, and the only building that St. Paul looked upon during his sojourn here of nearly two years. From this temple we took horses and rode to the gates of the citadel, about three miles distant, and two thousand feet high. This was the most impregnable fortress known to the ancients, called the "fetters of Greece" by Philip, and could be taken only by surprise or treachery, and even since the days of artillery can be taken from one side only, a pointed rock to the southwest from which it was battered and taken by Mohammed the Second. There are two or three sets of gates that must be passed ere one can reach the interior. Within the walls are the remains of a large town, perhaps not less than twelve thousand people once lived on this rocky pinnacle; none of the houses, however, remain intact, all have been partially or quite torn down. Two Mohammedan mosques remain, shattered as the rest. In the largest one about half-way from the gates to the highest point of the hill, two cows were quietly resting in the shade, chewing their cuds.

"Here is the spring at which Pegasus was drinking when taken by Bellerophon." At proper intervals along the walls many old cannon were distributed, but all at which they could belch forth their missiles of woe was gone.

Where two thousand years ago marble temples stood in honor of Venus, where was the Stadium, the Theatre, the Agora, the Lyceum and Academy, all was still; Mohammed's legions had likewise come and gone.

A few patches of houses (I will not say towns), disgraced the ample plains below, once teeming with cultured citizens, who excelled in painting and casting and working of glass as their neighbors at Athens did in sculpture, who probably were the authors of the bronze Hercules in the Vatican which cost Pius the Ninth, over ten millions of pounds.

A few crafts float in the harbors of the opposite seas, where once were forests of masts, whence sailed the first war galleys and whither came the commerce of all the Orient.

Looking northwest over the Corinthian gulf we saw Mount Parnassus, home of the Muses, mantled in snow above ancient Delphi,

"Where, save a feeble fountain, all is still."

Helicon and many other mountain peaks were in view, the mention of whose names calls to mind some tragic event in history, some metamorphosis of the mythologist, some immortal song of the poet.

We all gathered at the highest point and scanned the horizon round through our glasses, then the nearer landscape, then back into each other's eyes to read reflections that might find expression there. What melancholy emotions involuntarily arise in witnessing how the glory of man may vanish and come to nought!

We returned, reaching Athens about 7 P. M., and felt, as President Mills expressed it, that though he had to go over the road three times, it would not be too often.

The next day, in company with three of the gentlemen of the party that went to Corinth, we visited the American School of Archæology, History and Literature. We met Prof. Rolfe, a graduate of Amherst College, and for some time professor in the University of Ohio. Already he has gained an enviable place among modern archæologists, though he did not seem to be past twenty-five. We also met his accomplished young wife, a fit companion for a man whose chief association besides is with fragments of old stones exhumed from old city sites and tombs.

Prof. Waldstein is in charge of the school, and it seems to be in excellent hands. He will be remembered as the visitor who discovered the lost metope of the Parthenon in the Louvre at Paris, and came suddenly before the world as a discoverer, taking high rank as an archæologist, which position he has ever since most ably sustained.

From those gentlemen we learned that a student can live in Athens, have free use of the school, and meet all necessary expenses for about $12.50 to $15.00 per month.

We ascended Mt. Lycabettus hardby the city to the northeast, and enjoyed one of the finest landscapes on earth. Saving her temples, Athens is as beautiful, perhaps, as ever; so are her blue gulfs, her fields of wheat that skirt the suburbs, her groves of olive trees, her royal gardens, her wide well-paved streets, her marble palaces, her modern academies, one of which it is claimed has the finest *Aula* of any university in the world.

Athens that was did her share in making the civilization of the world that is, going in her mission by way of Rome and Constantinople, while Athens that is, at last is receiving back from the civilized nations, whom she so well served, the ideas of commerce, manufacturing, politics, literature and law.

CHAPTER XXIX.

THROUGH THE HELLESPONT TO THE SUBLIME PORTE.

We go from Piraeus, the harbor of Athens, to Constantinople by the Italian line of steamers. Now an Italian agent will always make a traveller pay more than the legitimate price of a ticket. On railroads, they only collect 5 *centimes* more than the price stamped on the face of the ticket, while I found, after going aboard, that I had paid three *lirae* or sixty cents more than the price as stamped on the face of the "billet."

We had a stormy sea until we reached the Dardanelles. I dreamed, the first night out from Athens, of embracing loved ones at home, and awoke to find myself holding tight to the sides of my berth to keep from falling out. A fellow-passenger told me, next day, that he was thrown from his (upper) berth to the floor of his stateroom, and considerably bruised. Bishop and Mrs. Fowler and their only son, C. H. Fowler, Jr., were on board returning from an episcopal tour through the mission fields of their (M. E.) church in China and Japan and on their way to the European mission conferences, one of which at Loftcha in Bulgaria, I hoped to visit, should time permit. Being about the ablest preacher of his denomination I hoped to hear him, but did not. What limited time we were together I enjoyed recitals of his experience as a christian and preacher. He enjoys a joke. He was one of the party when we visited, on donkeys, the ruins at Denderah, expressing pity for the donkey-boy, some one asked: "Why don't you take it time about with him, Bishop?" He replied: "There's a million of them and but one of me."

At ten o'clock next morning, we entered the mouth of the Dardanelles, the dead line of nations, and every foot of land to Constantinople has a thrilling history, associated with the building or burying of earthly empires. We first pass Tenedos, whither Homer says the Greeks carried their galleys to make the Trojans think they had retired from the siege, and where they built the wooden horse. We pass near that field where nothing but the death of faithful Patroclus could dispel the sullen gloom of Peleus' son and kindle his martial spirit into that quenchless flame that made him the hero of the first and greatest epic. Fine fields, fairly cultivated, stretch inland from the Straits and seem to be capable of large yield. Occasionally thin forests of diminutive growth adorn the landscape. We reach the towns of Sedur-Bahr on the left and Dardanelles on the right, where we have to halt and submit to an examination by the Turkish officials appointed by the government to examine all vessels passing that way to Constantinople and the Black sea. Near by we see where Leander and Lord Byron swam across, about three miles, the latter taking seventy minutes to make it. The distance is said to be three miles, while the current carries one a mile out of his course, making it necessary to travel four miles in all. Lord Byron and a fellow traveller, Mr. Ekenhead represented the current as strong, the water cold, though they made the shore without fatigue.

Some doubt whether the story of Leander be true, as

he would have to swim eight miles in going from Abydos to Sestos and returning. A tower, called Leander's tower, stands at the mouth of the Bosphorus between Stamboul and Scutari, built to commemorate this faithful brave and devoted lover.

Near Abydos, Xerxes had built his bridge of boats, fastened by cables of papyrus, for the transportation of the Asiatic troops to Europe, the first of which, by Mandraele, was carried away by a storm, which so enraged him that he murdered the architect.

The ancient site of Abydos is now occupied by a Turkish town called Nogaw Bauran; here Parmenio led Alexander's army across from Europe to Asia, and again the Osmanli Crescent crossed to be set up first on European soil, by Suleiman, A. D., 1360.

The day was very bright, which greatly increased the enjoyment of the sail through waters so renowned, where steamships from all nations pass hourly up and down. We fain would have driven our ship on faster, that we might enjoy the views presented by the borders of both continents, all the way to Constantinople, but night fell upon us as we entered the sea of Marmora (or marble). It is so named in consequence of the abundant supply of marble quarries along its coasts and in its Islands.

I can hardly hope to convey to my readers even a small conception of the beauty which the rising sun revealed on the morning of April 15th, as we came into the harbor of Constantinople. For more than an hour previous to our arrival we were on deck eagerly anticipating, from statements made by those on board and familiar with the city, somewhat of its magnificence.

In approaching the city on the sea of Marmora, we

pass Stephanos, where the English gunboats stopped the Russians approaching to the capture of the Turkish capital, in 1878, just too soon. Next is Makrikoi, (pronounced Makrikeue,) then a large factory town to the left and Scutari to the right—all suburbs of Stamboul. The sea contains many islands, a flying visit to seven of which claims one day of the hurried tourist's time.

The objects seen most distinctly at a distance as one approaches are the minarets of St. Sophia, the Mosque of Achmed and the Genoese Tower. These appear to be only a mite above a sea of indistinct objects all mingled together promiscuously—the outlines of this world-renowned metropolis. As we approach nearer and nearer, the parts of the mighty emporium stretch out on either hand like wings, and rising from the water terrace-like, extend far inland.

The sea is divided into two arms—one of which, to the right, extends twenty miles to the Black sea and is called the Bosphorus; the other, about six or seven miles long, is called the Golden Horn. That part of the city which is embraced by these two arms bears the double name of Pera and Galata. Pera is the name of the upper portion and Galata the lower. Rue de Pera is the name of the principal street of the city. Galata is connected with Stamboul or old Byzantium (of the Greeks,) by an American-built iron bridge across the Golden Horn. Immediately to the left is the old Seraglio grounds.

The city across the Bosporus on the Asiatic side is called Scutari, the Brooklyn of Constantinople, of which we shall have occasion to speak hereafter.

Our ship anchors just below Seraglio Point, surrounded by a hundred more, doing business in these waters to the amount of 7,000,000 tons annually, receiving and discharging tourists and cargoes from and to all civilized nations. A thousand minarets, each surmounted by a crescent, gleaming in the sun-light, rise above a city or cities magnificent in extent and in appearance from the deck of our steamer, and in power, also, if we judge by the length of time they have dominated these seas and shores, or by the dozen idle ironclads at rest in the Golden Horn, ready at short notice to sail in the national defence or to the conquest of any undefended nation whose tribute would be worth the cost of war.

Many are the factors that enter into the Eastern question, if it be any question, not the least of which perhaps is the providence that retains the dominancy of the "ever sick, but never dying man of the East," because his neighbors show no more readiness to uplift the masses than himself.

CONSTANTINOPLE.

CHAPTER XXX.

IN AND ABOUT STAMBOUL.

When I reached Cook's office, on the Rue de Pera, where good mail matter was in waiting, I met again Dr. Green, of Buffalo, N. Y., and Mr. Dogget, of Winooski, Vt., whom I had seen in Jerusalem. We took a carriage, and George Thomas for a guide. We went first to the Genoese Tower, built by the Italians when they were in possession centuries ago. It is on a hill in Galata, near to the British Post Office. It is a circular wall about twelve feet thick, if I remember correctly, and about fifty feet in diameter. One ascends by stone steps in the wall about two hundred feet, whence the view is very fine. We next cross the Golden Horn, pass *Publique Dette*—the Government School for Priests—into the Seraglio grounds, go through the Museum of Antiquities, see one fine piece of Statuary—Andreanus, the Greek victor—Cyprian pottery and Assyrian Antiquities, drive as near the Sublime Porte (that is, the lofty gate of the Seraglio, from which the name is given to the Sultan's realms) as they will allow, which is not near enough to pass through it, as we have no firman. In the grounds stands the largest tree I ever saw. It is a sycamore. We go hence to St. Sophia. It costs us two shillings each to enter and two piasters each for sandals to wear while within. Rugs and carpets of matting covered the floor, and a few Turks were praying, while others were laughing and talking. St Sophia was built for a Christian church, and the builder, when it was completed, was so elated at its magnificent appearance that he said: "Solomon, I have surpassed thee!" Some of the material was brought from Ephesus and other cities, and no doubt this was among the finest structures in existence when first built, as it is still.

We go to the Hippodrome, which contains an Egyptian Obelisk, Constantine's Tower, and the three brazen serpents, ten feet high and thirteen inches in diameter, which once "formed the interior of the Tripod of Delphos;" they are twisted together and have all been beheaded, the first one by Mahomet (not the prophet) when he took the city. We saw one of these heads in the museum. This is one of the oldest antiquities in existence, and speaks of the days when the Greeks looked towards Delphi as the Moslems do towards Mecca.

The Museum of the Janizaries next claims our attention; they were a mighty factor in the completion of the subjugation of the Byzantine empire. One sees the dress and armor used by each officer and servant. Their number was only 1,000 at first, chosen from among the Greeks as a body-guard to the Sultan, kept in position and faithful by receiving the spoils of war, they were increased to 40,000 and became a terror to Christendom in the East.

The Reservoir of 1001 columns is a wonderful structure; it contained three stories, each supported by 224 pillars, making 672 in all. Why it was called reservoir of 1001 columns I do not know. Two of these stories are now filled up; the third, about 25 feet under ground, is used to spin silk in. When used for water it contained 1,000,000 cubic feet, though that of St. Peter was six times as large. When we emerged from it a rough Turk who had seen us enter or who had been called by our guide, was on hand to receive *backsheesh* for so great and important a privilege as we had enjoyed.

We next visited Seraskierat, which contains the offices of the War Department, and the City Tower, which we did not ascend. Hardby is the Pigeon mosque, the court yard of which is darkened by thousands of pigeons daily. When a Turk is sick or in perils by the sea, he vows to Allah to go and feed the pigeons, if he but obtain deliverance; hence one can always see these Mussulmen fulfilling their vows much to the gratification of the pigeons.

Although we had engaged the carriage for the day, our coachman wanted his pay and to postpone till tomorrow the seeing of the Seven Towers and Palace of the Sultan's headquarters. After parleying over it for a long time we conquered and rode through the entire city of Old Stamboul, and back by the barracks of his majesty's troops and Topari or Artillery Mosque and Mosque of the Sultan, called also *Yildik* or Star. The interior of this is very imposing. The Sultan worships here once a week, on Friday. It is near to the Royal residence and surrounded by most splendid gardens, far up on the heights back of the city. Returning we stopped at the Bible house, and met Mr. Bliss, son of Dr. Bliss, whom we met in Egypt. He is the efficient young Secretary. Dr. Buckley learned from him that one could buy the air above residences, whereby the owner was prevented from building his dwelling any higher.

I was told that the Bibles they distributed are often torn to pieces by fanatical Turks; but a Mohammedan will never destroy a paper with the name of God on it, if he knows it; on the contrary, they will pick up and preserve every piece, however filthy, which contains that holy name. They cram these pieces into crevices between rocks or where the name will be preserved from further abuse. I heard a story of one thus preserving such a piece of Scripture in Jerusalem and had curiosity enough to read what was said about God, and was by it led to embrace Christianity. Nothing I have ever witnessed surpasses in sincerity and I may say solemnity, a Moslem at prayer, yet with all that it is not at all certain that he has any principle.

IN ASIA MINOR AGAIN.

April the 16th was set apart by us to visit Scutari, the Mohammedan and English Cemeteries, and Boulgourloo, on the Asiatic side of the Bosphorus. The steam ferry-boats start from the bridge that spans the Golden Horn, and are capable of carrying about one hundred and fifty passengers each, and they run about every fifteen minutes through the day. One man sells you a ticket, another punches it and a third collects. The boat is divided into two decks, first and second class, each of which is divided into two compartments—one for gentlemen, one for ladies; also on each side of the lower deck a room is cut off and labelled in English and Arabic, "Harem reserve." A man may take his wives in if it be unoccupied; if it be occupied, he is separated from them on the trip. I thought once, at Bebek, I should fail to get aboard at all, being met and stopped at every effort. I found that, without knowing it, I was trying to pass through a gate where only females could pass. "One must do in Turkey as Turks do."

Landing in Scutari we took a carriage for the Mohammedan Cemetery—one of the largest in the world, covering several square miles, and the tombs are crowded about as near together as they can be. Every grave was marked by a marble slab, or, I should rather say, post or column, for they were narrow and thick, often eight feet high, each having a head with a peculiar head-dress or turban worn by deceased during his life.

One is shown a canopy supported by six marble columns, beneath which is buried the favorite horse of Sultan Mohammed. Above all these wave tall and graceful cypresses, emblems of mourning.

Passing this, we soon reach the English Cemetery to the right. Not only the English sailors and inhabitants who die here are brought here for interment, but those of the English troops who fell in the Crimean war, sleep here also; and a granite shaft, forty or fifty feet high, stands in the midst of the grounds, raised in honor of England's fallen braves. It is approached from several sides by gravel walks, either shaded or bordered by several species of evergreens. Just outside is the hospital where is still shown the room and furniture of Miss Nightingale, who devoted her talents to the alleviation of human suffering.

About six miles from the landing at Scutari, we reach Boulgourloo, passing, on the way, several pretty towns and a few of the Sultan's summer palaces, for he has a great number of them. Boulgourloo is a high hill, covered with grass, sloping rapidly in all directions; it is one of the hills on which beacon fires were lighted from Tarsus to Byzantium before the electric telegraph.

From it the Emperors used to start to Asia on their hunting expeditions. The hill is several hundred feet high, and the forests having perished centuries since. one can see for a hundred miles over the sea of Marmora, studded with islands, and Kadi Koi, the site of Chalcedon of old, birth place of Zenocrates, and seat of the fourth general council, A. D. 451, which condemned the Monophysites; it was the starting point of generals, in olden times, to Persia and the East. It is more ancient than Byzantium (Constantinople). We see many miles over hills and plains towards the interior of Asia. On the other side the Bosphorus, adorned by a dozen towns, comes, by the aid of our glasses, within easy eye-shot. What shall I say of Constantinople, with her suburbs far enough away to lose all her objectionable aspects, and near enough to present her hundreds of mosques, palaces and public buildings, with the ships of all nations ever coming and going! Truly she sits a queen, and the most favorably located of any city in the world perhaps, if she only had a good citizenship, of progressive men in her back countries.

We very fortunately happened on this side on the most favorable day of the year; it is fifteen days until Ramazan, and the day the camels start to Mecca with the national offerings. They start from the Mosque of Achmed the first, and are taken thence to a boat. The boat brings them to Scutari, and two huge Bactrian camels, decorated with silk into which threads of gold and silver are woven and ostrich feathers until they are nearly covered up, wait to receive the presents; really the camels are meant for priests or dignitaries to ride upon, while thirty or forty mules are laden with two or three boxes and trunks apiece and the camels support large canopies that pitch forward at one step and backward at the next, as if they meant not to stay in position to grace the procession.

Thousands of people had gathered to witness the religious *fete;* all the piazzas and windows were full of excited spectators; about a hundred cavalry were on hand to keep the peace and guard the sacred treasures. The street that led down to the landing was so crowded that, fearing lest at the critical moment we should fail to be in a favorable position for seeing, we took a shop-keepers bench and stood upon it; but when the cavalry formed in line we were only about four feet in their rear, and the very horse that was in front of us became very restless, ran backward into our party, hurting several persons and upsetting our bench, almost breaking a boy's leg. While all this pageant was passing I had serious misgivings lest the fanaticism of these Turks should suggest something disastrous to us Christians, so few, and safeguards so far away, nor did I feel perfectly at ease until the crowd dispersed.

At two o'clock the booming of cannon informed us that the freight had started, and in a few moments it was landed, reloaded and hurried away. While it w s being brought ashore there was a mock gladiatorial contest.

The Ramazan is the Moslem Lent and lasts four weeks. During that time they neither eat, drink, nor smoke from sun-up until sun-down; the first thing after sun-down is to smoke; this they will do for an hour often, after which they eat. The camels start to Mecca two weeks before, so that the offerings may be on hand at the opening of Ramazan. We recrossed to the European side, made an excursion up the Golden Horn to the Sweet Waters, passing the magnificent red stone College of the Greek church, and completed the day.

CHAPTER XXXI.

CONSTANTINOPLE AND THE TURKS.

Wednesday, April 17th, was our last day in Constantinople. We went up the Bosphorus to the Black Sea, by the route which Jason went in search of the "Golden Fleece." The coast on either hand was lined with towns nearly all the way up. Ours was a mail steamer, and it was curious to see them deliver the mail and tickets. The former was carried in square boxes, locked with a hasp, staple and padlock. At every station the Captain would have the tickets tied up in a little bag about such as we have seen boys carry their marbles in, into which a stone weighing four or five ounces was dropped. This would carry momentum sufficient to land it, while he received a like wallet from each station, to be carried on, tossed aboard often after the boat was under headway. Failing to carry lunch I had to buy some bread, which gave me an idea I should else have missed. As I could not speak Turkish, and being alone (for my companions returned to the city, while I got off at Bebek to see our American College,) I stood near by the bread vender until I saw him sell a ring of it about as large as the ring used on a trapeze, say six inches in diameter, then I knew the price and bought myself, taking the bread and laying down two *metterlichs*. The idea I caught was the benefit of seeds sprinkled on the bread while cooking. I do not know the name of the seeds; they were about as large as cloverseed, and possessed a strong and very pleasant flavor. They also possessed an oily property, which made the bread more nourishing.

The college is about twenty minutes walk from the landing, and is reached by walking up a very precipitous hill overlooking the Bosphorus. The walk-way, however, is well graded and passes under that famous wall built by Mohammed II in three months, each workman doing more each day than had ever been done by one man in a day before or since. It was built in the shape of the Arabic letters which spell Mohammed's name, and as a rallying point from which to take Constantinople and destroy the Byzantine empire. I have seen no prettier location anywhere than Robert College enjoys. It overlooks nearly the entire length of the Bosphorus and far into Asia Minor beyond, whose bosom is covered with pretty towns and prosperous farm-houses in the midst of the green fields.

It is surrounded by a stone wall and a great variety of trees and shrubbery. The building is of stone and is large, commodious and well arranged; a four-story house, built around an open court, from which the ascent is made to the upper stories. After looking at the grounds and buildings sufficiently from without, I called on Dr. Washburn, the President; while waiting for him, an indelible impression was made upon my mind to the effect that the officers were very busy and the students equally as idle. Dr. Washburn I found to be a very polite, communicative gentleman. The students of the college were from Servia, Bulgaria, Austria and several other nationalities are represented including Jews, being either Greek or Catholic christians, instead of Turkish boys, only one or two of which, I believe, are in the college. The college is a power for good, though inferior to that of Beirut. The other high schools of Constantinople are said to be atheistic, which fact gains a sympathy otherwise denied this Protestant Christian college. They have one hundred and seventy boys enrolled. An orator alluding to its proximity to Mahomet Second's wall and towers, said: "It stands on higher ground than those towers. It dominates them. Its forces are spiritual and eternal. It shall see them pass away." This prophecy will doubtless be fulfilled. They were seven years securing a title to the property after it was purchased; such is the Turkish way of doing business and his fear of the Russ and Frank.

To-day is the Sultan's birthday; the masts of every Turkish craft are ornamented with streamers; the fronts of gardens and yards have lattice-work made of flowers and tinted paper woven into fanciful shapes; the branches of trees are hung full of bottles. The streets are crossed with ropes and twine woven into webs at places, all strung with candles and Chinese lanterns to be lighted at night. At 12 o'clock M. twenty-one rounds of cannon are fired.

Constantinople, a magnificent city, is at her best, doing honor to her ruler. Everybody seems to take pleasure in the occasion; though the Sultan is as much afraid of dynamite as the Czar of Russia.

At night the city, with all her suburbs, is illuminated; every one of her thousand minarets is blazing, and they look together like all the constellations of the skies had clustered just over the happy capitol. The Sultan's palace, just above *Yildik*, seemed from Galata across the Golden Horn, to be of crystal and illuminated with a hundred electric lights; and hundreds of inferior palaces, with mosques and military stations, far up on the heights in the suburbs, and private dwellings, all vied with each other in an effort to honor the Ottoman monarch.

No doubt thousands of barrels of kerosene were consumed, and the full moon lent all her mellow radiance to enhance the witchery of the scene. I stood for more than an hour beneath a spell, as it were. Pera, through which runs the Strand, or Broadway, and the city on both sides the Bosphorus, are behind me and out of sight; but Stamboul, rising terrace-like beyond the Golden Horn, is reflected from its trembling face, which almost doubled the grandeur, already everwhelming. I had never seen anything of the kind so splendid before; I do not expect to see it again on earth. Great is the power of a man or a system that sways millions of loyal souls, even though they be semi-heathens.

This ovation not only marks the high place the Sultan Abdul Hamid II holds in his subjects' esteem, but shows him entitled to be placed beside earth's potentates.

Again, we thought of the waste of labor and material, so much needed by the ignorant children of this ponderous empire, and asked the question, why all this waste upon one poor, perishing polygamist, who feels to be jeopardizing his life every time he goes out? And the answer comes back, for the sake of these same poor, needy wretches, who will not rest content without such remote, pampered, haughty, aristocratic masters. Of course oppression abounds, but this evil is less than those which arise from a consciousness of irresponsible freedom among a people incapable of self-government.

Give such a people pageants, illuminations, parades, sensuality and mystery about religion; make Cathedrals dark; read or sing prayers in an unknown tongue; excommunicate for reading scriptures and knowing truth, and it is no surprise to find anomaly in moral, social and political matters, such as a celibate priesthood on the one hand and a polygamous one on the other, resulting in scepticism and nihilism.

Time would fail to tell of all the strange experiences of a traveller here, or the interesting objects on every hand, or the habits or religion of the Turks. The facts that they do abstain from wine, do observe the rite of circumcision, do fast during Ramazan, show them capable of becoming exemplary christians. But they are cruel in the treatment of their wives, making them do almost all the work, consider the birth of girls a curse, and make them begin to wear veils at eleven or twleve years of age.

If a man wishes a wife he must speak to his father to secure one for him; if he likes her he keeps her, if not, he returns her to her father; and if he be able to support two he gets his father to look him up another. No courting among the Arabs.

Their salutations are unsurpassed by any people for grace and significance. An Arab meeting or parting with a friend will raise his right hand to his forehead, drop it to his lips, then to his breast, which means, I revere you with my mind, speak well of you with my lips, and give you a place in my heart. One might go far to find more delicate politeness. On parting the first says: *Yallah salaam!* May you go in peace. The other responds: *Salaam*, i. e., peace. The ordinary salutation is, *En harak sa'id*, i. e., "May you have a rich day." The response is equivalent but the words different, and is: *En harak mabarak!* If an Arab wishes to carry a point he will stoop to conquer; he will kiss your hand repeatedly, lay the back of it against his forehead, on the top of his head, and kiss it again.

A story is told of a Turk as follows: A neighbor wished to borrow his donkey and was told the animal was not at home; pretty soon the animal brayed, said the neighbor: "There, he is at home." "I won't lend anything," said the Turk, "to a man who believes a donkey's voice in preference to mine!"

If you approach a female unveiled, who usually keeps her face veiled, she will either pull the veil over her face, and hold it in her mouth or turn her head till you pass.

Often in the warmer climates of Egypt and Palestine the males and females seem to be dressed alike, looking at them from the rear; a tunic or something like a sheet of white cloth is worn over the whole body, head and all; the men often wear clothes like an American, often a skirt which fastens to each leg below the knee and a coat about his body. The women have a great variety of dress, including trousers. Mothers of the poor learn their children to say *backsheesh* before they learn to say mother. I have seen them send babies out to meet us not three years old, who understood their business. They will come out, babe in hand, point to it and say "he" or "she christian, *backsheesh*, Howadji!"

A lady told me that while at Marsaba, in Palestine, she ordered a donkey boy to wash out the kyathos and bring her a nice drink of water; he put some water in the vessel, went up to a donkey, thrust the end of the donkey's tail into the kyathos and mopped it out and brought her a nice drink of water! Using him as a cup-towel! Very convenient that; it can be hung out to dry and preserved for future use.

While there are about 1,000,000 inhabitants in Constantinople our guide said there were 1,500,000 dogs. I I have counted eight in one pile, sleeping like hogs. These are nearly all of the same species, a kind of cross between the cur and Shepherd dog. They are religiously scrupulous about the treatment of canines. Every man fee s the dogs in front of his door, though he lays no claim to them; he will also defend them when endangered. The dogs of one street or section live in harmony among themselves, but will not tolerate strange dogs; they unite to ostracise any visitor; all seem to understand the proper boundaries of their real estate and allow no trespassing. Friday is Moslem Sabbath and on that day they publicly feed dogs.

The Mahometans are fatalists. When misfortunes overtake them they say, *Kismet Dur*—It is fate. They do not think the trouble could have been averted by any effort of theirs.

Oriental cities are generally built in a very compact manner because it is more economical and affords greater defense in time of war, few of the streets are broad enough for vehicles to pass, they are often built on hillsides, also, because of the better defense thus secured. So that instead of the carts and drays used in Occidental cities, men carry the baggage and freight from wharves to stores and warehouses. A thick pad is fastened over the shoulders falling down below the hips, a box of merchandise often weighing three or four hundred pounds rests on this while the man goes in a stooping attitude, a long rope reaches around the burden behind and around the bearer's forehead. The limbs of these human freight cars are generally bare, and evidence the greatest possible muscular development.

They say that Satan, "Stoned Devil," against whom they pray five times daily, is the genius that inspires all mechanical wisdom.

They punish apostasy with death, unless the apostate recant at once. When Mohammed began his brilliant career, he told his followers the world was divided into two parts, viz: *Dar ul Islam* and *Dar ul Harb*—that is, House of Islam and House of War. "House of War," said he, "is for God. God gives it to you." What such a motto and its inspiration wrought, Christendom knows but too well. He predicted the capture of Constantinople 700 or 800 years before it was done. It was not Mohammed's purpose to destroy Christians and Jews. He called them *Kitablees*, or people with a Book, meaning the Bible—his system being a degenerate Judaism grafted to Arabic habits. His followers, however, did not adhere to this part of the plan. Jerusalem was the first city that fell into their hands, and Charlemagne, to whom the Kalif sent the keys of the Holy Sepulchre, secured from them safety for Frank merchants in Syria and Egypt.

Dr. Menzies' *Turkey, Old and New*, says:

"Mussulman conquest is rapid and splendid and followed by precarious and incurable decadence."

The Turks had a standing army when such a thing was unknown in Europe. But Europe was laying broad and deep the foundations for mightier conquests than the "gorgeous East" had ever known, or could ever attain, until they too should follow the ways of the western world.

The following is a summarized estimate of the Turks by one who travelled throughout the Ottoman Empire.

"They are hospitable, charitable generally, sometimes generous; the lower classes are honest, their greatest merit; not so with the upper classes; but one may rely on their solemn promise. They are ignorant, presumptuous, vain and bigoted, proud without any feeling of honor, and cringing without humility, cannot resist money or the prospective benefit of a lie.

In Government and administrative duties they are tyrannical and overbearing, in religion dogmatic and intolerant, in fiscal measures mercenary and arbitrary, and ignorant of their own history as they are of others. The higher classes are inferior in character, probity and honor to the lower. Their virtue is that of the Savage, who is generous because nature supplies his wants, and charitable because of the uncertain tenure by which he holds his goods; poor and removed from temptation he is honest, but entrusted with office he becomes a thief. He plunders the poor and propitiates the rich by bribes, hence offices are sold to the highest bidder."

Constantinople is the headquarters for such missionary work as is carried on in Turkish territory. Our Consul there is a Jew, and secures for our Missions more clemency than his Christian predecessor, so I was informed at Bierut. He put the Missions on the same basis as all other American enterprises. Dr. Hamlin, founder of Robert College, relates an experience which illustrates the power of christianity even among Mussulmen. While superintending a bakery that supplied the English army with bread, he bought on thirty days time, ten thousand dollars worth of flour from a Turkish merchant, on his credit as a Christian Missionary. I visited the Sailors' bethel here and was present at one service, and had a gracious season of prayer with a sailor who had not walked for several weeks, on account of rheumatism, and was glad to hear that he came down stairs the next day.

As I looked at this degraded people, I was saddened

beyond expression; they looked like sheep, having no shepherd. I often longed for a voice that they could understand, that I might tell them good news, and that the christian church could but catch as a watchword Mahomet's own, "This part is God's, God gives it to you," and give and go and continue giving and going until the mighty work of preaching the gospel to every creature is done.

CHAPTER XXXII.

THROUGH ROUMANIA, BULGARIA, SERVIA, HUNGARY AND AUSTRIA.

At 9 o'clock, P. M., I left Constantinople for Vienna. After buying my ticket I was seized by two burly Turks unable to speak English more than to say *"passe-port."* Now, a pass-port is seldom required on entering Turkish dominions, but always on leaving, so I had secured a *Teskereh* (Turkish pass-port) for Constantinople; just such a one as even a Turk would have been required to have if visiting there from some other place, but I had not had my American pass-port *vised*, i. e., passed through the hands of a Turkish Consul and had his permission to travel in Turkey written on it. So I produced my *Teskereh;* they read it, handed it back, and demanded: "Passe-port." Now, if I had given them my American pass-port, not *vised*, they would have fined me two or three dollars and detained me, perhaps, as many days. So I did not produce that, but handed back the *Teskereh* again, which they refused, saying: "Passe-port," "passe-port." Not producing the other, one of them snatched the *Teskereh* out of my hand, which I snatched back as quickly, and turned and walked away. I had learned the tricks of Turks during two months in Egypt, Palestine and Syria, and knew they were only after backsheesh. Had I fallen into the hands of the ruffians on entering their country for the first time, I would have had to pay out and been detained several days besides. When the train rolled off I felt a burden roll off with it. One is ever ill at ease for fear these Arabs will practice some new, successful trick upon him. There is no trouble to one using Cook's or Gaze's tickets, but sometimes I traveled without them—did not have one then.

The distance from Constantinople to Vienna is one thousand and fifty miles, the time forty-seven hours. I left the brilliantly illuminated city at nine o'clock, P. M. Two or three young Germans got on the same car, and I made an effort to get into the same compartment with them, first, because I was going towards Germany and I would practice speaking a little, and second, because I was afraid to ride with two or three Turks all night in a car locked up, and in a car from which there was no possible egress and no hope of aid if it should be needed. I had purposely assumed a garb that was calculated to allay all suspicion that I might have anything worth seizing, and enjoyed more ease in consequence on this transcontinental ride.

The cars on all European railroads are dispatched in the same way, as follows: Two alarm or signal bells are rung a few minutes before the cars are ready to start; when the time expires a third bell is rung, the conductor blows a whistle like a dog whistle, the engineer responds with a single whistle from his engine, the cars moving off at the same instant. There is no getting off or on after the last bell is rung.

As we said we took the cars in old Stamboul and skirted the city by the seashore. It was twenty minutes ere we passed the last emblazonry of the Sublime Porte and shot out into the darkness towards the west and home.

Unable to converse with the two or three passengers that were in the section of the car with me I was left to my own reflections, and many were the thoughts that coursed through my brain about these Turks, so strange in religion, in habit, in speech, in dress and all their customs; and the mind went on to kindred subjects, the conditions of the human race, their multiform ways, creeds, colors and characteristics. But much is common to them all. All thirst for more. All have some form of religion. All are "made of one blood for to dwell on all the face of the earth," and perhaps God sees a greater good in them all than we can see or are ready to believe. Musing thus the hours wore on and tired nature sank into the arms of Morpheus. There are no sleeping accommodations on this line, except on the train that leaves on Sundays, but I left on Thursday.

Next morning we reached

ADRIANOPLE,

the last Turkish town. Other travelers carried their baggage to the custom house from the train. I did not. I had not seen it on that fashion as yet. So in a few minutes the officers searched the train, and I expected trouble, but found none and experienced such a sense of relief at being rid of these bugbears as only those who have travelled in the Orient are able to appreciate.

As we hurried through a very fertile looking plain the Balkan mountains, about twenty miles from our way, were covered with snow. The fellaheen were ploughing with six-ox teams to iron plows, made by civilized mechanics, which promised to put new life into the agricultural interest of lands so long depressed under Turkish rule. We passed the breastworks that mark the spot where many a brave Servian bled and died in 1877-'78, striving to free themselves from the galling yoke of Turkey. Large herds of sheep were pasturing near the road in Turkey, Servia, and Roumelia.

This long railroad has different cars and different officials for every state through which it passes, and we knew when we ran into a new territory by the change in the uniform of the railway and military officers. The Servians and Bulgarians wear very heavy caps of felt with long knap, also the red stripes down their trouser legs was about two inches wide while that of the Turks was only one-fourth to three-eighths wide; all soldiers wear their national coat of arms. The first day I took dinner at Tzaribrod. This is the country where people live so long. Near here, Peter Czartan lived 185 years, and Kamartzik, of Polotszk, 163 years, and between here and Constantinople, an old Turk still lives, aged 150 years, supported by the Sultan's generosity. If one of these old gentlemen should declare that he was Adam, no living man, from his own personal knowledge, could deny it. The names on signs here were almost all Russian, as well as the style of the people's dress.

I noticed in passing through Bulgaria, the water conveyed to several mills through races around hillsides until it had reached the point to be applied when it was emptied from the race into a hollow log about twenty feet long through which it was precipitated against a paddle wheel.

On the evening of April 18th, the snow was falling and there was promise of a cold, sleepless night. I had just fallen into a good slumber when quite a stir of passengers awoke me. All must go with all their baggage again to the Bulgarian customs officers to be examined and have our passports restamped. My shoes were thin, the rain and snow were falling fast, the fire had died out in the stove that was this time under the coach, warming the car by a pipe that ran through from bottom to top. So I moved slowly and my baggage was rather heavy for a single man to carry. There were no lights about and I was nearly lost in the darkness, unable to speak a word comprehensible to the people there. There were two or three doors or windows lighted up by dim lamps within, and in one of these I saw people moving about; to that one I went to find the low counter for the reception of a traveller's baggage. Passing these guardians at the outposts of the nation who register every passenger's name, place from which he comes, and to which he is going, (because 'eternal vigilance is the price of liberty') and regaining my car, I wrapped myself in my Arab *bist*, and slept till the morning sun showed us the flushed river Save at the junction of which with the Danube we see the beautiful city of Belgrade, into which we run and get a fine breakfast at the railroad restaurant.

Once more our luggage and passports have to be exhibited, and once more on the cars we feel easy. We cross a high trestle over the Save and stop at Semlin, still in sight of Belgrade, and are ordered once more to give the representatives of the Austrian Empire sufficient reasons why we should hope to enjoy so great and important a privilege as to pass through their country. It is not enough that a man is of a lawful age, he must be well recommended also.

From Semlin to Pesth the road soon crosses the Danube and then runs north between the rivers Theiss and Danube, about seven hours through a marshy plain all the way. Many ponds of water, miles in extent, and not over two feet deep, lay along our way. The farm house, all through Hungary, reminded me of those of the Dutch I had been used to at home. The cattle are some species of long-horns; often their horns seemed to be three feet long, or more.

We stopped only about an hour or two in

BUDA-PESTH,

and had only time to get an idea of the general appearance of the Hungarian capital, and hurried away to Vienna, Wien they call it in German. I found two Hungarians aboard the cars who had lived a long while in America. One was going to Vienna to see his wife and baby. To hear him speak of his baby reminded me of the father of " dat Young Yawcub Strauss." Following his advice I stopped at the hotel Wimberger, near the West Bahnhof, and was well pleased, even when I reckoned with mine host and Co. Generally two or three to a dozen servants are on hand when a traveller leaves, each expecting a gratuity.

CHAPTER XXXIII.

VIENNA.

It would require a whole book to give any adequate idea of the "most splendid capitol of Europe." It is an old city, originally settled by Celts, afterwards, it became a Roman military station. Marcus Aurelius died there. It was besieged by Attila and afterwards by the Turks. It has been the seat of the house of Hapsburg for more than six hundred years.

Vienna owes its beauty to a circumstance. It was once a walled town, but all the space having been taken for buildings and streets within the walls, the space around them was taken until there was more of the city outside than inside the walls.

The ancient city within the walls is called the *Stadt*, and numbers about 50,000 inhabitants, while the entire city numbers about 1,000,000. As the bulk of the city was thus exposed, it was determined about thirty-two years ago to tear the wall away, the space occupied by the wall was converted into a street about two or three hundred feet wide, laid off into boulevards and streetcar lines. It is called Ring-Strasse.

The *Stadt* is the fashionable quarter. The Hofburg, or imperial palace is there as well as those of the nobility. There is the Graben or street containing the finest stores, the banks, leading churches, museums, galleries, etc.

Around the Ring-Strasse (Ring Street) are situated the National Museum, two large stone buildings covering about four acres each, and between them Maria Theresa Platz, where her bronze statue is seated in an imperial chair surrounded by statesmen, generals, poets, sculptors, physicians and musicians as Loudon, Khevenhueler, Lichtenstein, Daun, Kaminitz: Haugwitz, Mozart, Haydn and others.

Next is the Treasury, after which is the Parliament building, the facade of which presents three gables adorned with statuary representing the country at peace: these are supported by fifty Corinthian columns and eight pilasters. Sloping walks, guarded by *gens d'arms* go up to the great porches. The interior is arranged after the same model as that of the United States at Washington. The top is surmounted by eight chariots drawn by two and four horses. It is said to have cost 8,000,000 florins. We noticed some master-pieces of frescoing, done by Kruppen-Carl: Maria Theresa, after the seven years' war, Founding of St. Stephens, and From the Cradle to the Grave, the original, no doubt, from which came the chromos and engravings of the same, so numerous in the United States. Next to this is the *Rathhaus*, or city hall, one of the finest in the world, costing 17,000,000 florins, (a florin purchases about as much labor as a dollar, but is less than 50 cts.) The ceiling of one room, the grand reception hall, cost 48,000 florins and a single chandelier cost 35,000 florins. The floor is made of oak mosaics oiled.

The *Rathhaus* is situated in the rear of a square laid off in pretty walks and thick-set with shrubbery.

Next to the *Rathhaus* is the *Votivkirche* (Votive church) erected in commemoration of the Emperor's escape from assassination in 1853. Very near by is the University. The departments are all in the same room, and labeled

Law, Theology, Medicine, &c. The *Aula* contains the statues of Maria Theresa, and Rudolph, the founder. The library occupies nine stories, having floors of iron bars about the size of plastering laths turned edgewise to admit the free transmission of light. It is said to contain 1,000,000 volumes, besides several thousand *incunabula* (first books printed) some fine books of parchment costing 1,400 florins per volume when new. They contain very rare, highly colored pictures. All these are seen in glass show-cases. Crossing the *Ringstrasse*, we pass the New Opera, a very imposing structure externally, enter the *Volksgarten*, a small park containing the Theseum, a small Temple built like the Temple of Theseus at Athens, and to hold Canova's marble group of Theseus slaying the Minotaur. Passing through the *Volksgarten* we see the Opera House, Bank, *Academia*, Kunstler Haus, which is quite a picture gallery, filled with visitors. One picture, by Falkenburg, unfolds to a protestant philosophic mind one cause of the universal social and moral obliquity that predominates here. The picture is that of a young woman, with rather flushed face, kneeling behind an old man clad in the attire of a Catholic Priest; his head inclines to catch the words she tremblingly whispers in his ear; we pause to hear them; "*Pater peccavi!*" (Father I have sinned). Forgiveness is easily obtained, and the way is paved for repetition.

The educating influence of such pictures in these conspicuous places is past estimating, especially when they are praised by the great and learned.

The art galleries of Europe are largely what Catholic priests have made them; the people are very largely influenced by the galleries. If chastity is barely known it is because it is not desired. The innate sense of purity is assisted just enough by the church to forbid that the sale of indulgences and the confessional should cease, while human nature has all the encouragement that the lewdest genius can suggest. It is a positive injury for any one to visit these places whose character is not formed. * * * * Men of prestige should cry out against the lewd in art, unless the modesty that is praised be false and have no foundation in nature and the fitness of things. We in America are following in the wake of our ancestors. Are we only behind them in reality or following them astray?

French Infidelity, German Rationalism and Russian Nihilism are only natural reactions—protests against the unnatural and illegitimate assumptions and teachings of Roman Catholicism in France and Germany and Greek Catholicism in Russia.

Beside the *Kunstler Haus* stands the elegant *Music Freund*, adorned with the marble busts of Gluck, Haydn, Mozart, Beethoven, Schubert, Schumann, and many others. A little further is Christ's church and Beethoven's monument in Bronze.

All these places which I have mentioned are situated on an arc of the circular street called the *Ringstrasse*, and suggest how splendid an appearance it must present. The whole of this street runs between lofty mansions, hotels, museums, galleries and beergardens fitted up like parks.

I attended service in St. Stephen's church, Stephen's Platz or square, said to be one of the noblest gothic edifices in Europe. The Catholic worship is all alike to me, and it is not necessary to explain it to those who have seen it, and hardly possible to those who have not.

I ascended the tower, over 450 feet high, there being only two church steeples higher in the world, those of *Strasburg* and *Cologne*.

I went to the Augustine church to see Canova's monument of the Archduchess Maria Christina, said to be one of his noblest works. The tomb is triangular, and built of marble. The inscription above the door is in Latin—UXORI OPTIM.E ALBERTUS—*to the most excellent wife of Albert.* Above this inscription an angel supports a cartouch bearing her name and profile; another approaches bearing a palm; a female figure and two children enter the door bearing an urn and wreaths; to the left another female figure leading an old man; to the right an angel reclines on a sleeping lion. The figures are life size. In the Loretto Chapel of this church are the silver urns that contain the hearts of many members of the imperial family.

The Capuchin church contains two leaden boxes, in which are the ashes of Maria Louisa and the Duke of Reichstadt, second wife and only child of the great Napoleon. This unfortunate son fell as far short of as his father transcended parental expectancy. Two squares away, in the Treasury Museum, is the royal cradle, trimmed in satin, pearls and gold.

We noticed a barefoot (not an uncommon thing) Capuchin priest sitting near the sidewalk reading on Sunday morning, and stopped to learn that he was so posing to arrest passers by, who should thus be made to read the conspicuous advertisement of a "panoptican show" going on in rear of him. His trick was a success.

All these Austrians go to church. I noticed little children, not over three and four years old, at church and worshipping, just as the old people did, kneeling before the crucifixes, images and paintings of Christ as they passed. All attend early and say their appointed number of prayers, and the remainder of the Sabbath, say after nine or ten o'clock, is converted into a holiday. They go by thousands into the country on excursions, as hundreds of tram-cars run daily, while all who do not go to the country go to the Prater or other *beergarten*. The Prater is the great place of concourse. I went out Easter Monday, and I and a Presbyterian minister who witnessed the scene, estimated that there were no less than 100,000 people in the Prater that day. It is a magnificent park, laid off into walks and drives, containing many theatres, circuses, *beer-gartens* "flying Dutchmen, lady orchestras and other catchpenny places of amusement."

To say this number drank not less than 5,000 barrels of beer that day would appear extravagant until we state that we have it on good authority that one *beer-haus* in Munich consumes 1,000 barrels daily, a quart being the smallest amount sold at one time. The average daily consumption is two quarts per capita for the entire population.

A tram-car climbs from the city to the heights on the west by means of a cog-wheel; we ascended and had a nice view of the city and her environs. It is novel to an American to see little boys of 7, 8 and 9 years carrying side arms and dressed in uniform, and of all ages carrying canes. They appear to be following the precept as they understand it—train up a child in the way he should go and when he is old he will not depart from it. They want a soldier out of every man, and so begin on him in time. And while these youngsters are in the cities and towns of Europe flirting with city girls, their sisters are at home doing all the farm work. It was a daily sight in Vienna to see pretty girls driving two-horse wagons from the country, when no doubt their brothers were in the Austrian camp. It was the same going from town to town on the cars—the women were cultivating farms everywhere. Alas, when a nation must thus waste its productive forces in order to feel secure, while all the delicate sense of woman, that makes her queen of home and clothes her with native charms, is blunted by reducing her to a serf, with the task of feeding the family and supplying tax sufficient for the nourishment of her son, husband or brother and the government besides.

It was really amusing to see large dogs hitched to one-horse wagons loaded with milk or vegetables, to lighten the draught otherwise falling upon the market-woman.

We took one morning to visit *Shoenbrun*, the magnificent summer palace of the Emperor two miles from Vienna. We counted 165 windows on one side, which enables one to have some idea of its size. It is in harmony, externally and internally, with the style of Francis Joseph. All the entrances are guarded by *gens d'armes*, and though in this is like all European palaces, we are glad of the contrast in this respect between it and the White House.

A pretty park, covering more than a thousand acres, surrounds Shoenbrun. It is laid off into many pretty walks and drives and beautified by fountains filled with fishes. Seats are placed at proper intervals, and it did me good to see the poor people walking through these royal gardens or resting by these beautiful spouting fountains. One drive, about a mile in length, has a row of small oak trees on each side that seem to have been cut perpendicularly by a great plane, and then about twenty feet above the ground, by a horizontal plane; looking down this avenue from one end there seems to be a solid wall on each side of the drive; not one twig an inch long projects beyond the plane.

In one museum I saw figures in wax illustrating many diseases. The flesh seemed to be purposely cut away so as to expose the various organs affected in these diseases, and often many figures were reproduced to show the progress of the diseases; bones were broken, often projecting through the flesh, polpoid growths were being extracted; eyes, ears, nose, throat and all were diseased and being relieved. The nervous, veinous, arterial and muscular systems with the viscera were all shown, each to itself. One hardly knows which to admire most, the one who dictated or the one who executed so skillfully for such an exhibition.

The squares of Vienna are adorned with many equestrian statues. Belvedere gallery is the largest in the city and claimed my time one half day. Raphæl's Madonna à la Verdure is here. Titian has a Madonna here, Corregio a Ganymede and an Io. One of the best pieces is an Altar piece representing the Catholic, Greek, Jewish, Mohammedan and Brahmin faiths.

It has been the custom for more than 250 years for the Austrian Emperors and their wives to wash the feet of twelve old men and twelve old women of the city on Friday before Easter, every year. They also send a *table d'hote* dinner and a bottle of wine to those whose feet they have washed. The suicide of the *Kronprintz* this year cast such gloom over the royal family as to forbid festivities, and the ancient custom was unobserved.

The Austrians are a healthy, good-natured looking set, fond of show and pleasure, and mostly have blue eyes. They are all Catholics, and badly priest-ridden. I copy a few extracts from a confidential circular placed in my hands:

The object of this communication is to give a few particulars of a quiet work for the Lord which has been carried on for some time at ———, province of Austria. The indiscriminate publication of details in Christian journals is an impossibility, as in consequence of the lack of religious liberty in this country, all aggressive evangelistic effort, especially that of an undenominational character, is practically prohibited, and it is only by acting with the greatest prudence and by keeping carefully within the letter of the law that such work can be done. We therefore earnestly request those Christians into whose hands this may fall to regard the communications it contains as *confidential*, and to exercise care that the circular may not fall into the hands of Jesuit spies, who are constantly on the watch for any streak of light on this priest-ridden land, and whose influence upon the authorities and people at large is so great that they often succeed in putting an end to all efforts.

Public Gospel meetings as they can be held in England, France and Italy, being forbidden in Austria, we can only have private gatherings in our own dwelling, with a limited number of people, whom we must invite personally by cards.

The great centre of attraction in our meetings is *the Bible*. By far the majority of our attendants had never seen a copy of the Word of God ere they came to us.

CHAPTER XXXIV.

THROUGH GERMANY, DOWN THE RHINE.

Our train rolled out of the grand *Westbahnhoff* on the clear, crisp, frosty morning of April 24th, bound for *Frankfort-on-the-Main*. I took a slow train because they often stop over two, four and six hours, giving the hurried tourist time to see many places he would have to pass by if on the limited express; also the slow trains are used by the common people, while the fast trains are chiefly used by the wealthy, and I wished to see all I possibly could of the middle and lower classes. The rich are about the same the world over.

Soon after leaving Vienna the mountains of Styria and Tyrol appeared far off to the left and covered with snow seemed to lift a warning hand that Switzerland was too cold and must be passed by. All day we fly over the most pleasing landscapes; all the land that is cleared is in a fine state of cultivation. If it is clothed in verdure every foot is occupied; if it is fallowed every inch is broken; if a canal passes through it does not monopolize; just so much as is necessary is taken for the water, the remainder is utilized in some other way. If some is left to sustain its native forest, the decaying trees and shrubs are removed and every part presents the finish of agricultural and horticultural skill, and nature herself has woven these landscapes into lovely shapes as deft fingers do the drapery of dress. Baedeker says of this section, "No other district in Germany offers such a variety of charming scenery within so small a compass."

PASSAU,

the first town reached in Germany, at the confluence of the Inn and Danube, is a beautiful town that really looks more rustic than city-like. We spent an hour here looking round and getting rid of Austrian *florins* and *kruetzers* for German *marks* and *pfennigs*.

I met a gentleman here who spoke English; we took a compartment together to Nuremburgh. He was a native Russe, and spoke freely of the efforts made by Russia to capture Servia and Bulgaria by flooding those sections with political and religious (Greek) literature from Moscow and other great centers of Russia, and expressed himself as of opinion that they were about ready to ally themselves to Russia.

We pass, near

REGENSBURG,

the *Walhalla* or Temple of Fame, called also *Deucher Ehren*, modeled after the Parthenon at Athens, built fifty or sixty years ago by Louis I, of Bavaria. The entablature is adorned with sculptures by Wagner, illustrating Germany's ancient history. Below are a hundred busts of eminent Germans. The grounds about the building are admirably laid out, and command a fine view. The whole is on a height overlooking the Danube and city.

I stopped four hours in

NUREMBURG,

which gave me time to see the old high-gabled houses

with stone balconies; the double wall, 800 years old, whose lofty tower called the *Burg* I climbed to get a better view of the town and its environs. The *Rathhaus*, or town hall, was about to be closed for the day, but a few *pfennigs* turned the key backwards, and I saw within. It is a rare building and has connection with famous deeds. It contains Albert Durer's best works in frescoes, and a very fine painting of himself painting Maximilian the Great; also a fine portrait of Faber, of lead pencil notoriety. There is the lion of "Red-wine and White-wine" fame, and I sat in the Royal chair of Leopold I. The *Shoene Brunnen*, or beautiful fountain, deserves the name.

In the valley of the Pegnitz, where across broad meadow lands,
Rise the blue Franconian mountains, Nuremberg, the ancient, stands.

Quaint old town of toil and traffic—quaint old town of art and song,
Memories haunt thy painted gables, like the rooks that round them throng:

Memories of the Middle Ages, when the Emperors, rough and bold,
Had their dwelling in thy Castle, time-defying, centuries old.

And thy brave and thrifty burghers boasted, in their uncouth rhyme,
That their great imperial city stretched its hand through every clime.

Everywhere I see around me rise the wondrous world of Art,
Fountains wrought with richest sculpture standing in the common mart;

And above Cathedral doorways saints and bishops carved in stone,
By a former age commissioned as apostles to our own.

Here, when Art wast still religion, with a simple, reverent heart,
Lived and labored Albrecht Dürer, the Evangelist of Art:

Here Hans Sachs, the cobbler-poet, laureate of the gentle craft,
Wisest of the Twelve Wise Masters, in huge folios sang and laughed.

But his house is now an ale-house, with a nicely sanded floor,
And a garland in the window, and his face above the door:

And at night the swart mechanic comes to drown his cark and care,
Quaffing ale from pewter tankards, in the master's antique chair.

Not thy Councils, not thy Kaisers, win for thee the world's regard;
But thy painter, Albrecht Dürer and Hans Sachs, thy cobbler-bard.

Thus, O, Nuremberg, a wanderer from a region far away,
As he paced thy streets and court-yards, sang in thought his careles lay:

Gathering from the pavement's crevice, as a floweret of the soil,
The nobility of labor—the long pedigree of toil. —*Longfellow.*

From Nuremburg we ran down to

WURZBURG

on the Main, reaching there a short while before day Having to leave at sunrise, and as there was a good restaurant in the Station, I did not go to a hotel; here I received the first native hospitality I had known for many weeks. An attendant at the depot invited me to his room and supplied me with water, soap, towel and a comb, which conduct I supposed was designed to secure a small perquisite; this he refused, however, when offered, and only received it when I insisted. I was anxious to go across the Main and visit the monument of Walter of Vogelweid, the Minesinger of whose will Longfellow says:

> "And he gave the monks his treasures,
>   Gave them all with this behest:
> They should feed the birds at noontide
>   Daily on his place of rest;
>
> Saying, 'From these wandering minstrels
>   I have learned the art of song;
> Let me now repay the lessons
>   They have taught so well and long.'
>
> "Thus the bard of love departed;
>   And, fulfilling his desire,
> On his tomb the birds were feasted
>   By the children of the choir.
>
> "Thus they sang their merry carols —
>   Sang their lauds on every side;
> And the name their voices uttered
>   Was the name of VOGELWEID."

The town is also noted for the manufacture of fine wines from the vineyards seen along the railway, and for the medical department of its University. There were three Japanese students in the Station who had been smoking and drinking beer all night.

We dashed down and across the Main, through tunnels, over bridges, through green fields and forests of maple, cypress and oak, and reached

FRANKFORT,

the home of one of the Rothchilds and birthplace of Goethe, at 8 o'clock, A. M.

The Ariadne, Danneker's masterpiece, in Bethmann's Museum, is a solid piece of Marble representing this beautiful daughter of Crete as left by Theseus and found by Bacchus, seated on a lion. She sits sidewise on the beast looking over her right shoulder. The poet-sculptor clothes her with that happy freedom from care that we welcome in any face, and that laxity of restraint for which the artist refuses any substitute. Leaving the Ariadneum I mistook the directions of the keeper, and was soon lost; having only my German to fall back upon, I asked many a time, the best I could, the way to the Städel Gallery, and sometimes got plain directions, accompanied by appropriate motions of the head and hands, the latter of which conveyed more intelligence to my mind than the best German: often I would pause in front of a fellow-pedestrian with my stereotyped, *Wo ist Stadel Museum?* He would very often look straight at me, as if astonished, and reply: "*Ich verstehe nicht, mein Herr.*" "I do not comprehend, sir." Again I approached some one who was evidently a stranger, like myself, he would merely shrug his shoulders and pass on. (All Europeans shrug the shoulders when asked a confusing question.)

> "To sit on rocks, to muse o'er flood and fell,
> To slowly trace the forest's shady scene,
> Where things that own not man's dominion dwell,
> And mortal foot hath ne'er or rarely been,

> To climb the trackless mountain all unseen,
>   With the wild flocks that never need a fold
> Alone o'er steeps and foaming falls to lean—
>   This is not solitude, 'tis but to hold
> Converse with nature's charms, to view her stores unrolled.
>
> " But in the city's hum, the din, the shock of men,
>   To hear, to see, to feel, and to possess
> And roam along the world's tired denizen,
>   With none to bless us, none whom we can bless.
> Minions of splendor shrinking from distress,
>   None who, with kindred consciousness endued,
>   None who if we were not would smile the less
> Of all who followed, flattered, sought and sued,
>   This is to be alone; this, this is solitude."

I instinctively carry my reckoning, like the lower animals, but lost it altogether in Frankfort, and only began to find myself after I had gone over the "Cock and Devil" bridge, as it is called, because the architect consigned the first living thing that should cross it, to the bottomless pit; this proved to be a cock, a large figure of which is placed on one of the pillars that extends several feet above the floor, also one of Charlemagne is near by. Like the Seine at Paris, and the Thames at London, so at Frankfort the Main runs between stone walls and over a macadamized bed. Once over this bridge I had to go down the river half a mile to the museum, and the tops of steeples and other high objects all became so adjusted in my mind that I had no farther difficulty.

The Stadel gallery contains several Madonnas (portraits of the Virgin Mary) which are classed among noted paintings, an altar-piece by FRA ANGELICO, and imitations of the *Venus de Medici*, Laocoon, Wrestlers, &c. The Brazen Shield of Achilles by Schwanthaler is a master-piece. A very fine painting of the Ten Virgins must have suggested the lines of Owen Meredith:

"One still as death, hollowed her hand about her lamp,
For fear some motion of the midnight, or her breath
Should fan out the last flicker.
Rosy clear the light oosed through her fingers o'er her face,
There was a ruined beauty hovering there.
Over deep pain, and dashed with lurid glare—
A waning gloom."

The *Kaisersaal*, which contains frescoe portraits of all the German emperors from Konrad I, 911, to Francis II, 1806, and the clock given by Napoleon I, claimed me an hour, after which I went to the *Dom* to see the Dead Christ, by Van Dyck, and an altar-piece in wood, representing the crucifixion. I made a hurried visit to the beautiful *Palmgarten*, the monuments of Schiller and Gutenberg, and left for Heidelberg, passing Darmstadt, in which one sees from the cars the war monument of Ludwig Einster, 1870-1.

Almost every foot of lard is cultivated from Darmstadt to Heidelberg; it is rented out in small patches; often one farmer has a lot fifty yards wide and three hundred long in wheat, beside that and about the same size, one is newly ploughed for corn or some other crop. The land for many miles is laid off this way, and I was told that one man had possession of only a few acres. In the distance to our left several towers rise on the heights.

CHAPTER XXXV.

HEIDELBERG, WORMS, DOWN THE RHINE TO COLOGNE.

At nightfall the old University town of

HEIDELBERG

is reached, made up of 16,000 Protestants, 9,000 Catholics and 2,000 Jews. After a good night's rest I took a guide and went to the Molkencur, a very high mountain overlooking the city and valley. My guide pointed out one of the largest cement factories in the world, the valley over the Neckar where the students fight duels two or three times a week, a church half Catholic and half Protestant, each denomination worshipping in it every Sabbath, and the old castle, which has been destroyed by the French, by lightning, and is now in the hands of the ever successful destroyer, Time. Heavy fogs advised us not to ascend to *Konig's Stohl*, as the view would not repay the toil.

We will go down from this splendid observatory to look through the historic castle. It is reached by crossing a draw-bridge, over a very large moat, then through the gate in which hangs still the ponderous portcullis, and we are in the open court, where sixteen of the electors of Palatine, done in stone, look down from their niches in the lofty walls. In a museum of antiquities, seen for twenty *pfennigs*, there are many old swords and all the machinery of ancient battle, keys almost as heavy as a pick, mugs, moneys, postillion boots truly monstrous model of the castle *Molkencur*, Konigs Stohl and plan of the city made of cork by a cook, securing for him a fortune. Below is the great Tun, holding 50,000 gallons of wine; it has eighteen hoops 8x10 inches, the two at the ends being 8x14 inches. It has been filled three times, the last time was in 1769, by Charles Theodore elector of Bavaria. On the top is a platform where about six or eight persons can dance, which they did on the occasion of filling the *Tun*.

The great university founded by Rupert Carolo, elector of Palatine in 1487, contains his bust in the *aula*, or assembly hall. Around the front of the gallery are the names of many of their noted professors, while the ceiling has female figures representing Theology, Law, Medicine and Philosophy.

I went from H. to Maintz, stopping two hours in

WORMS

to see the monument of Martin Luther on the Luther Platz. He is standing with upturned face on which is depicted intelligence, conviction, courage, purpose. In his left hand he holds the Bible; his right is closed and rests on the Bible; below him are cut in the stone the words:

> Hier Stehe Ich.
> Ich Kann nicht Anders.
> Gott Hilf mir! Amen!

which mean: Here I stand. I cannot retract. God help me! Amen!

The artist was most happy in the execution of his

task; one seems to be in the presence of the living hero of 1521. I saw nothing else while traveling that so electrified me as did this statue.

There is no grander exhibition on earth than a man to whom God has committed a trust not recognized by his cotemporaries perhaps, but known to himself, and having the courage of his convictions amid all opposition and persecution, intent on doing his part at all hazards. No doubt the world is a greater debtor to moral than to physical courage. It is in such birth-throes that correct thought and right sentiment burst the prison bars of dogmatism and custom and leap into life to emancipate nations and races.

It is a very interesting ride of an hour to

MAINTZ.

Farm houses are thick; gardens, pastures and stock are fine; at every station country lasses unload large cans of milk for the city. A bar or rail is put up at every railroad crossing, and the sentry presents arms while the train is passing. Every private soldier salutes every officer he passes, though they may be on opposite sides of very wide streets, filled with carriages or wagons. This often requires several hundred salutations a day.

Maintz is one of the best fortified cities in Europe, and contains many fine monuments. The Cathedral is said to be the richest in monuments of any in Europe. I only took time to hurry through it. The Tablet to Fastrada, wife of Charlemagne, and Schwanthaler's monument to Frauenlob, the pious minstrel of the Holy Virgin, were all I noticed. Cars run on both sides of the Rhine, but we preferred to take a steamer. The Rhine has been written about so much that I hesitate to say anything; the scenery to Bonn, birthplace of Beethoven and seat of a University, is wild and attractive; the perpendicular hills are crowned with old towers, the sloping ones ornamented with terraces, growing fruits and grapes. The Rhine and its fels and towns have many a legend of ancient hero and heroine, as Siegfried and Brunhilde, of Rinbod and the Maiden offered to the monster of Drachelfels and Lurlei, Bishop Hatto and the Mouse Tower, Hans Winkelsee, and scores of others. In all their romances and songs the river of Germany has mingled its "chorus sweet and clear."

Across the Rhine Julius Cæsar built his bridge, and along its banks history has been making ever since.

We reached

COLOGNE

about sundown. I stopped within one square of the Cathedral, thought by some to be the grandest Gothic structure in the world, being 500 feet high; it has one door or portal (on the south) that cost $500,000; it has a chapel called the Chapel of the Three Kings, said to contain the bones of the Magi!

I attended the Church of England services on Sunday, which seemed designed for, as they were only attended by visitors. The Sabbath is used as a holiday, after the early morning service, say nine to ten o'clock, in Cologne as in Vienna. I went to the Cathedral before breakfast on Sunday to find it almost filled at that early hour. They had the finest music I ever heard, which was kept up nearly all day; when one division of the choir would sing until exhausted, another would be called on.

I went to St. Andrew's (Catholic) Church before breakfast Monday morning. About 200 children were at prayers, with about a dozen ladies, all led by a little girl not over ten years old. She would utter several invocations, pause and be followed by the congregation repeating the last sentence or uttering a responsive prayer. They had stepped into this church on their way to school, as they do every morning, and as their minds are developed their hearts and habits are fixed about the altars of the church.

The church of St. Peter has an altar-piece, Rubens' "Crucifixion of St. Peter," which is thought to be very superior; the head is downwards. Near by, at No. 10 Sternengasse, is shown the house in which Peter Paul Rubens was born, 1577, and in which Maria de Medici died in 1642, having been driven by the heartless Richelieu, for whom she had obtained the cardinalate from her Parisian home.

The *Rathhaus*, about six hundred years old, is a splendid city hall, dedicated to the Cæsars. The bronze equestrian statue of William III, places him high above the men who graced and supported his *regime*, and others of the cult of Blucher and Von Humboldt.

At 12 M., on the day after reaching Cologne we took the cars for

BRUSSELS,

arriving at 9 o'clock the same evening, passing on the way *Aix-la-Chapelle*, the birth-place and favorite residence of Charlemagne, and where for several hundred years after his death the German emperors were crowned.

At this place both Charlemagne and his wife Fastrada

died. He was buried in the octagonal nave built by himself in a marble chair. About a mile or two from the railway one can see the *Frankenburg*, a hunting-seat of the great Charles. It is said the water surrounding the Castle was a lake, into which his wife's ring was thrown.

> "Thou knowest the story of her ring,
> How, when the court went back to Aix,
> Fastrada died: and how the King
> Sat watching by her night and day,
> Till into one of the blue lakes,
> Which water that delicious land
> They cast the ring drawn from her hand;
> And the great monarch sat serene
> And sad beside the fated shore,
> Nor left the land forevermore."
>
> —*Golden Legend.*

We pass Liege, a factory town, and the first in Belgium. A train with 200 passengers dashed in from *Spa*, the oldest watering place in Europe, of any note. As it only costs from one to three cents per mile to travel in Belgium, and as it is the most populous country in the world for its size, there is much travel. *Chaude Fontaine*, another watering place, was on the line of our road and looks somewhat like Piedmont Springs, in Burke County, N. C. A large new hotel was in course of erection. The entire face of the country in Belgium is as pretty as a picture. The morning after reaching Brussels I went out to see the field of

WATERLOO,

twelve miles from the city. A large mound has been built in the center of the field, about 800 feet west of where Wellington's headquarters were during the fatal day, and very near the position of the impregnable square, behind which was the road into which fell

"Rider and horse, friend and foe, in one red burial blent."

The top of the mound is reached by ascending 200 steps. It is surmounted by a granite base of huge proportions, on which stands a cast lion looking towards France with one fore-foot resting on a globe. This signifies so much to the Frenchman that my guide said only few of them visit Waterloo at all. I was very fortunate in having a guide well posted on the history of the movements made by all the leaders in that crisis of the world's history.

Napoleon had approached to within a few hundred yards of Wellington's position, when Blucher arrived. Wellington had all the advantage in position from one side of the field to the other. But such battles are determined by the Friend of the nations and *not* by the " heaviest artillery."

Some one has said that Napoleon never wrote an important document without using the word " glory," as if that were his talisman, and Wellington likewise always used the word " duty." And on this field of carnage the world has been taught the superiority and triumph of *duty* over *glory*.

CHAPTER XXXVI.

THREE WEEKS IN LONDON.

Leaving Brussels, one hour sufficed to reach Antwerp, a well fortified town on the Scheldt, on the borders of Holland. Next morning at six we were seated in an English railway carriage on British soil and enjoyed a peace of mind that was new. I felt like talking much, like one after a long fast enjoys a sumptuous table d'hote, and indulged freely with a Londoner and an English-speaking gentleman from Vienna. The country along our route was cleared of timber, as in most European States, but the farm-houses and farms were more like those I had been used to at home. Soldiers ubiquitous on the Continent were missed here.

At nine o'clock I stood on one of the streets of the busiest metropolis of the world, inquiring for a 'bus that would take me to Smith's Temperance Hotel, Southampton Row. I was directed to go to the Bank, near by. There are scores of banks in London, but only one is known as "the Bank." From that point omnibusses go in all directions and every one or two minutes, for one penny a mile. Every one goes loaded, and the number of pedestrians does not appear to be diminished. In fact so dense is the travel on the main thoroughfares that it is often difficult to leave a store for want of a place in the throng, but once in one is moved along almost involuntarily. This is true any day on Cheapside, the

Strand, Oxford street or Holborn. On these streets police are stationed at every crossing in the center of the street to direct vehicles to the left side, order them to stop and move along, and give every one a fair opportunity to change his location, a privilege his individual self-assertion is often inadequate to obtain.

"The thing that most astonished me about London, and that I had been least prepared to see there, was the amazing activity in the streets. A New Yorker born and bred, who has seen the principal American cities, fancies that there can be nothing in the world like Fulton street and Broadway.

"London is full of Fulton streets and Broadways, and in them and in all the other streets the cabs and hansoms fly about in such a hot and apparently reckless way that I always felt while I was there that the only reason I did not read of a hundred 'run over' accidents every morning in the papers, was that it would be doing violence to the organic principles of the London press to print the news. I confess I was more than half afraid to cross the crowded streets, and with a fear which is engendered in New York in few places and on few occasions. I was assured by the citizens that they are all so accustomed to project their coat tails at right angles to their bodies and to invoke divine aid between the flying hoofs of horses, whenever they need to cross a street, and that they are as adept at it as an American lightning rod man is at dodging missiles. Yet I observe that Dickens, in his Dictionary of London, thinks it worth while to suggest that the only way to go from curb to curb is to make up your mind what course you will take and then stick to it, because then the London cabbies will divine your intentions. To change your mind while en route is to confuse the cabmen, and make your return to America be in the form of freight. Then, again, I found that in the Western end of the Strand—that is down by Temple Bar and the Law Courts —200 more or less mangled bodies are sent to the Charing Cross Hospital every year."

There are several elevated railways, and London underground is said to be honey-combed with railroads. There is one place where 1200 trains pass daily, or one nearly every minute. These are necessary to accommodate the vast numbers of a city that is a microcosm.

"It contains more Roman Catholics than Rome itself; more Jews than Palestine ; more Irish than Dublin ; more Scotchmen than Edinburg; more Welchmen than Cardiff; has a birth in every five minutes and a death in every eight minutes ; has seven accidents in it every day in its 7,000 miles of streets ; has 124 persons every day, and 45,000 annually, added to its population ; has 117,000 habitual criminals on its police register, and has 38,000 drunkards annually brought before the magistrates."

There are 5,500,000 inhabitants occupying nearly 790 square miles. Allowing a third for streets, parks, gardens and the Thames, there would be 17 persons to the acre. If four houses were built on every acre, there would be a family of four to every house, and enough over to make four cities as large as Raleigh. As many of the wealthy have large yards and gardens and small families, one can conjecture how densely must be populated the poorer districts; often fifty or more are crowded into one tenement dwelling. This is a fruitful source of both crime and disease, and the wiser heads are trying to devise means for the amelioration of these evils. "What shall we do with our cities?" has long been a question among European philanthropists and economists. Investigation reveals that there are no people in London whose ancestry can be traced back four successive generations in the city. One way of checking the evil is to open up large public parks and gardens, but the desire to be near their work and to diminish rent on the part of the poor, and the increased income from rents, influences the wealthy to crowd as many as possible into every house that is for rent, and thus misfortune and Mammon sway to the ignoring of the good laws ordained of God for man's well being. Those who most need to obey the laws of health are ignorant of them, and have not the power if they had the wisdom to observe them. Those who know of them and have the power to see them observed more generally, have not the disposition to help any but themselves.

They have in London what is known as the "sweating system," by which is meant that a person who has credit gets work from tailors or others, and gets those persons to do this work at a very small price, who have no credit and who, to make their wages cover their necessary expenses of living, crowd together in tenement houses until the heat radiated from their bodies, and the air, robbed of oxygen by frequent inhalation, make a condition worthy of the appellation. It presents one of the evils to be combatted by philanthropists in the overcrowded city.

"The report of the Committee of the House of Lords on Sweating has just been presented. It is affirmed that the chief factors in the Sweating System are not middle-men or foreign labor or the extensive use of machinery. The system is shown on the contrary to be the issue of inefficiency in the class of workers, early marriages, and the tendency of the residuum in large towns to form a helpless community and to accept a low standard of life. But, in the main, the system is ascribed to the excessive supply of unskilled labor, and the work of married women, who are willing to employ the intervals of domestic duty at a low rate of wages which to single women would mean starvation. The report places little reliance on legislation, though it suggests that all home-workers should be registered and open to authorized inspection, but it looks hopefully toward an increased sense of responsibility in the employer and improved habits on the side of the employed. Surely John Wesley's panacea of all evils, social, industrial, political is still the true and only one—the spreading of scriptual holiness throughout the land."

There are many institutions built by charity, for poor children. I saw representatives from sixty-six institutions for the governing and training of destitute and criminal children. It was in St. James' Hall. They numbered 600, and were trained to sing, march, and perform in pantomime with almost perfect precision. I also attended a meeting of the "London Society for Prevention of Cruelty to children" held at the Mansion House, with the announcement that "*The Right Hon. the Lord Mayor will Preside.*" This announcement always secures a full attendance. The meeting was addressed by H. E. Cardinal Manning, (whose appearance and bearing are very similar to those of Dr. Closs, during life), Hon. A. F. Mundilla, M. P., A. K. Rollit, M. P., and others.

The sights of London are too numerous to be catalogued, a list of the most interesting is kept at all the hotels for gratuitous distribution; to write them up would be to write almost a history of England. The May Meetings, including over 130 different Societies for the good of Christian, Jewish and heathen men, women and children were holding their annual meetings, and were of great interest because I wished to learn how the English churches met and carried their responsibilities.

As Bishop Marvin said, the English have their own way of doing things. At all of the meetings which I attended, about twenty, everything was cut and dried beforehand. The questions to be discussed were printed. The mover of every motion, and the one appointed to second it. and the words of the motion were all on a printed circular. The speech of the putter of the motion was sometimes read. No place is allowed for extemporaneous speechifying. Generally effort was made to secure the endorsement of my Lord, so and so, by putting him in the chair or announcing that he would be present.

These Lords and bishops have a monopoly and are conservative enough to keep as far as possible the first places at a distance from all whose qualification to fill them comes by any other way than by inheritance or court favor.

They put on the greatest imaginable stiffness and behave as if they thought the matter at hand were worthy to monopolize the world of thought for a decade or two. The audience appear to accept the interpretation put upon it and cheer to the echo such periods as are commonly used all over our country, and cry " Hear, hear," to ordinary truisms. Their preparation always prevents confusion and I judge they moved so slowly only because their common people were so far behind. In the matter of collections, however, they are ahead of us. I never attended any service in church or public hall that a collection was not taken, nearly every one contributing.

What I have said does not imply that Great Britian has not led the world in literature, poetry and government, as well as in religion. She has. If her form of government is not equal to ours, in our judgment it is in their opinion superior, and may be superior when we consider the character of the subject. Our forefathers brought away the best conceptions of goverment then existing and the best class of citizens the world could thne furnish with which to maintain such a government when it should be formed.

England has done more than we in the matters mentioned above, but she has been many centuries at it. I told a patriotic Briton that we expected to have as many Poets and Literati after awhile as England. He said we did not have one whose name was as great, and who had lived before the world so long as Shakespeare. I told him just to wait until we lived to be as old a people as the British and he would see what he would see!

At these meetings it was plain to be seen that a war was going on between the established church and the dissenters. At several meetings of the church of England in Exeter Hall, whenever evangelistical efforts er e reported such as they were driven to adopt by dissenters there would be cheers loud and long. Frequent disparaging references were made to dissenters, while the dissenters were loud in their complaints against an oppressive system that had to be supported by all the people, many of whom did not believe in its polity, nor all of its doctrines. In Joseph Parker's church an order of court that had been issued for selling some poor man's property for taxes due the established church was exhibited and much enthusiasm aroused against such a condition of things. Rev. Mr. Cleal said in City Temple at this same meeting that he had known the names of pupils taken in the day schools to compel them to attend the Sunday Schools of the English church. He said "Our opponents are hard to oppose because they drift in the spirit of the age."

The dissenters are hopeful of a change and are faithfully bearing the testimony of Jesus.

There are many Churchmen who are uneasy lest the Pope shall make great inroads into England, he has already said: "England is doing well." The "Tract Movement," converted thousands to Romanism. The Queen's private Sacretary is a Catholic, and wise people know what that means. The alarm has been great enough to call forth much comment in the *Churchman*, specially on the occasion of Her Majesty's visit to a convent while in Spain, and a poem which had a wide circulation, a stanza or two of which I copy :

> To-day the *curse* is in his *heart*,
>   The while with *lips* he blesses;
> *Infidel—Godless* England sees
>   No harm in his caresses;
> The maudlin men of "Modern Thought"
>   Can grip no Standard truth;
> And Jesuits in the English Church
>   Have Romanised our youth:
> The very throne has bowed itself
>   At Leo's trampling feet;
> *Can* God do *otherwise* than let
>   *Such* sin with *sorrow* meet?
>
> Beckon him on!! This *blessing*-Pope,
>   He holds Victoria *vile*,
> And fain would give her "*Moonlight*" *fare*,
>   As in the Sister Isle;
> "No faith with heretics," is *still*
>   The Papal undertone;
> And Englishmen are *fools*, who think
>   That Rome has *kinder* grown;
> "*Kill, kill*," she says; let *Manning's* words
>   Our sad attention win,
> Or *life* or *liberty* goes out
>   When Leo's *power* comes in.

Victoria has a hard time, I presume; while everything nearly seemed to indicate the greatest love and devotion. Each party is very jealous, and objects to any patronage being given to the others. Her policy seems to be to do at Rome as the Romans do. In Scotland she attends the Presbyterian church, in Spain the Catholic, at home the Episcopal.

One can see why she should defer to so great an extent to the Catholic church, when one remembers that Ireland is so largely Catholic and that 50,000 of her troops are

Catholic, besides those who live on English soil, and the further fact that her Majesty's interest in the East is protected by the Catholic in the jealousy he bears towards the Greek church of Russia and the Slavonic States. All eastern people are ruled through their religion, and to be stable in power the monarch must properly estimate all the factors involved in the problem of ruling. The Queen can afford to smile upon the church of Rome for the returns. The leaders of Society forgive her if their principles oppose, for their standing depends upon her patronage as well. And if the Jesuit is far more diligent and successful in improving every occasion than the Protestant, nobody deserves so much blame as this same fault-finding Protestant. The propagation of any religion depends upon the operation of natural laws (on the human side) which are as much the property of one individual or sect as of another.

Protestantism needs to learn the value of printer's ink, as the Politician and Jesuit know it, as well as the worth of devotion to the task in hand.

Mr. Spurgeon has learned this lesson and not only has written a great many books, but has organized a thorough system of Colportage, the annual meeting of which it was my privilege to attend in his Tabernacle; it is working well. Mr. Wesley learned it, and wrote and sold books—cheap books—with what result is known too well to be repeated here.

CHAPTER XXXVII.

SIGHTS IN LONDON.

At several meetings of the Wesleyan Methodists I learned that they are trying to carry their share of responsibility in supplying the people with the gospel. I was present at the opening of Cleveland hall, which is a Methodist church. The same meeting was protracted and many souls converted.

The West End Mission is supplied by Revs. Hugh Price Hughes, who is second only to Spurgeon as a popular leader among dissenters, and Mark Guy Pearce, his colleague, both of whom I heard preach.

I attended several services in City Road Chapel, in the church of John Wesley. It now has two preachers, one of whom, the Rev. Mr. Murrill, kindly showed me through Mr. Wesley's house. His study was a small room not over 7x8 feet. In it is the quaint old teapot from which he gave his preachers a cup of tea on every Sunday morning; part of the spout is broken off and on each side is burned in blue letters a stanza used as a blessing before and after meals. One reads as follows:

> "Be present at our table, Lord—
> Be here, be everywhere adored,
> And in thy mercy grant that we
> In paradise may sup with thee."

The room in which Mr. Wesley died is a small room.

CITY ROAD CHAPEL, WESLEY'S CHURCH—FRONT VIEW.

INTERIOR OF CITY ROAD CHAPEL.

In it are his writing desk and library, his clock and his chair. Mr. Murrill said that Cyrus Field had offered $2,500 for the writing desk and $500 for the teapot; but no sum could purchase them. I was present at a tea-party in the parlor of the church and was invited to address the meeting. I also made a talk to their Sunday School, and preached in the evening in the Mission Chapel. In the rear of the church is Wesley's tomb, which is very unpretentious, consisting of a base about four by eight feet and about four feet high; on this rests a shaft six or seven feet high, with the single word Wesley on one side. Since my visit a tomb like the accompanying cut has been built. Around him lie Clark, Watson, Benson, and many others noted in Methodist history. Tablets to the memory of the Wesleys, Fletcher, Dr. A. Clarke, Joseph Benson, Coake and others, are in the walls of the church behind the altar and on either side.

Across the street is Bunhill Fields Cemetery, once the chief burial place for non-conformists, but now disused. It contains the tomb of Watts, DeFoe, Bunyan, whose tomb has the figure of "Pilgrim," with a load upon his back. A large upright marble slab, near the centre of the grounds, contains the following:

HERE LIES THE BODY OF
MRS. SUSANNA WESLEY,
WIDOW OF REV. S. WESLEY, M. A.,
YOUNGEST DAUGHTER OF REV. S. ANNESLEY, D. D.,
MOTHER OF NINETEEN CHILDREN,
OF WHOM THE MOST EMINENT WERE JOHN AND CHARLES, THE FORMER FOUNDER OF THE SOCIETIES CALLED METHODISTS.

In sure and steadfast hope to rise
And claim her mansion in the skies;
A Christian here her flesh laid down,
The Cross exchanging for a crown.

WESLEY'S TOMB.

Of the noted preachers in London I heard Spurgeon, Canon Farrar, Hugh Price Hughes, Mark Guy Pearce, Newman Hall, Joseph Parker, and the Bishop of London. At the May Meetings I heard some dozens of preachers from the country, and Missionaries from the foreign fields. Besides the Colportage meeting in Spurgeon's Tabernacle, I was present on two Sundays when he preached; both sermons were superior as to matter and delivery. His church has two elliptical galleries, each holding about 1,000, while the body of the house holds 4,000. It was full on both occasions. His voice was pitched on the proper key to fill the auditorium, and sustained throughout. He preaches an hour, and uses great variety of style both in sermonizing and in his delivery. He comments on the lesson before the sermon and pronounces the benediction without song or prayer, after the sermon. He aims at immediate results, and preaches with great earnestness and unction.

As nothing else in the world is so great as a really great man, I called to see him one afternoon for a few minutes. I said, Mr. Spurgeon, I am an American stopping for a short time in London, and thought I would like to form your acquaintance. He smiled, extended his hand and remarked: "Well, you have seen a great somebody, indeed." After a short pleasant conversation I arose to leave, when he said: "May the Lord bless you and give you a safe voyage home."

I attended a prayer meeting in a room of the Tabernacle, which is held every Sabbath from 10:30 to 11 A. M., when prayer is offered for the Holy Ghost's presence and power to rest on Mr. Spurgeon, the members of the church, visitors and the unconverted who may attend.

This was to my mind an explanation, largely, of how, for thirty years this great man has been so efficient in his Master's vineyard.

Mark Guy Pearce is a Perfectionist, and, while sensational, believes in the presence of the Holy Spirit and his willingness to do now all we need to have done if we are but willing and anxious. He preaches with much feeling. His colleague, H. Price Hughes, is very sensational. He attracts and controls large audiences. He is a great leader.

On the last Sunday I spent in London, in the afternoon I heard Canon Farrar preach in Westminster Abbey, and scores of people were turned away for want of even standing room. He read his sermon, and it was a piece of splendid composition for which he is so renowned. He has a mellifluous voice, and his delivery was splendid considering the reading.

Joseph Parker's City Temple, Holborn, is a most elegant church, with lecture room, study and parlors. He is a topical preacher; his style is elevated and stately; he is a grand man to look at. The discourse to which I listened was not above an average, but was enlivened occasionally by some startling statement or comment apropos of the discussion. Speaking of Esau he said: "Has it come to that! Life reduced to repentance—repentance vain! Disembowelled life! An epitaph of two words, Born—Died! Alas what doth temptation!" He uttered no uncertain sound on the subject of future punishment: "God says thou shalt surely die. Satan says thou shalt not surely die. Reject, young man, any theory that promises any probation beyond the grave."

There are many noted churches in London—City Road

INTERIOR OF WESTMINSTER ABBEY—CHOIR.

Chapel, already noticed; Westminster Abbey, which contains the dust of kings, queens and warriors, painters, poets and sculptors, statesmen, philosophers and theologians, all honored with appropriate tombs, tablets and epitaphs. One is shown the Jerusalem chamber, where King James' and the revised versions were translated. A whole day is necessary to half way see over the ponderous pile; while one might read, reflect and study there for a lifetime without exhausting the subjects of interest.

St. Paul's is the third largest church in the world, and is also a receptacle for such heroes as Wellington, Nelson, Sir Christopher Wren, the architect who built it, Reynolds, Samuel Johnson and others, making it a kind of "National Temple of Fame."

The Bow Church on Cheapside is one of Wren's best works. There is a dragon on the top of the steeple 9 feet long. Persons born within hearing of the Bow-bells are Cockneys, i. e. true Londoners, (B.)

Newgate, Ludgate, Billingsgate were named after the old gates that led through the wall when this was a Roman town, and mark the old city limits, now miles from the suburbs.

The Tower, which covers 18 acres, has four objects which every visitor should not fail to see, viz:

1. The Crown Jewels in the Wakefield Tower. Among many other coronets is that of Queen Victoria, containing 2783 diamonds. They are confined like lions in a circular cage of iron about ten feet in diameter. Crowds of people gather here daily to behold the dazzling gems, regalia, scepters, &c., valued at £3,000,000 or about $15,000,000.

2. The White Tower, the old original Norman keep or prison, with walls 15 feet thick, containing a very large

collection of old armor, such as was used during several hundred years.

3. Leaving the White Tower, the space in front is called Tower Green. In this are buried the victims of jealousy and revenge. In the middle of it one sees a small square paved with granite to indicate where the scaffold stood for the execution of Queens Anne Boleyn and Katharine, Margaret, Lady Jane (Gray) and many other royal unfortunates.

4. The Beauchamp Tower on the west, whose walls are full of inscriptions, cut in the stone by the unfortunate wretches incarcerated there, repays a visit.

The Bridges, the Equestrian Statues, the Monuments to statesmen, warriors and discoverers, the British Museum, National Gallery, South Kensington Museum, Madame Tussaud's Waxworks, with the Zoological Gardens, Parks, Palaces, Houses of Parliament, Place of Justice, with strangely clad justices and barristers, Banks, Halls, and so on, would require many weeks to see and understand.

The public ground called a *Square* in America is called *Circus* in London, *Piazza* in Italy, *Place* in France, and *Platz* in Germany.

The dogs in Turkey are curs or Shepherd dogs, or a mixture, in Vienna the Mastiff predominates, and is worked to the market wagon, in London the Pug seems to be in the ascendency and is always led about by a string.

The large Norman draught-horses, as in France, Germany, Austria and Belgium, are used in England also.

The streets are kept clean by regiments of boys, carrying wooden scoops and stiff brushes, moving rapidly from point to point as their task requires, half bent, the scoop sliding. When full it is emptied into an iron box by the sidewalk, several feet high. These boxes are duly visited by wagons.

Often one sees a boy or man with colored crayons making beautiful pictures on the smooth stones of the sidewalk. You cannot but pause to admire them, stretching for many yards, and often the product of real genius. You will soon see in large letters: "WILL YOU NOT CONTRIBUTE TO AID A POOR AMBITIOUS YOUTH?" or some other phrase, asking alms.

On almost every square small stands face the street where milk is on sale. At these one can get a quart of milk for 5 cents, and plenty of bread for a hearty meal for two cents. There are commissioners appointed to buy milk daily from these stands, testing its quality to protect the purchaser from imposition.

Their police regulations in all their details are equal to the best to be found in the world, probably.

The movements of the royal family are chronicled in England about as famous persons are in America. It was announced one morning that the Queen would take the cars, from Paddington Station, for Windsor, so I, with multitudes of others, went out of my way to see her. Great crowds gathered on all the street-corners, requiring many police to preserve order. Her face was flushed, she seemed excited, but I was unable to determine whether it was from modesty, irritation at the poor order kept by the guards, or a fear of bombs, or something altogether different. The pageant was not overpowering, yet somewhat greater than a Presidential turnout.

CHAPTER XXXVIII.

SCOTLAND—ABBOTSFORD, EDINBURGH, GLASGOW.

After a sojourn of three weeks in London, every waking hour of which was turned to the best account, I bought a ticket to Glasgow by way of Melrose (called the Waverly Route) and Edinburgh, passing on the way Peterboro the Proud, York the Ancient, Durham with its castle and cathedral encircled by the river Wear, and Newcastle father on, where I spent about four hours, which enabled me to see the old castle, built by the son of William the Conqueror, and Stephenson's great bridge over the Tyne and his monument, reaching

MELROSE

about 6 o'clock, P. M. I met in the Abbey a gentleman from West Virginia. We remained until about dark and listened to the custodian, who never tired showing the resting places of those buried within its walls and telling of their heroic deeds, such as Douglas, King Robert Bruce, whose heart is buried there, Michael Scott, the famous Wizard, Murdoch, the first Master of Melrose Lodge A. F. and A. M., which, with Kilwinning is said to be the oldest in Scotland, and of many others:

> "Within the pile no common dead
> Lay blended with their kindred mould:
> Theirs was the hearts that prayed or bled,
> In cloister dim or death-plain red,
>   The pious and the bold."
>
> "The pillared arches over their head,"

the finest in finish of any I saw anywhere, engaged our attention quite awhile. "There is one cloister, along the whole length of which runs a cornice of flowers and plants, entirely unrivalled, to my mind, by anything elsewhere extant, I do not say in Gothic architecture merely, but in any architecture whatever." Just east of the Tower Base is a stone in front of a large window in the perpendicular style and just by the tomb of Michael Scott the "Wizard" of the "Lay," on which Sir Walter used to sit for hours meditating and composing, often till late at night, for,

> "If thou wouldst view fair Melrose aright
> Go visit it by the pale moon-light.
> When buttress and buttress alternately
> Seem framed of ebon and ivory;
> When silver edges the imagery,
> And the scrolls that teach thee to live and die;
> When distant Tweed is heard to rave,
> Then go—but go alone the while—
> Then view St. David's ruined pile;
> And home returning, soothly swear,
> Was never scene so sad and fair!"
> —*Lady of the Lake.*

Next morning we went up to Abbottsford, called the "Romance," Sir Walter's home, built on the grounds where was the scene of the last feudal conflict of the Borders; near by is Dryburgh Abbey, the Eildon Hills, "for weirdly deeds renowned," Ettrick Forest and the "dowie dens o' yarrow," and only half a mile to

> "Where gallant Cessford's life-blood dear
> Reeked on dark Elliot's border spear."

This was the last battle of Melrose, the last great clan battle of the Borders, fought 1526, for the body of James V.

Sir Walter greatly enlarged this estate and planted on

it 2,000 sweet briers, 3,000 each of laburnums, scotch elms and horse chestnuts, loads of hollies, poplars, filberts and 100,000 birches. Mr. Rokeley called it a "Caledonian Eden." It is situated about three miles from Melrose, on the banks of the Tweed. It is a fairy glen, favorable for study, with the mumuring Tweed, impending hills, flowers, ferns and forestry to inspire his genius. As Rae-Brown says:

> "Scott, with a poet-painter's skill,
> Immortalized lake, tree and hill,
> Till Scotia seemed the brightest gem
> That shone on nature's diadem."

One is shown his armory, a fine selection, containing the pair of pistols carried by Napoleon Bonaparte at Waterloo, with many other valuable relics; his library of 20,000 volumes and many fine paintings; his study, with his desk, book-holder and the room in which he died, containing a bronze cast taken while he lay in state. Other things than arboriculture also occupied the acquisitive Laird of Abbotsford. Writing to his sister-in-law (Mrs. Thomas Scott) he says: "In despite of these hard times, which affect my patrons, the booksellers, very much, I am buying old books and old armour as usual, and adding to what your old friend Burns calls

> "A fouth of auld nick-nackets,
> Rusty airn caps and jingling jackets,
> Wad haud the Lothians three in tackets
> A townmont guide;
> And parritch pats and auld saut backets
> Afore the flude."

We spent one day—the Queen's birthday—in the learned city of Edinburgh. Queen Street is thought by many to be the finest street in the world, but the crowd

SIR WALTER SCOTT'S MONUMENT.

was so great one had to struggle to get along instead of leisurely admiring objects of beauty around him.

We ascend Calton Hill, which gives an extended view, embracing the city of Leith, Arthur's seat and the harbor on the Firth of Forth. An iron globe passes up and falls on a percussion cap discharged by electricity from the chronometer at Greenwich; this fires a cannon precisely at 12 o'clock, M., every day. Here also are the incomplete National, Nelson and Stewart monuments. Below the hill on the way to Holyrood is the monument to Robert Burns, at the unveiling of which his mother said: "He asked for bread, but they gie him a stein," meaning the stone material of which it was composed.

The Castle which covers 7 acres, and has endured many sieges, where James I. of England or VI. of Scotland was born, containing the ancient regalia of Scotland consisting of a crown, sceptre, sword of State, and the Lord Treasurer's rod of office, the room of *Mary, Queen of Scots*, Queen *Margaret's* Chapel, the smallest church in the world, perhaps, *Mons. Meg,* a historic cannon of 1497, with the Highlanders crowned with helmets plumed with Ostrich feathers worth $25, and tartan frocks that reach only to the knee, the rest of the leg and foot being bare, and the Scott monument below costing $2,000,000, with its churches and schools, all would tempt one to linger in this classic town, but only one more day remains for Glasgow and the country between ere the S. S. *State of Nebraska* will sail for New York and bear me to my native land.

Glasgow claims to be the third city of Great Britain, and is indebted for her prosperity to her facility for uniting commerce and manufactures. Four things consumed my time for one day: the Cathedral, which has one of the finest crypts in existence, with 33 columns and 20 pilasters supporting the ceiling, and stained glass windows from Munich; the Necropolis, just over the "Bridge of Sighs," that holds, with many others, the ashes of John Knox. On a single Doric column rising above his remains we read that the regent said at his funeral: "Here lieth he who never feared the face of man." Many events connected with the reformation in Scotland are inscribed on the monument and a fine statute of Knox surmounts the shaft. We spent a few hours in the Hunterian Museum of the University, which has a fine natural history collection; and the shipyards on the Clyde, where are made the great ocean-going steamers; fully one hundred, of various sizes, were in course of construction, made throughout of iron. They are built on an inclined plane, on a line cutting the shore diagonally, and are launched stern foremost.

We went through a large factory which employs several hundred blind people, who were weaving, making brooms, brushes, sieves and many other useful articles, all executed with surprising precision and dispatch.

Many emigrants sail from Glasgow to America. About 200 were on the *State of Nebraska.* Fully 2,500 people were on the wharf to see her sail and bid friends adieu; some wept, some laughed, while others cheered.

There is a solemnity about the sailing of a steam-ship laden with passengers bound for some foreign land. What fate awaits them, who can tell? Many have gone with as gleeful spirits as they, never to be heard of again.

Slowly we moved down the Clyde by the great shipyards. By and by we passed Greenock, birthplace of James Watt, and where Burns' Highland Mary is buried; on the opposite side, almost in sight, is the Whistler's Glen, where Donacha Dhu and the poor boy of Effie Deans rendezvoused as Scott relates in "Heart of Midlothian." Soon we run into Gourock bay "where the yacht clubs fit out their crack cutters, yawls and schooners for the summer races." It is said to be a lucky bay to sail from, especially if ballast be taken from Granny Kempoch, a rock on the cliff at Kempoch Point. Across from Gourock bay Loch Long branches off, on an arm of which (Loch Goil) Lord Ullin vainly called to his eloping child and her Highland chief

"'Come back! come back!" he cried in grief,
'Across this stormy water;
And I'll forgive your Highland Chief,
My daughter, oh, my daughter!'

'Twas vain; the loud waves lash'd the shore,
Return, or aid preventing;
The waters wild went o'er his child,
And he was left lamenting."

"Holy Loch is separated from L. Long by Strone Point projecting into the Clyde, here the scenery is Alpine, with precipice, crag, pyramidal hills, contrasted with others whose smooth, verdant sides swell into aerial heights. Particularly fine is Argyll's Bowling Green. It is a matchless amphitheater with downy fronts and lofty summits." Across the Firth to the left rise the Renfrewshire and Ayershire hills, land of Burns. Rothsay, a favorite watering place, was passed; here stands a castle dating back to 1098, where Robert II. resided for a time and where he died. It contains a stair known as the "Bluidy Stair" where tradition says a deed of horror occurred.

> The morning woke on the Ladye's bower,
>   But no Isabel was there;
> The morning woke on Rothesay tower,
>   And bluid was on the stair.
>
>   *   *   *   *   *   *   *
>
> And aft in the mirk and midnight hour,
>   When a' is silent there,
> A shriek is heard and a Ladye is seen
>   On the steps o' the Bluidy Stair."

The Firth of Clyde widens out and the shades of night shut out from our vision the enchanted land of Scott and Burns, of Wallace and Bruce, of McLeod and Knox.

We awoke to look upon Erin's emerald isle. Our ship spent a day at Larne, completing her cargo, affording passengers opportunity to run up to Belfast and spend a few hours.

Late in the afternoon our vessel was loosed from her mooring and steamed northwards through the north channel skirting the picturesque coast of Ireland homeward bound.

One of the pleasant features of a sea-voyage is the number of nice people one meets. I was very fortunate on this trip. There were five ministers aboard, two of whom were Methodists, three were Presbyterians. We were eleven days crossing, including two Sundays. On one of these Mr. Langley, of Canada, preached, and I on the second. During the day there was music and many kinds of games for those fond of amusement, and a good library for those who wish to read, while others write letters, still others look for whales and icebergs. We had two concerts and charades at night. It fell to my lot in one of these to feebly portray the desirable qualities and inexhaustible resources of our own Southland, and urge on all those seeking homes in the new world the benefits of locating amongst us.

I greatly enjoyed the association of Dr. Hobbs, a young alumnus of Johns Hopkins, who had been to Germany to study there. He belongs to the U. S. Coast Survey and is the author of a learned treatise on the " Rocks occurring in the neighborhood of Ilchester, Maryland." I enjoyed no less the acquaintance of the Rev. B. Langley and wife and the Rev. Jas. Lanman and wife whom I first met on the Luther Platz in Worms.

On the morning of June 5th we passed Sandy Hook, the Statue of Liberty, and soon stood on American soil.

My heart thanked that faithful Friend under whose protecting hand our ship had reached this shore in safety and whose defenses had been about me since January. I had travelled so many thousands of miles without accident, sickness, loss of any kind, (except a package sent home), or even missing a single connection by rail or steamer, or receiving a line of news from home to rob my journey of enjoyment.

> "'Tis sweet to hear the watch-dog's honest bark,
> Bay deep-mouthed welcome as we draw near home;
> 'Tis sweet to know there is an eye will mark
> Our coming, and look brighter when we come."

FINIS.